Kuno Meyer

The Voyage of Bran, Son of Febal, to the Land of the Living

An Old Irish Saga. Vol. II

Kuno Meyer

The Voyage of Bran, Son of Febal, to the Land of the Living
An Old Irish Saga. Vol. II

ISBN/EAN: 9783744732451

Printed in Europe, USA, Canada, Australia, Japan

Cover: Foto ©Thomas Meinert / pixelio.de

More available books at **www.hansebooks.com**

The

Voyage of Bran Son of Febal

to the Land of the Living

AN OLD IRISH SAGA

EDITED AND TRANSLATED BY

Kuno Meyer

With Essays upon the Irish Vision of the
Happy Otherworld : and the Celtic
doctrine of Re-birth : by

Alfred Nutt

VOL. II

𝕲𝖗𝖎𝖒𝖒 𝕷𝖎𝖇𝖗𝖆𝖗𝖞

No. 6

THE VOYAGE OF BRAN

VOL. II

The Celtic Doctrine
of Re-birth

Alfred Nutt

With Appendices : the Transformations of Tuan
Mac Cairill, the Dinnshenchas of Mag Slecht
Edited and Translated by

Kuno Meyer

Published by David Nutt in the Strand

1897

GRIMM LIBRARY. No. 1.
GEORGIAN FOLK-TALES. Translated by
MARJORY WARDROP.
Cr. 8vo, pp. xii+175. 5*s. net.*

GRIMM LIBRARY. No. 2.
THE LEGEND OF PERSEUS. By EDWIN
SIDNEY HARTLAND, F.S.A.
VOL. I. THE SUPERNATURAL BIRTH.
Cr. 8vo, pp. xxxiv+228. 7*s.* 6*d. net.*

GRIMM LIBRARY. No. 3.
THE LEGEND OF PERSEUS. By EDWIN
SIDNEY HARTLAND, F.S.A.
VOL. II. THE LIFE-TOKEN.
Cr. 8vo, pp. viii+445. 12*s.* 6*d. net.*

GRIMM LIBRARY. No. 4.
THE VOYAGE OF BRAN, SON OF
FEBAL. Edited by KUNO MEYER. With
an Essay upon the Happy Otherworld in
Irish Myth, by ALFRED NUTT. Vol. I.
Cr. 8vo, pp. xvii+331. 10*s.* 6*d. net.*

GRIMM LIBRARY. No. 5.
THE LEGEND OF PERSEUS. By EDWIN
SIDNEY HARTLAND, F.S.A.
VOL. III. ANDROMEDA. MEDUSA.
Cr. 8vo, pp. xxxvii+225. 7*s.* 6*d. net.*

PREFACE

THIS second instalment of my studies in connection with the *Voyage of Bran* appears later and is less extensive in scope than was anticipated by me. I had hoped to bring out vol. ii. within a year after vol. i.; I had intended to trace the re-birth conception throughout the Aryan-speaking world in the same way as I have traced that of Elysium, and then to discuss the relation of both to similar conceptions in the earlier civilisations of the East as well as in barbaric and savage communities of the present day. The failure of my hopes accounts in some measure for the curtailing of my plan; to carry this out in its original form would have involved, in view of the scanty working-time at my disposal, another year's delay. It seemed advisable, therefore, to restrict myself to the essential part of my scheme—the exposition and discussion of the Irish evidence —and to reserve the important but secondary question of origin for future investigation.[1]

I would again emphasise my wish to have my work judged in the first place as a contribution to the history of mythic literature among the Irish. In this respect I venture to think it has some claim to the attentive con-

[1] A further reason for modifying the original plan will be found in the last chapter.

a 2

sideration of scholars, and should prove of assistance to fellow-students.

I wish to renew my expression of indebtedness to the scholars already mentioned in the preface to vol. i., in particular to M. d'Arbois de Jubainville, Professor Erwin Rohde, and Dr. Whitley Stokes. A somewhat lengthy examination and criticism of M. d'Arbois' views on the Tuatha de Danann mythology entered into my original plan. Here again it seemed best to content myself with setting forth my own theory.

Professor Kuno Meyer has laid me under deep obligation by careful persual of the proof-sheets, by many important suggestions, and by the appendices of unedited Irish texts, which will give this volume a value in the eyes of philologists to which it could not otherwise lay claim. I have also to thank Dr. Jevons for kindly reading over the chapter in which I discuss the classical *testimonia* and enabling me to correct and amplify the argument based upon them. I must state, however, that this chapter contains much to which he would not yield unqualified assent. I mention this lest I should seem to lay upon him the responsibility for possible errors of my own.

My critics have treated me with a leniency and appreciation that demand my grateful recognition. Many helpful suggestions were made, notably by Mons. L. Marillier, Professor York Powell, Mons. Henri Gaidoz, and Dr. F. B. Jevons. Some of these I have been able to utilise in the present volume; the larger number had reference to that

part of my scheme which, for the present, I have dropped.
One point, however, which could not be dealt with in the
body of the work, but which involves important questions of
method, may be briefly glanced at here.   My friend, Professor W. W. Newell, protested at the close of his notice in the
Journal of American Folklore against the use of the terms
Celtic or Aryan as applied to anything else save languages.
'It is not at all certain that there exist either Celtic or
Aryan legends,' he says.   If the adjective be held to imply
a monopoly of the legends in question, I agree.   But I have
never used the terms criticised in this restrictive sense, and
I do not think there is any danger of such a misleading
interpretation becoming current.   I do hold, on the contrary, that there is a sense in which we may legitimately
speak of Aryan myths or Aryan institutions as opposed to
Semitic myths and Semitic institutions, or to the myths and
institutions of any other well-defined groups of men.   It is
not implied that such myths or institutions are the exclusive or even the special possession of either Aryans or
Semites ; it is enough that a majority of Aryans or Semites
should possess them and should impress upon them differentiating features.   In the same way, within the Aryan
group I hold it perfectly legitimate to speak of Celtic
myths and institutions.   Here again I imply no exclusive
possession, but I do most emphatically imply differentiating
features, and differentiating features common, in a greater
or less measure, to the various Celtic-speaking peoples.   The
existence of these differentiating features in Celtic romance,

custom, and belief, on the one hand, the presence of a common Celtic tone, temper, and colouring on the other hand, can, so at least it seems to me, only be denied by those who are ignorant of the facts, or who are incapable of rightfully apprehending their significance. And I furthermore emphatically urge that within the Aryan group the test of speech is not the sole, perhaps not even the most important test of kinship. Philologically, Celtic is most closely allied to Italic; in other respects the Celt seems to me to have closer and more varied affinities with the Greek.

As regards the general question of the relations of Aryan to the older Oriental culture I have expressed myself fully and plainly in the final chapter.

In conclusion, I would urge increased study of the Celtic past by the English-speaking communities. They are pledged to it alike by filial piety and by political expediency, for the Celtic element in their civilisation is considerable, and, though it may somewhat change its form, it is not likely to decrease. As far as the purely scientific aspects of the study are concerned the facts speak for themselves; as far as its beauty and interest are concerned there again the facts speak for themselves. But I rest my advocacy of the fostering of Celtic studies upon other than scientific or æsthetic grounds; I believe it to be a task, patriotic in the highest sense of the word, as tending to sympathetic appreciation of a common past, to sympathetic union in the present and future of all the varied elements of a common nationality.

ALFRED NUTT.

July 1897.

CONTENTS

THE CELTIC DOCTRINE OF RE-BIRTH

CHAPTER XIII

THE MONGAN LEGEND

CHAPTER XIV

IRISH RE-BIRTH LEGENDS

CONTENTS

CHAPTER XV

THE RELATION OF IRELAND TO CHRISTIAN AND CLASSIC ANTIQUITY

CHAPTER XVI

AGRICULTURAL RITUAL IN GREECE AND IRELAND

CHAPTER XVII

THE TUATHA DE DANANN

CHAPTER XVIII

THE CONTEMPORARY FAIRY BELIEF OF THE GAELIC-
SPEAKING PEASANT

CONTENTS

CHAPTER XIX

SUMMARY AND CONCLUSION

APPENDICES OF IRISH TEXTS

Edited for the first time and translated by

Prof. KUNO MEYER

THE VOYAGE OF BRAN

THE CELTIC DOCTRINE OF RE-BIRTH

CHAPTER XIII

THE MONGAN LEGEND

The object and methods of the investigation—The date and peculiarities of the Mongan story; the statements of Bran's Voyage and of the glossator; the testimony of the eleventh century prose texts; the poem ascribed to Muru of Donegal; the annalistic references; the nature and value of the Book of Fermoy text—Comparison of the reconstituted Mongan legend with the Mabinogion of Pwyll, Prince of Dyfed, and Manawyddan, son of Llyr—Date and nature of the Mabinogion discussed—Mongan and Finn—The legends of Mongan, Arthur, and Finn, discussion of their relation to each other, and of the relations between Goidelic and Brythonic heroic myth—Reconstitution of the myth underlying the three cycles of heroic romance—Sketch of the Mongan saga in Irish literature; elements which it yields for the re-birth conception.

In the preceding chapters, in which are studied the origin and nature of the two leading and mutually complementary conceptions found in the old Irish romantic legend, *The Voyage of Bran*, I dealt with the Irish vision of the Happy Otherworld, and reached the following provisional conclusion: Substantially pre-Christian, this vision finds its closest analogues in the earliest known stage of Hellenic belief, and forms with them the most archaic Aryan presentment we possess of the divine and happy land.

A

I now propose to consider the conception of reincarnation or rebirth. In the case of the Elysium vision there
was an *a priori* possibility that the Irish accounts were simply
distorted reminiscences of Christian Heaven and Paradise ;
here too the surmise of Christian influence is at least
possible. The chief Christian dogma may well have
borne unexpected fruit. Stranger results have followed
from the contact of higher and lower cultures. The lines
of my investigation will thus be much the same as in the
Elysium section. After a careful examination of the
Mongan stories with a view to determining how far they
are early in date and archaic in character, I shall adduce
and study Irish parallels. The question of Christian
influence, notably of the doctrine of the Incarnation, will
then be briefly glanced at ; the conceptions involved in
the obscure Pythagorean and Orphic systems of Hellenic
antiquity must be noticed, and their possible bearing upon
Celtic belief discussed. Ritual, custom, and folklore must
then be cross-examined to check results derived from written
texts. If, as I trust, the history of the Irish rebirth conception can be set forth with some certainty, and its nature
elucidated, the conclusions already reached in the Elysium
section cannot fail to be either confirmed or invalidated.

In this, as in the Elysium section of my study, my object
is to place and account for, historically, certain Irish legends.
I start from these, and the illustrative material I bring
together will be found, I trust, pertinent in reality, though
it often seem remote from and disconnected with the starting
point. On the other hand, I deliberately discarded in the
first volume much that would necessarily find a place in
a general history of the Elysium conception, but which did
not, in my opinion, fit in with the proper mode of investi-

gating the particular manifestation of it I had in view. I shall follow the same course in the following pages, at the risk of at times appearing to neglect facts and considerations germane to my subject.

The stories of which Mongan is the hero, as also the historical notices concerning him, printed in vol. i., have already yielded the conclusion that there existed, as early at least as the tenth century, tales about a Mongan son of Fiachna, a noted wizard, a son of Manannan, and, by some accounts, a rebirth of Finn, son of Cumall. This sufficed for my purpose at the time, but a minuter scrutiny of these stories is now necessary.

THE MONGAN REFERENCES IN BRAN'S VOYAGE.

The poems contained in Bran's Voyage are the oldest portion of the text, dating back as they do to the eighth or possibly to the seventh century. What have they to say of Mongan? His real father is Manannan, son of Ler, who will come to parts dwelt in by Bran, will journey to the house of the woman of Linemag, and will lie with Caintigern ; of his progeny shall be a very short while a fair man in a body of white clay, whom Fiachna shall acknowledge as his son, who shall be the delight of fairy knolls, have the power of shape-shifting, be throughout long ages an hundred years in fair kingship, be slain by a son of error, be fifty years in the world, be killed by a dragon stone from the sea in the fight at Senlabor, be taken by the white host under a wheel of clouds to the gathering where there is no sorrow (Quatrains 49-59, vol. i. pp. 24-28).

The prose text of Bran's Voyage states that Manannan appeared to Bran, telling him ' it was upon him to go to Ireland after long ages, and that a son would be born to him, even Mongan, son of Fiachna' (p. 16), a passage which introduces the idea, absent from the verse, of a considerable lapse of time between Bran's journey to the Otherworld and Mongan's birth.

The statements of the verse are evidently not homogeneous, and the passage concerning Mongan's death has apparently been coloured in a Christian sense.

It will be recollected that Prof. Meyer traces all existing MSS. of Bran's Voyage to a transcript, probably made in the tenth century, from an older text. The glosses which accompany the present text are probably of the same date, *i.e.* the tenth century, as this lost archetype MS., and it is interesting to see how the tenth century scribe understood the dark allusions of the poem he was copying. Thus (Quat. 49) when Manannan announces that he will go to the woman of Linemag, the scribe adds the gloss: 'Conception of Mongan.' The statement that Manannan's progeny will be 'a fair man in a body of white clay' elicits the gloss: 'Mongan, son of Fiachna.' Quatrain 55 seems to have puzzled the scribe. 'He will be throughout long ages an hundred years in fair kingship,' says the verse; *i.e.* 'post mortem' comments the glossator, adding, moreover, 'he will be famous without end in futuro corpore,' glosses caused, possibly, by the wish to reconcile the statements of this quatrain with the very definite life-span of fifty years assigned to Mongan in Quat. 58. On this quatrain again is a gloss, 'in corpore,' showing how distinct in the glossator's mind was Mongan's other- from his mortal life. The line in the same quatrain, 'a dragon stone from the sea will kill him,' is glossed: 'this is the Death of Mongan,[1] a

---

[1] This is a reference to a story thus entitled, a story which has not come down to us.

stone from a sling was thrown at him.' So far Bran's Voyage. It affords clear evidence, I think, to the idea of an earthly chief being the son of a superhuman father, and endowed, in consequence, with superhuman qualities and attributes. We may further conclude, that already in the tenth century certain passages were interpreted as testifying to the continued existence after death of the god-begotten hero, and that the lack of homogeneity in the account of Mongan, which strikes the careful reader of the ancient poem, also struck its earliest known commentator, inducing him to supply glosses of a reconciling and harmonistic nature. Again we may fairly assume that the poem made little chronological distinction between Mongan and Bran, whilst the later prose fixes a gulf between them, a fact doubtless due to the assignation of Mongan to a well-defined historical period in the interval that elapsed between the composition of the verse and prose portions.

THE PROSE TALES CONCERNING MONGAN.

With the obscure and scanty hints yielded by our text must be compared the statements in the prose texts which Professor Kuno Meyer has printed and translated from the Book of the Dun Cow.[1] These tales *must* be as old as the early eleventh century, and were probably redacted at the same time (late tenth century) as the hypothetical archetype of all existing versions of Bran's Voyage, *i.e.* they belong to that period of comparative calm following the troubles of the Viking invasion age, when the remains of older Irish story-telling were being gathered up, transcribed, in part

[1] Vol. i. pp. 44 *et seq.*

remodelled.   The tales, briefly recapitulated, are as follows :—

The tale entitled *Compert Mongáin* (Mongan's Conception) gives him as father Fiachna Lurga, sole king of Ulster, an ally of Aedan (king of the Scotch Dalriada, who reigned from 574 to 606).   The hero's birth is due to the favours accorded Manannan by Fiachna's wife in return for his promise to save her husband's life.   The queen's name is not given, nor is aught stated of the son to be born except that he should be famous.

In the *Story of Mongan* [1] the king appears on friendly terms with the dwellers of various fairy knolls, to whom he sends a messenger, laying upon him strict injunction to take naught from his hosts beyond what he had been sent for.

The *Cause of Mongan's Frenzy* [2] relates, in obscure and confused fashion, a visit of Mongan and his court to Faery, a visit of much the same kind as those of Conn and Cormac described in the first volume.   It is probably the introductory prose opening to the rhapsody which Mongan brought back with him from Faery, and which was given in the now lost tale of Mongan's Frenzy.

The *Story from which it is inferred that Mongan was the son of Find mac Cumaill and the Cause of the Death of Fothad Airgdech* [3] relates how Mongan, to save his and his wife's honour from a bard to whom he had given the lie and who had threatened to bespell his land in consequence, is helped by Cailte who comes (from the dead), addresses Mongan as Find, and substantiates the truth of his story.   The tale ends thus : ' Mongan, however, was Find though he would not let it be told.'

---

[1] Pp. 57 *et seq.*   [2] Pp. 56 *et seq.*   [3] Pp. 45 *et seq.*

In these stories Mongan is always associated with
Rathmore of Moylinny; in two of them his relations with
his wife are emphasised; in two of them he is on intimate
terms with the *sid* or fairy folk; in two of them he is
brought into contact with a poet, Forgoll.

It is, I think, evident that these stories cannot have
their sole origin in the verse portions of Bran's Voyage.
Whilst there is general agreement as to the birth, character,
and attributes of Mongan, the details are so dissimilar, the
independence of either account is so obvious, that the
hypothesis of common derivation from an earlier and more
complete Mongan legend at once suggests itself. If we
turn to early notices of a professedly historical nature the
surmise that such a legend existed is strengthened. The
verse preserved by the eleventh century Tigernach, and
ascribed to the late seventh century Ulster kinglet, Benn
Boirche, an ascription which is possibly correct, connects
Mongan's death with Islay as does Quat. 56 of Bran's
Voyage. To a similar statement of the tenth century
historian, Cinaed ua Hartacain, less weight might be
attached, as it possibly rests wholly upon the authority of
Benn Boirche; but, as we shall see later, it is important in
another connection. The eleventh century annalists are
the first to cite the name of Mongan's slayer, Arthur, son
of Bicor of Britain, but the tradition may certainly be
relied upon as genuine. As Professor Zimmer has pointed
out, the name Arthur occurs several times, both among the
Northern and Southern Kymry at the close of the sixth
and beginning of the seventh centuries.[1]

---

[1] Nennius Vindicatus, p. 284.

So far we have dealt with *testimonia* which can be dated with some precision, and which are all anterior to the middle of the eleventh century. Among the *testimonia* of uncertain date is one which, could we accept the traditional ascription, would be of first-rate importance. The fourteenth century MS., Laud, 615, has preserved some verses ascribed to Muru of Fothain,[1] who died A.D. 650, in which is told how Mongan came 'to converse with Colum Cille from the flock-abounding Land of Promise.' Another poem in the same MS.[2] professes to give the hero's greeting to the Saint, part of which, as already noted by Professor Meyer, is substantially the same as Quatrain 25 of Bran's Voyage. In view of the well-known practice of Irish writers to father their own productions upon earlier celebrities, it is safer to suspend judgment on the date and authorship of these verses. It is noteworthy, however, that they contain an idea foreign, save indirectly, to Bran's Voyage as well as to the prose tales preserved in the Book of the Dun Cow. Mongan is represented as being himself an inhabitant of the Land of Promise. This, it may be urged, is a natural development of the supernatural parentage assigned to him in the legend. True—provided it be added : at an early stage in the history of the legend. Thus, in Greek myth, Menelaus is transported to the Isle of Rhadamanthus solely because of his kinship through Helen to the gods. Some such idea may well underlie the representation of Mongan as Lord in Faery, but if so it is decisive testimony to the archaic character of the Mongan legend. For in the later stage of legend, when the historical-heroic have superseded the purely mythic elements, divine parentage by no means necessarily ensures access to the divine land.

[1] Vol. i. p. 87. [2] Vol. i. p. 88.

Another point worth noting in connection with these verses is the clear distinction they make between the Christian heaven and the Land of Promise. Mongan comes from the latter and goes to Heaven under Colum Cille's protection :

> 'Mongan found not any help
> When he went to see Heaven,
> But his head—great the profit !
> Under Colum Cille's cowl ' :

strong witness, these words, both to the might of the pagan hero to whom Heaven could be opened, and to the essential paganism which necessitated his being smuggled in under the cowl of the greatest of all Irish saints save Patrick.

In any case, this view of Mongan as a dweller in the Land of Promise is also found in those undated verses, quoted by Professor Meyer,[1]

> ' O Mongan, O Manannan,
> Your wandering is not frequent
> In the land with living heart,' etc.

which contain, perhaps, the most exquisite of the many exquisite names the Irish poets gave to the western wonder-isle of their longing fancy.

MONGAN IN THE ANNALS.

In view of the foregoing facts, the passage quoted in vol. i. (p. 139) from the Irish annals found in Eg. 1782, and translated by Mr. Standish Hayes O'Grady, annals dating back certainly to the twelfth and probably to the eleventh century, acquires a fresh significance. ' Albeit,' says the annalist, ' certain dealers in antiquarian fable do

[1] Vol. i. p. 85.

propound Mongan to have been son of Manannan and wont
to enter at his pleasure into divers shapes, yet this we may
not credit, rather choosing to take him for one that was but
a man of surpassing knowledge, and gifted with an intelligence clear, and subtle, and keen.' Here we may see the
outcome, so far as the official science of the day was concerned, of the long evolution of the Mongan legend with
its two different modes of representing the hero, one purely
romantic (resting, as I shall hope to show, upon an older
mythic basis), one historic. The annalist has no doubts;
the romantic tales are but 'antiquarian fables,' the real
Mongan is the sixth to seventh century Ulster kinglet. But
another, and for us far more important conclusion, must be
drawn from his statement, for which the extant bulk of
Mongan romance affords so little justification. He must
have been familiar with many tales besides those we have
glanced at, tales too in which the attribute of shape-shifting,
so strongly insisted upon in Bran's Voyage, but absent from
the stories preserved by the Book of the Dun Cow, must have
been prominent. Have any remains of this legend cycle,
known to the twelfth century historian, but unrepresented,
directly, in pre-twelfth century MSS., come down to us? If
so, in how far do they faithfully represent the older saga?
These are questions which must be answered before a
sketch of the Mongan legend and of its evolution in Irish
romantic literature can be essayed.

MONGAN AND DUB-LACHA.

In the first volume of this work Professor Kuno Meyer
has printed and translated[1] from a fifteenth century MS.,
the Book of Fermoy, a story entitled 'The Conception of

[1] Pp. 58 *et seq.*

Mongan and Dub-Lacha's love for Mongan.' In its present form, the story is probably little, if any, older than the MS. which has preserved it. Not only the actual form of the speech, but style, expression, literary convention, betray a far later date than that of the tales found in the Book of the Dun Cow. But, as I have so frequently pointed out, the fact that an Irish story was rewritten in the thirteenth or fourteenth century by no means implies that it may not preserve the structure and incidents of a pre-eleventh century tale with almost absolute fidelity. In so far as a presumption exists, it favours the retention of the older tale in essentials if not in accidents. We may therefore apply ourselves to the consideration of the Book of Fermoy story without any prejudice based upon its comparatively late date.

I do not propose to summarise here a story already printed in full, and which must be read through to enable appreciation of the following discussion. The first portion of the tale covers practically the same ground as the eleventh century Conception of Mongan. Comparison between the two is interesting. In the eleventh century tale the amorous god appeals to the wife, in the fourteenth century tale to the husband. The wife only yields under menace of danger to her husband ; the husband is easier going, 'I would not let one single Irishman fall on account of that condition,' says he. In the one tale, then, the husband, in the other the wife, ignores the supernatural parentage of the wonder-child. In the younger tale the device is precisely the same as in the Arthur or Hercules birth stories—the wife receives the god in the guise of her husband. The earlier tale plunges at once *in medias res* ; the later one has an elaborate introduction, intended, it would seem, for it is obscure, to provide an opportunity for Fiachna's danger and the intervention of the amorous god. The personages of this introduction are well-known figures in Irish bardic romance; the Black Hag who makes a demand she knows cannot be satisfied, in order to have the chance of sending the hero upon an expedition full of danger ; the King of Lochlann who can only be cured of illness by the flesh of one particular cow; the venomous sheep which ravage the hero's army, the equally venomous hound which overcomes them. In the earlier tale we have only a general prophecy concerning the fate of the supernaturally begotten child; the later tale tells us that he was carried off to the Land of Promise by his father when *three nights* old. The earlier tale only knows a Mongan, the later one a servant-companion and a lady-love begotten the same night as himself, and possibly of supernatural parentage likewise.

In all these respects the later tale, as will at once be apparent to students of storyology, has a more *märchenhaft* character. Reference need only be made in this place to the first volume of Mr. Hartland's Legend of Perseus, in which will be found a vast array of examples of the theme —the magic birth of one, two, or three heroes destined to be companions in after adventures—from all ages and countries, whilst the carrying off of the wonder-child is a commonplace of the European folk-tale, specially prominent and traceable far back in Celtic romance. Before discussing the significance of this fact, the remainder of the tale must be examined.

Mongan having lost his wife to the King of Leinster through one of those rash promises which are so frequent in early Irish fiction, is enabled to visit, and finally to recover her, thanks to his skill in magic. Aided by his foster-brother, who plays the part of a Sancho-like chorus, he gains access to his wife in the guise of a monk, confessing her in a manner familiar to students of mediæval κρυπτάδια, and finally carries her off in the likeness of a Connaught prince, having left in her place with the King of Leinster a hideous hag whom his magic had turned for a night into the semblance of Erin's fairest damsel.

The lateness of certain traits, *e.g.* the transformation of Mongan into a monk, must not lead us astray. The prominent fact in the story is insistence upon that shape-shifting power of Mongan, celebrated by the eighth century poet of Bran's Voyage, noted by the twelfth century annalist but unrepresented, directly, in those Mongan stories known to be as old as the eleventh century. Here is strong ground for presumption that our tale does reproduce in essentials, modernise certain details as it may, a genuine episode of the original Mongan legend. We can strengthen the presumption by comparing the Book of Fermoy Mongan story as a whole with two Welsh tales belonging, undoubtedly, to the earliest stratum of Welsh romance. If the comparison yields proof that on either side of the Irish Channel have been preserved mythico-romantic fragments, relating partly to the same group of superhuman beings, and presenting largely the same incidents in their career, it will I think be granted that the Irish fragments, if written down later than the Welsh ones, must be nevertheless at least as old as they. The Welsh stories in question are the Mabinogion of Pwyll, Prince of Dyfed, and Manawyddan, son of Llyr.

MONGAN AND THE MABINOGION.

The former tells how Pwyll met, whilst hunting, Arawn, a prince of Annwvyn (or 'Faery'), how the two, at Arawn's request, to atone for an unintentional insult on Pwyll's part, changed shapes ; how Pwyll reigned a year in Arawn's stead undetected even by Arawn's wife ; how he slew Arawn's foe, and, on returning to his own country, was known ever afterwards as Pwyll, Prince of Annwvyn.   At the time, he was unwed, but later he was wooed by a supernaturally wise and beautiful maiden from Faery (even as Connla and Oisin were wooed), by name Rhiannon.   At the marriage feast he grants incautiously a boon to a stranger who turns out to be Gwawl, an old lover of Rhiannon's, and who promptly claims her at Pwyll's hands.   Rhiannon urges compliance to save her husband's honour, but obtains a year's respite from Gwawl.   At the end of the year Pwyll, instructed by Rhiannon, appears disguised as a beggar, and by means of a trick wins Rhiannon back from Gwawl, and takes her to his own land.   The son she bears is carried off on the night of his birth, and Rhiannon, accused by her women of having slain and eaten him, is doomed to degrading penance.   But the boy is left with Teirnyon, a retainer of Pwyll's, a mare of whose had foaled that night, and as he watched, a gigantic claw came through the roof to carry off the foal.   Teirnyon hewed off the claw, the monster fled, leaving the boy behind.   He is brought up as Teirnyon's son until he has reached youth ; then his foster-father, seeing his likeness to Pwyll, and bethinking him of the story, takes him to Pwyll's court, proclaims Rhiannon's innocence, and his foster-son, acknowledged as Pwyll's heir, in due course succeeds the latter, his name being Pryderi.

The Mabinogi of Manawyddan takes up the chain of events at a later stage.   Pwyll is dead.   Pryderi, his successor, and Manawyddan are two of the seven heroes who escape from Ireland with Bran's head after the disastrous failure of Bran's expedition to avenge the wrongs of his sister Branwen. For seven years after their return they had stayed at Harlech listening to the song of the three birds of Rhiannon, and fourscore years they had passed at Gwales in Penvro—'they regaled themselves and were joyful . . . and of all they had heard of they remembered nothing . . . nor of any sorrow whatsoever . . . nor were they more weary when first they came, neither did they, any of them, know the time they had been there.' But at last they opened the fated door and must needs return to earth. These things are told of in the Mabinogi of Branwen, daughter of Llyr, which links together the Mabinogion of Pwyll and Manawyddan.

When the latter opens, Manawyddan has lost his inheritance during the expedition to Ireland and the after-years spent in Faery. Pryderi then bestows upon him his mother, Rhiannon, and the four, Manawyddan and Rhiannon, Pryderi and his wife, Kicva, live happily together. But a friend of Gwawl's, Llwyd, son of Kilcoed, has not forgotten the old wrong done unto Gwawl by Rhiannon and Pwyll, and, in revenge, by art-magic he wastes their land and drives them forth. For many years they wander through Britain supported solely by the skill of Manawyddan, who is a master of every craft. At length Pryderi and Rhiannon are lured into a magic castle of Llwyd's and there kept captive. For a year longer Manawyddan supports Kicva by his craft of shoemaking, then returning to their own land they plough and sow and await the harvest. But Llwyd's enmity has not slumbered. His wife and the women of his court, changed into mice, devour the grain as it ripens ready for the sickle. Manawyddan determines to watch, and succeeds in catching Llwyd's wife, as she, being pregnant, cannot escape quickly as her companions. By threatening to slay her Manawyddan obtains the release of Rhiannon and Pryderi, the unspelling of the land, and a promise from Llwyd to seek no revenge.

It needs no pointing out that the action of these stories passes in the same realm of romantic fancy as the Irish tales concerning Mongan, and those which narrate Irish visits to the Happy Otherworld. We are in a kindred wonder-world of magic singing birds, of feasts in which years pass as an hour, of damsels immortally fair and gracious, of magicians who assume all shapes at will. But more; the incidents and episodes of the fifteenth century Irish Mongan are found in the Welsh tales, different as sequence and connection may be. Pwyll is lured into Faery, as is Mongan's father, Fiachna. Mortal and immortal change shape, though in the one case the immortal, in the other the mortal wife is deceived. Pwyll's son is carried off on his birth-night, as is Mongan when three nights old. A foal is born the same night as Pryderi under circumstances that link together the fate of man and beast, as a comrade servant is born the same night as Mongan. Pwyll loses his wife for a year as Mongan does his, and wins her back by a trick, involving disguise, as also does Mongan.[1]

These parallels, all between the stories of Mongan and Pwyll, justify the surmise of some kind of connection between the stories. The case is immensely strengthened by consideration of the Mabinogi of Manawyddan. For Manawyddan, son of Llyr, is undoubtedly the counterpart in Welsh literature of Manannan, son of Ler, in Irish litera-

---

[1] In the *Academy* of Aug. 15, 1896, Prof. Rhys equates Rhiannon and Etain, in which latter name he surmises a Rigetain. In view of the facts noted above, the suggestion acquires some force.

ture. His union with Rhiannon, the fairy mother of Pryderi, the damsel from the Welsh equivalent of the Irish Land of Promise, the owner (like Cleena, in Teigue, son of Cian) of the magically sweet singing birds, thus assumes a new and most significant aspect. The two are really of the same kin, and from the same divine land. Behind the Welsh tale, as we now possess it, we may dimly con-jecture a form in which Manawyddan and Rhiannon, lord and lady of the god land of the living heart, were the real father and mother of the wonder-child Pryderi, the latter being the real hero, as is his Irish counterpart Mongan, of the adventures related of his father Pwyll. How significant in this aspect the action of Manawyddan in his struggle against Llwyd ! It is not merely the mortal wife of his old age, but his immortal companion and his own son whom he has to deliver out of the hands of his magician foe.

The same transference of incident and attribute from father to son which I conjecture to have taken place in the Welsh tales, has also, most probably, taken place in the Irish Mongan legend, Mongan being morally, as he may once have been physically, a reincarnation of Man-annan.

It will, I think, be conceded that the Welsh and Irish stories owe their likeness to origin in a common body of mythic romance, the chief actors in which were the sea-god Manannan, and a supernaturally begotten semi-mortal son of his. It will further, I think, be conceded that the Irish story preserved by the fifteenth century MS., the Book of Fermoy, whilst younger in tone and colouring, less close in details to the hypothetical parent myth, yet reproduces its general outline and march of incident more faithfully than do the Welsh tales. In other words, the Irish story is sub-

B

stantially as old as, not to say older than, the Welsh Mabinogion.

But what the age of these? A question we must answer, or we are simply explaining the unknown by the more unknown. I have said above that they undoubtedly belong to the earlier stratum of Welsh romance. This 'undoubtedly' derives, however, no justification from the MS. tradition. The oldest MS. of the Mabinogion cannot be carried farther back than the end of the thirteenth century. In claiming an earlier date we rely upon the critical canon that no literature, even that of the most self-conscious and deliberately archaising age, our own for instance, entirely escapes the influence of the time. If the Mabinogion proper (*i.e.* the four stories of Pwyll, Branwen, Manawyddan, and Math) had been composed, or even entirely remodelled, in the late twelfth or thirteenth century, they could not have failed to be influenced by the French romantic form of the Arthur legend, which became known in South Wales in the second half of the twelfth century, mingled with and modified the genuine native form of the legend, and, in especial, gave it that note of universality which enabled it to interpenetrate and assimilate other legendary cycles, which had hitherto preserved a distinct individuality in the national consciousness. That the four Mabinogion ante-date the year 1100, so far as their contents are concerned, is the opinion of most experts.

Granted they belong to the eleventh century or early twelfth century ; granted their subject-matter is kin to that of Irish mythic romance, there are divers ways of accounting for this kinship, and upon the explanation favoured will largely depend our estimate of the real antiquity and origin of the Mabinogion. The subject-matter of these tales is, as Professor Rhys has said, the fortunes of three clans of supernatural beings : the children of Llyr, the children of Don, the family of Pwyll. We cannot fail to recognise the Irish Tuatha de Danann, or Folk of the Goddess Danu, a leading chief among whom is Ler, father of Manannan.

Now Brythons (represented by modern Welshmen) and Goidels (represented by the modern Gaels of Ireland and Scotland) may have had a common fund of mythic fancies, developed by each section of the Celtic race in its own way. On *a priori* grounds there is no objection to be urged against the hypothesis, which amply accounts for the likeness in essentials and marked variation in details of the legends we have considered. Nor does it necessarily exact throwing them back to prehistoric (*i.e.* in this connection to pre-Roman) times. As is well known, a considerable Brythonic immigration took place, in the fourth and fifth centuries, into Wales from the Northern Brythonic district (which was roughly equivalent to Scotland south of Clyde and Forth and England north of Humber). These Brython invaders may well have brought their traditions with them, .and that these should resemble those of the Goidelic inhabitants of the opposite coast of Ireland need cause no wonder.

But the very fact of this fourth to fifth century invasion of Wales by Brythons, who supplanted an existing Goidelic population, suggests another explanation. The Bishop of St. Davids, in his *Vestiges of the Gael in Gwynedd*, treats this Goidelic population as the first wave of Celtic immigration into Britain, whilst for Mr. Skene it merely represents temporary and foreign invasion fròm Ireland affecting the coasts rather than the interior.[1] But both scholars agree in referring the Mabinogion, not to Wales as the

[1] Cf. the Introduction to the Four Ancient Books of Wales.

country of the Kymry (Brythons), but to the period when Mona and Arvon were possessed by a Goidelic population, the legendary kings of which are the main actors in these tales. Professor Rhys has recently developed the views of the Bishop of St. Davids. It was not, according to him, until the fifth to sixth centuries, that the Brythons obtained definite supremacy over the earlier Goidelic population, which may well have preserved its speech for some time longer. The Mabinogion are the mythico-heroic traditions of this Goidelic people inhabiting Wales down to the sixth century, translated into the Brythonic speech of their conquerors, and filtered through a medium of Brythonic culture and historic conditions.

There is much that is fascinating in this hypothesis. It accounts for the apparent archaic pre-Christian character of the Mabinogion more satisfactorily than does the preceding view, according to which they were imported into Wales in the fifth century by the Brythonic invaders from North Britain. For these invaders of Wales belonged probably to a long Romanised and Christianised population, and had doubtless sloughed off their pagan beliefs (though this is by no means so certain as some writers assume). Many peculiar features of the Mabinogion are undoubtedly most easily explained, if they are regarded as the mythic traditions of one race arbitrarily fitted into the historic traditions of another. On the other hand, the scanty, obscure, and controverted historical facts upon which the hypothesis rests can hardly be said to afford it sufficient support, while the philological facts relied upon by Professor Rhys await expert criticism.[1]

[1] In a paper read before the Hon. Society of Cymmrodorion, Professor Meyer has argued against the theory on the ground of its

A third hypothesis remains. The Irish, as was shown sufficiently in the first volume, had developed, by the early seventh century, a great school of story-telling, which flourished vigorously down to the Viking period (beginning of ninth century), reviving a century later, after the storm and stress of the Scandinavian invasion had passed, when it gathered up and retold the ancient tales and stories which we find in the great vellums of the eleventh and twelfth century and later MSS. From the beginning of this period, not to speak of a far earlier date, the relations between Wales and Ireland were close and continuous. We know by the existence of actual translations from the Irish, that Welsh literature was affected by that of Ireland. We may conjecture that at any date up to the end of the eleventh century Irish story-tellers may have delighted Welsh hearers with their romantic fictions, and have formed Welsh disciples who retold the foreign legends, fitting them into the framework of their own land and its history. This hypothesis would account for what seem grave alterations in the very essence of the mythic legends preserved in the Mabinogion, and for the fact, which I was the first to point out in my study on the Mabinogi of Branwen,[1] that the Mabinogion apparently betray familiarity with the great North sea sagas of Siegfrid and Gudrun-Hilde, which may well have become known on either side the Irish Channel in the tenth-eleventh centuries.

I need not stop to discuss which of these hypotheses has the most in its favour. For even if the last be accepted, it still throws back the Mabinogion to the early eleventh

variance with the known history of the period. For the purposes of my thesis it matters little which view be accepted.

[1] Folklore Record, vol. v.

century, and the Book of Fermoy Mongan (which preserves in part the same traditions in a form partly more genuine) to a yet earlier age.   In other words, the tale for which we have only a fifteenth century MS. voucher, may be considered equal in age (so far as the contents are concerned) with those preserved by the oldest Irish vellum, the Book of the Dun Cow, copied at the end of the eleventh century from far earlier MSS., and its subject-matter may be used with equal confidence for working back to the earlier forms of the legend.

MONGAN, FINN, AND ARTHUR.

I trust that the result of this comparison between Gaelic and Welsh mythic romance may be deemed interesting and important enough to justify another comparison of the same kind before essaying to sketch the growth of the Mongan legend.   The parenthesis I am about to open may seem unduly lengthy, but its contents are, I think, germane to the point at issue.

Mongan then is a son of Manannan—the supernatural being endowing his mortal offspring with superhuman attributes and capacities.   But Mongan is also a re-birth of Finn, son of Cumall, or rather, to put it as the Irish storyteller does, Mongan was Finn, though the latter had been supposed to be long dead.   Now, as I have repeatedly pointed out,[1] the chief parallelism between Irish and Welsh heroic saga is furnished by the stories of Finn among the Irish and of Arthur among the Britons.   In the circumstances of their birth and upbringing, in the unfaithfulness of their wife

---

[1] Cf. more specially Transactions of the Second Int. Folklore Congress ('Problems of Heroic Legend'), and *Rev. Celt.* vol. xii. ('Les derniers travaux allemands sur la legende du Saint-Graal').

with their favourite nephew and knight, there is marked similarity. But if we enlarge the area of comparison by adducing the Mongan story, as, considering the identity of Mongan and Finn, we are entitled to do, the similarity is still more marked. For the birth stories of Mongan and Arthur are substantially the same, allowing for the fact that in the Arthur legend traits and incidents are translated out of mythic into human conditions, whilst the final passing of Arthur to Avalon assumes an entirely fresh meaning if we regard the mythic Arthur as the Brythonic counterpart of the Goidelic Mongan, owing his mortal origin to the lord of the magic wonderland whither he passes after his span of mortal life is ended. That such may have been Mongan's original fate we may surmise from the verses which associate him with his divine father as dwellers in the land of the living heart. But just as the Brythonic myth, fitted into the framework of the historic Arthur saga, lost the pristine significance of the birth incident, so the his-toricising of the Gaelic myth, by fusion of the mythical and historical Mongans, may well have obscured the original form of the death incident.

If it be admitted, as it can I think scarcely be denied, that the groups of mythic-heroic legend associated respec-tively with the names of Finn-Mongan in Ireland and Arthur in England, are largely made up of identical tradi-tional material, and may, in fact, be regarded as variant forms of a common heroic myth, this substantial identity may be explained by either of the three hypotheses we have just considered in the case of the Mongan-Pryderi parallel. Arthur may be the Brythonic counterpart of the Goidelic Finn-Mongan, or he may be the British-Goidelic form of the hero of whom Finn-Mongan is the Irish-Goidelic form,

or the heroic romance connected with his name may be a
Welsh imitation dating from the ninth to the eleventh centuries of similar Irish stories. The third hypothesis is at once
open to the grave objection that the Arthur saga, in both
its historic and its romantic form, is clearly indicated in the
Historia Brittonum of the South Welsh Nennius writing
at the close of the eighth or in the early part of the ninth
century, whilst it is extremely likely that in this portion of
his compilation he is embodying documents which may be
a hundred years older. If this argument were not considered sufficient it could, I think, be amply proved that
the peculiarities of the Arthur romance, as we know it from
the twelfth century Geoffrey, and the somewhat later
romance writers, are quite inconsistent with the theory of
comparatively recent importation of the romantic elements
which it contains.

Let us look at the matter a little more closely. Here
are three groups of legend, partly historic but mainly
romantic, similar or identical in important respects, associated each with definite historic tribes and territories. If
we adopt the traditional chronology associated with the
heroes of these legends and arrange the groups accordingly,
we have :

(*a*.) The Finn group, associated *chronologically* with an
Irish chieftain of the third century of our era, *topographically*
rather with Southern and South-Western Ireland, although
some of the earlier notices seem to refer him to that West
Scottish district with which, at a later stage, he is so prominently connected ; these notices, however, seem to involve
the parallelism of Finn and Mongan.

      Finn is a posthumous child, reared in the woods,
the destined avenger of his father, possessor of

magic gifts and powers, deserted by his wife for his favourite nephew and warrior.

∴ The oldest witness extant to the Finn legend may date back to the eighth century.[1] A considerable number of testimonia belong to the tenth and early eleventh centuries. But the legend as a whole only becomes really popular in all Ireland from the eleventh century onwards, from which date it competes with and finally supplants the Ulster cycle of Conchobor and Cuchulinn.

(*b.*) The Arthur group associated *chronologically* with a Romano-British chieftain, who fought with considerable success against the invading Germanic tribes at the close of the fifth and in the early part of the sixth century; *topographically* (1), with the North-Western Brythonic district, covering the western half of Southern Scotland and Northern England; (2), with South-West Britain (the romantic element of the legend being located in South Wales as early as the eighth century).[2]

Arthur owes his birth to shape-shifting on his father's part—*i.e.* it is practically the same as Mongan's, whilst his life-story largely resembles Finn's, in so far as his wife's unfaithfulness and its attendant circumstances are concerned. Arthur has supernatural kindred and passes into Faery at his death.

[1] Waifs and Strays, vol. ii. p. 403, where I cite a verse from the gloss on the Amra Choluim Cille, referring to Grainne's love for Diarmaid, quoted for the purpose of explaining the meaning of two words which had become obsolete in the eleventh century.

[2] In the mention of the Twrch Trwyth story found in the Mirabilia embodied by Nennius in his Historia Brittonum, and in Nennius's allusion to a lost saga of Arthur's son Amhir, whose grave is located in modern Herefordshire.

∴ The earliest extant witness to the Arthur legend is, as we have seen, possibly of the seventh, certainly of the eighth, century. The legend must have been known and popular in the Northern and Southern insular Brythonic (or, as they came to be called, Kymric) districts in the ninth, tenth, and eleventh centuries; it must have been popular in the continental Brythonic district (Brittany) at least as early as the beginning of the eleventh century, as it was carried by the Normans to Italy in the second half of that century, and they could only have learnt it from their Breton neighbours. But, as a whole, the legend only secures wide acceptance and popularity from the early part of the twelfth century onwards.

(*c.*) The Mongan group, associated *chronologically* with an Ulster chieftain slain in 615, *topographically* with the extreme North-West of Ireland.

> Mongan is a son of the sea-god Manannan, or a re-birth of Finn son of Cumal. The supernatural character of his birth is ignored by one of his mortal parents; his boyhood is spent with his divine father in Faery; he is a notable wizard and shape-shifter; he loses and recovers his wife (born the same night as he, perhaps of the same divine begetting, in which case she=Arthur's sister with whom he has, un-knowing, incestuous intercourse) by art magic; he has dealings with the fairy folk.

∴ The Mongan legend, as we have seen, is testified to as early as the eighth century (the verse portion of Bran's Voyage). It must have been very popular in Northern Ireland in the ninth to eleventh centuries, but after the twelfth century it disappears almost entirely from Irish story-telling.

It is significant that the latest of the three groups, in so far as the traditional historic date of the hero is concerned, the one also connected, historically, with the least important tribe, by far, also, the least important of the three in its influence upon romantic literature at large, is that which contains the largest proportion of mythical elements and which works those elements into the most connected sequence. Does not this fact justify afresh the view that in proportion as mythic saga is interpenetrated by or assimilates a larger mass of historic fact, whether it be the life-history of an individual or of a race, or the changes in topographical distribution of several races, in so far it sheds or transforms its mythico-romantic elements, which, instead of being the latest, are really the earliest among its constituent parts ?

The facts which have briefly been submitted to the reader will doubtless be held to disprove the theory that any one of these three legendary cycles is the original, and that the similarity between the other two is due to simple copying. Such a theory must necessarily start with the Mongan cycle, which is at once the most archaic and the earliest recorded. It would, I think, pass the wit of man to frame an intelligible account of the process by which fictions, devised to honour an obscure Ulster chieftain, spread into Britain on the one hand, throughout Southern Ireland on the other, and associated themselves with heroes of far greater importance and of an earlier age. In setting forth a different theory I will endeavour to gather up the scattered threads of investigation into the history of the Mongan legend, and to present the main outline of that history in connected form.

Earlier than and underlying the heroic legends of Finn, Arthur, and Mongan, I assume that among the Celtic-speaking inhabitants of these islands, Goidels and Brythons both, there was current the tale of a wonder-child, begotten upon a mortal mother by a supernatural father—reincarnated in him, or transmitting to him supernatural gifts and powers —associated with his father in the rule of that Land of Faery to which he passes after his death. Such a tale would be a natural framework into which to fit the life-story of any famous tribal hero. Identification might arise from, or at least be facilitated by, identity or likeness of name, possibly again by likeness of circumstance. Once the identification was established, the legend would be subject to two sets of influence, one purely romantic, derived from and further developing the mythic basis; the other historic, or quasi-historic, anxious to accommodate the traditional incidents to the known facts of the hero's life. The popular story-teller would discard the historic framework, save a few vague names of persons, places, or battles; the professed antiquary would gloss and rationalise the mythic incidents, torturing them into conformity with the facts known to him. Between these extreme modes, every variety of treatment might be looked for.

This hypothetical *a priori* reconstruction can be amply verified by an impartial examination of the literature which has preserved to us the legends of Finn and Arthur. In both cases we note a constant struggle between romantic tradition and pseudo-historic record. There exists, too, a curious analogy between the legend itself and its life in history and literature: the god animates the mortal, endowing him with strange and mystic powers, with the gift of shape-shifting, bestowing upon him the boon of deathless life in the Land of Youth and Promise : so, too, the ancient myth quickens the record of some mortal hero's story, lifts it above the limits of time and space, endows it with the power of transformation to suit altered conditions of tribal history, bestows upon it the immortality, more surely the attribute of the great heroic romances than, perhaps, of any other creation of man's fancy. How strikingly is this the case with Finn and Arthur, of whom one became the representative of pan-Gaeldom, the other the type and standard-bearer of mediæval Christendom, whilst the tale of their deeds, centuries and centuries after their death, had power to influence alien generations, to originate new growths of artistic emotion and expression. Such, too, might have been the fate of Mongan but for historic circumstances which can, I think, be definitely indicated.

The hero of this mythic romance was known to the Celtic tribes inhabiting North-West Ulster as Mongan.[1] This I assume because the fact that the historic Ulster chieftain, slain in 615, bore this name, seems to have been one of the reasons why he stepped into the shoes of his mythic namesake. There may, of course, have been other reasons, some similarity, for instance, between the life-history of the real Mongan and the familiar legend. Mongan may have been a posthumous child, or a bastard, skulking for his life in youth, winning his chieftainship

---

[1] Mongan is not a real full-name. Like Willie for William, it is a shortened hypocoristic form (of endearment) of a longer compound name, the first element of which was Mong. The second may have been anything, but the only male name beginning with Mong known to me is Mong-find, *lit.* 'white mane,' K. M. A most suitable name for the sea-god's son, and if Mong-find was the original name it is possible that while one element persisted in North Ireland the other (Find) survived in South Ireland.

under circumstances that struck the popular fancy and recalled the older story. We can but conjecture. We can, however, indicate another reason for bringing down the earlier hero from his mythic wonderland and locating him in North-East Ulster at the close of the sixth century. One of the very strongest witnesses to the genuine character of Irish mythic romance and to the passionate hold it had on the imagination of the Irish race is afforded by the repeated efforts to bring the older heroes within the pale of the new faith. Mongan did not escape a tendency, manifested in the case of Conchobor and Cuchulinn, of Cormac and Finn. And with him the legend assumes a peculiarly pregnant and ingenious form. The lord of the old pagan wonderland of delights is sent to the Christian heaven, doubtless to proclaim its vast superiority, whilst testifying to that precognition of the faith among the pagan Irish, which similar legends endeavour to establish. A hero, specially beloved and renowned among the Northern Irish, his guide and safeguard, must be none other than the greatest of North-Irish saints, the best-beloved, too, of the bardic class, Columba of Hy. But Columba's period, the middle of the sixth century, was well known, and a later age, receiving, with naïve credulity, the legend of Mongan's visit to Heaven under Columba's guidance, and seeking to realise it, would naturally cast about among the saints' contemporaries for the hero of the story. A famous Ulster chief, of the same name, whose lifetime partly over-lapped Columba's, who may well have come in contact with the saint in his own youth, whose life-history, as I have hinted, may have vaguely recalled incidents in the accounts of the mythic Mongan, naturally offered himself. The identification once firmly established, the actual life-story

of the historic Mongan became a potent factor in remodelling the legend; the birth-story was definitely associated
with his parents, Fiachna and Caintigern (although it lost
little, if any, of its mythic character), the form in which it
has come down to us being undoubtedly determined by real
events in Fiachna's life; the passing of Mongan into Faery,
on the other hand—which, we can hardly doubt, was an
essential feature in the purely mythic legend—was supplanted
by the actual death-story of the historic Mongan. For some
reason, which will probably always remain unknown to us,
the incursion of a British chieftain resulting in Mongan's
defeat and death at Senlabor in the year 615, strongly
affected the imagination of the Ulster story-tellers. But
save in the historic setting given to the birth-story, save in
the substitution of historic for mythic circumstance in the
death-story, there is but little trace of historic fact in the
Mongan legend as it has come down to us. The bulk of
it is formed by romantic commonplaces, based upon,
developing and remodelling incidents in the original
mythic legend.

How does this view agree with the known facts of the
literary history of the legend? Columba dies in A.D. 592.
Within fifty years of his death the legend of his having
extended his protection to a mythic hero of his own tribe,
to Mongan, lord of the Pagan Elysium, enabling him thereby
to visit the Christian Heaven, obtains currency, and is
noted in the verses of Muru who died in 650. At this time
the identification with the historic Mongan, slain in 615,
had not been thought of. Muru may well have known
the latter, and may, even in his early youth, have known
Columba himself; in any case he almost certainly knew
that the saint predeceased the chief, and could not there-

fore have summoned the latter from the Land of Promise. But within the next fifty years the legend of the meeting of saint and semi-divine hero led to the identification of the latter with the historic Mongan, and the story, as we have it, was called into being. Now we understand why in Bran's Voyage the Mongan episode is introduced at all, and at such disproportionate length. The old importance of Mongan as lord with his divine father in Faery was still vaguely present to the story-teller's mind; the most famous incident, for the story-teller, in Manannan's career was probably his begetting the wonder-child Mongan; a tale wholly concerned with the over-sea Elysium and unconnected with the great heroic cycles could hardly fail to mention both Manannan and his son. But the legend, as Bran's Voyage relates it, has definitely assimilated the historic elements derived from the life-story of the historic Mongan. The process involved may well have taken eighty to a hundred years, so that taking 640 (conjectural date of Muru's verses, which testify to the unhistoricised Mongan legend) as a starting-point, we can hardly place the composition of the verse portion of Bran's Voyage much before 740, a date already assigned, on other grounds, in the first section of this essay.

The foregoing hypothesis likewise accounts, I would maintain, for that connection between Mongan and Finn, apparent even in the scanty remains of the legend that have come down to us, and otherwise inexplicable. This connection is vouched for not only by the purely romantic text which makes Mongan a re-birth of Finn, but by the pseudo-historic notice due to Cinaed ua Hartacain, the leading Irish historian antiquary of the tenth century, which brings into close juxtaposition the deaths of both heroes. Warranted by no other circumstances, historical, geographical, or literary, that we can detect or surmise, this connection, vague and casual as it is, is explicable if we admit an original mythic connection between the two cycles, consisting in the fact that both heroes are largely hypostases of the same semi-divine personage.

In the after-history of the legend we trace that conflict between historic record and romantic convention I have already spoken of. In the stories preserved by the Book of the Dun Cow the romantic side predominates; in the passage of the eleventh to twelfth century annalist the would-be historical point of view is sharply asserted.

As it comes before us, the Mongan legend is essentially North Irish. The mythic hero was in all probability an object of especial veneration to the northern tribes; it is the great saint of the northern race to whom the legend ascribes his reconciliation with the new faith; it is a northern cleric (Muru of Donegal), to whom we owe our knowledge of the legend; it is in the Book of the Dun Cow, that vellum copied in a northern monastery from an earlier compilation of Flann of Monasterboice, the greatest scholar of North Ireland in the early eleventh century, that are preserved the romantic tales concerning the hero. Now for several hundred years the headship of the Irish race was to be found in the north; the head kingship was almost hereditary among the descendants of Niall of the Nine Hostages (*floruit* A.D. 322–404); in so far as any one Irish heroic legend could claim to be the common possession and the great treasure of the whole race, it was the Ulster saga of Conchobor and Cuchulinn. Such was the state of affairs from the end of the fourth to the middle of the tenth century—predominance of the North in the political as in the literary sphere. Then comes a great change. Brian of the Munster Dal-Cais clan wrests the head kingship of Ireland from the O'Neils. The centre of political gravity is shifted from the North to the South. To this political there corresponds, I believe, a literary revolution. The Finn story, which I take to be essentially South Irish, acquired, in addition to the considerable popularity it already enjoyed, official recognition from the bardic class, intent upon pleasing the new holders of power and purse, and gradually superseded the older Ulster cycle as the national Irish heroic saga. Thus whilst the Mongan story, a Northern legend, enjoyed literary favour consequent upon the predominance of North Irish chieftains, it was overshadowed by the superior claims of the great cycle, of which Cuchulinn, *fortissimus heros Scotorum*, was the protagonist; when that predominance ceased it was killed by the competition of the Finn saga, the tribal legend of the new masters of Irish polity, of the new dispensers of literary favour. Such are the historic causes which prevented its attaining the same rank as the kindred legends of Arthur or Finn.

I said *killed*, and the word is hardly excessive, for the Mongan legend ceased to be a formative factor in Irish romance after the twelfth century. Yet, by a lucky accident, an extensive fragment took the fancy of a fourteenth to fifteenth century Irish story-teller, and, rewritten in the taste of the day, has been preserved to us by the scribe of the Book of Fermoy.

The foregoing discussion, unduly long though it may seem, was indispensable. We purpose investigating the nature and origin of certain Irish beliefs and fancies, our evidence for which is largely contained in the scanty extant remains of the Mongan cycle. A clear idea must first be gained of the general position of the cycle in the evolution of Irish mythic romance. It would be presumptuous to speak of proof in regions of research where the facts are alike scanty, obscure, and insufficiently studied as yet, but I have, I trust, succeeded in establishing a strong presumption in favour of the archaic and original character of the Mongan texts. This presumption I base not so much upon the texts themselves, though I firmly believe that to an impartial student the internal evidences of age and authenticity will appear neither few nor light, as upon their relation to other mythico-romantic texts, and upon the way in which they have come down to us. That we have in the Mongan story a local, historicised variant of an older mythic legend, dating back in its present form to the first half of the eighth century, akin to, but neither derived from nor itself the origin of the romantic cycles connected with Finn in Ireland, with Pryderi in Goidelic Britain, with Arthur in Britain, a variant deprived, by well-known historic causes, of expansive and transformative power, and ultimately overshadowed out of existence by the kindred Finn saga —by this theory alone can I explain the appearance, the growth and the decay of the legend in Irish romantic literature.[1]

[1] As use has been made of the verse ascribed to Muru of Donegal, a seventh-century Irish cleric, I must again point out that the language, metrical peculiarities, and style of this little poem, as well as of the numerous poems ascribed to or associated with Columba, among which it is found, do not warrant an earlier date than the thirteenth century. But I must also point out that, although the Muru poem fits admirably into my hypothetical reconstruction of the evolution of the Mongan legend, yet the hypothesis nowise depends upon its being a product,

A firm basis being thus secured for further investigation, we must now proceed to study parallel Irish stories which have come down to us from the pre-eleventh century period. It may be well, however, to briefly review the evidence of the Mongan cycle as to the nature of the re-birth conception.

Supernatural beings (*e.g.* Manannan), themselves deathless, have the power of begetting children with mortal women, of endowing their offspring with supernatural attributes and powers, in especial with that of shape-shifting. Heroes (*e.g.* Finn Mac Cumaill) may, after a lapse of several centuries, be born again into the world, retaining the memory of their past existence.

Both of these *motifs*—divine *cum* mortal parentage, re-

even as far as the tradition which it embodies is concerned, of the seventh century. It can be put on one side altogether without affecting the general validity of my argument. *A fortiori* it is quite indifferent to me whether it is, formally, a seventh-century poem or a thirteenth-century pastiche. But I am exceedingly loth to believe that it and the poems among which it is found can be *inventions* of the thirteenth century without any basis of older text or of oral tradition. Why should a thirteenth-century cleric poet have taken the trouble, or where should he have got the idea, of *making up* a legend about Columba and Mongan, and even if this possibility be admitted, *could* he have invented the contents of the legend? There is nothing, as we have seen, in the extant Mongan saga to suggest such an idea or to yield the materials for its embodiment. Such a question must be determined by the balance of probability, and all the probabilities to my mind favour the view that the cleric poet who wrote down in the thirteenth century poems ascribed to Muru and Columba, had before him far older poems the substance of which he reproduced, or was acquainted with a definite oral tradition concerning the relations between Columba and Mongan. I also believe that in ascribing the poem to Muru, the author, whoever he was, followed tradition, and if a tradition existed it seems to me it must be of early date.

birth with memory of past existence—are introduced so casually into the tales that they were evidently either quite familiar to author and hearers, or were retained from a far older mythico-romantic system on account of the traditional sanctity attaching to them.

CHAPTER XIV

IRISH RE-BIRTH LEGENDS

The birth-story of Cuchulinn—The birth-story of Etain—The Begetting of the Two Swineherds ; summary of story, and discussion of its date and nature—Conclusions drawn from these stories—The birth-story of Conall Cernach—The transformations of Tuan mac Cairill—The birth-story of Aed Slane—Comparison of the Irish stories with the Welsh *Hanes Taliessin* ; vindication of the archaic nature of the Taliessin story—Amergin and Taliessin : early Celtic pantheism—Nature of the re-birth conception as found in Celtic romance.

THE stories now to be examined are far from possessing the intrinsic merit of the Voyages to the Otherworld discussed in the first volume. They have engaged the attention of no such original and charming artists as the unknown story-tellers to whom we owe Cuchulinn's Sick-Bed or the Adventures of Teigue Mac Cein. As a rule fragmentary and obscure, the central incident is not infrequently glossed over and rationalised away so that it is difficult at first sight to distinguish its true character. This is notably the case with the Birth-Story of Cuchulinn, the first among these tales to demand notice, from the importance of its hero as from the antiquity of its record. For among the many MSS. that have transmitted it to us one is the Book of the Dun Cow, that oldest Irish vellum, copied at the close of the eleventh century from compilations of the earlier half of the same century.

38

The Birth-Story of Cuchulinn is extant in two versions, neither of which is in its original form, and one of which has come down to us mingled with and distorted by the other. I give each version in outline; where desirable, in full detail.[1]

Version A.—Dechtire, sister of Conchobor, fled one day and, with her, fifty damsels. Neither from the men of Ulster nor from Conchobor did they ask leave. Track nor trace of them was not found for three years, nor was aught heard of them. Then they came in bird guise to the Plain of Emania, and they devoured everything and left no blade of grass standing. Great was the grief of the men of Ulster at this sight. Nine chariots were harnessed to pursue the birds, for 'twas a custom of theirs, bird-hunting. Conchobor was there, and Fergus, Amorgin, and Blai Briugaid, Sencha and Bricriu. The birds flew before them to the south, past Sliab Fuait, etc. Night fell upon the warriors of Ulster; the bird flock vanished; the men of Ulster unharnessed. Fergus set forth in search of shelter and came to a little house. Therein he found a man and a woman who greeted him. Fergus asked for food, but was not given any because his comrades were outside. 'Come to this house with thy comrades, and they shall be welcome.' Fergus rejoined his companions and brought them with him, men and chariots, and they went into the house. Then Bricriu went out and heard somewhat, a low plaint. Guided by the noise, he went towards the house he saw before him, a house great, fair, and magnificent. Entering by a door and gazing in, he beheld the master of the house,

---

[1] The story has been edited by Prof. Windisch in the first volume of *Irische Texte*, and translated by M. Louis Duvau, *Rev. Celt.* vol. ix. Cf. also Zimmer, L. U. pp. 420-425.

a young warrior, handsome, of noble mien, who spake to
him thus: 'Come in, Bricriu.' 'For my part,' said the
woman, 'thou art welcome.' 'Why does thy wife greet
me?' said Bricriu. 'It is for her sake that I, too, greet
thee,' [said the woman]. 'Are you missing any one at
Emania?' said the man. 'In truth, yes; fifty damsels
these three years.' 'Would you know them if you saw
them?' 'If I did not, it is only because one may forget
or be doubtful after three years.' 'Try and recognise them,'
said the man, 'the fifty damsels are here; this woman in
my power is their mistress, and she is Dechtire. They it
is in bird shape who came to Emania to lure the men of
Ulster hither.' The woman then gave Bricriu a crimson
mantle with fringes, and he went forth to rejoin his comrades. On his way he bethought him: 'As to these fifty
damsels whom Conchobor is seeking, I shall deceive him
about having found them here.[1] I shall hide that I have
found them, and only speak of the house full of fair women.'
Conchobor asked Bricriu what of his search? 'I came to
a fair and brilliant house, and therein I saw a queen, noble,
gracious, of right royal mien, with fair, curling hair; a
group of women, lovely and well clad; the master of the
house brilliant and generous.' 'He is my vassal,' said
Conchobor, 'he lives on my land; bid his wife come and
sleep with me this night.' But no one save Fergus would
go on this mission. He was welcomed, and the woman
went with him, but she complained to Fergus she was in
travail. Fergus told Conchobor this, and a delay was

---

[1] Read (Windisch, *Ir. Texte*, p. 144, l. 30): 'In cóeca ingen si tra,'
al se, 'testo ar Conchobar, dobér múin n-immi a fagbáil sunn.' As to
the meaning of the phrase dobér múin n-immi, see Stokes, *Rev. Celt.*
xiii. p. 473, s. v. múin.—K. M.

granted her on that account. Then each of the men
of Ulster went to bed with his wife, and all slept. When
they awoke, they saw somewhat, a little child in Conchobor's lap.

[The remainder of this version describes how the Ulster
warriors put forward their claims to act as foster-father to
this child.]

Version B.—The mysterious birds come to ravage the
plain of Emania. Nine cars are harnessed for the pursuit,
in one of which Conchobor takes place with his maiden
sister, Dechtire, who serves as his charioteer. Among the
other warriors are Conall Cernach, Fergus, Loegaire the
Victorious, Celtchar, and Bricriu.[1] Full of beauty was the
bird flock and their song. They sang as they were flying.
Nine times twenty were they, linked two and two by silver
chains ; at the head of each group of twenty flew two birds
of noble plumage, linked by a chain of red gold. These
birds flew apart till nightfall, preceding the hunters to the
end of the land. Night fell upon the men of Ulster, and
thick snow fell. Conchobor bade his men seek shelter.
Conall Cernach and Bricriu find a new house. Entering
they see a man and woman, who greet them. Returning to
their comrades, Bricriu declared it was beneath them to go
into the house, where they would find neither clothing nor
food. Yet they went in, and took their chariots with them.
*And hardly were they in the house with their chariots, and
their horses, and their arms, but there came to them all manner
of good things, meats known and unknown, so that they never*

[1] The redaction of this version is probably later than that of Version
A in so far as the list of Conchobor's companions is concerned. Conall,
Loegaire, and Celtchar are 'common form' in the more highly-developed
texts of the cycle.

had a better night.[1] The master of the house then told the
men of Ulster that his wife was in travail. Dechtire went
to her, and she gave birth to a son. At the door of the
house was a mare which gave birth to two foals. The men
of Ulster took the child. The father gave him the two
foals. Dechtire brought him up. In the morning, house
and birds had vanished, and the warriors found themselves
in the east of the land. They returned to Emania, taking
with them the child, the mare, and the two foals. The
child grew up and, falling ill, died. Great was Dechtire's
grief. On her return from burying him she asked for drink
in a vessel of brass. Drink was brought her. As she
raised the vessel to her lips she felt a little beast come
with it, and she drank it in. She slept afterwards, and
at night she saw somewhat, a man neared her and spake
unto her, telling her she was with child by him. He
it was who had carried her off with her companions,
he had led them in the shape of birds. He was the
child she had reared; now he was about to enter her
womb, and would take the name of Sĕtanta. He was
Lug, son of Ethne.

[The version then tells how the men of Ulster were
shocked at Dechtire's pregnancy, thinking the father must
be Conchobor, who had done violence to his sister when
drunk. She is married to Sualtam. The child she bears
is named Setanta. The oldest MS. which has preserved
this version, the Book of the Dun Cow, then relates the
strife of the Ulster warriors to foster Setanta, which is also
found in Version A.]

It is evident that we have here three separate accounts

---

[1] This passage is only found in full in the later MS., though it is presupposed by the Book of the Dun Cow text.

of the parentage of Cuchulinn, the greatest of Irish braves. (1.) He is a re-birth of the god Lug, who lures his mother Dechtire to Faery, commits himself as a child to her care, and, when he dies in this shape, passes into her under the form of a little beast which she drinks (Version B). (2.) He is the son of Dechtire and an unnamed lord of Faery, who transforms her into a bird, carries her off to his home, and, after three years, when she is on the point of giving birth, sends her in bird-shape to lure her brother and his chief warriors, to whom the child, when born, is committed (Version A). (3.) He is the son of Dechtire and Conchobor. This account is implied in the definite statement of Version B, that the men of Ulster suspected Conchobor.

It is furthermore evident that neither version has come down to us in an original form. Notably Version B, as we have it, presupposes Version A in Lug's statement to Dechtire that he had carried her off with her companions in the shape of birds, whereas, according to existing texts, he had done nothing of the kind. I have given Version A. in sufficient fulness to be spared the need of pointing the traces, obvious to the careful reader, of abridgment and contamination.

If now we turn to the MS. tradition of the story we gain valuable hints as to the age and nature of the incidents it relates, and concerning the way in which Irish mythic romance has been transmitted to us. Version A is found in a fifteenth century MS., Eg. 1782. Version B is likewise found in this MS. and *also* in the Book of the Dun Cow, which further, as already pointed out, contains the strife of the Ulster warriors over Cuchulinn's fostering, found in Version A. In the Eg. form of Version B it is missing.

If we compare that portion of Version B common to the fifteenth century MS., Eg. 1782, and to the eleventh century MS., the Book of the Dun Cow, we find that the fifteenth century text is much superior. Not only does it contain details, barely indicated or slurred over by the eleventh century text, but in many passages it has preserved what is obviously the true reading where the Book of the Dun Cow text has been corrupted by transpositions or other scribal errors. Finally, as we have seen, Version A (only known to us from a fifteenth century MS.) is presupposed by Version B, found, in a corrupt form, in an eleventh century MS.

I have dwelt upon these facts at some length, as they afford an admirable instance of truths always to be borne in mind when studying mediæval Irish literature. The date of the MS. affords no certain clue (save as a *terminus ad quem*) to the age of the text which it may contain. The oldest MS. may yield a text substantially younger than that of MSS. centuries later in date. The absence of a text from the older MSS. affords no decided, or even strong, presumption against its possible antiquity.

Having thus cleared the ground for a consideration of the versions upon their merits instead of upon their nominal date, we may form some idea of the evolution of the legend as it offers itself to us in extant Irish literature. Of the three forms of the birth-story presupposed by our texts it is by no means certain that the one which ascribes Cuchulinn's birth to incest between Conchobor and Dechtire is necessarily the youngest. The existence of a parallel incident in the allied heroic legends of Arthur and of Siegfried testifies clearly to a mythic original for a trait now existing only in heroic guise. The mythic prototypes

of Conchobor and Dechtire doubtless belonged to a stage
of thought in which the horror, felt at a later date, for
incest was wholly missing.

The Irish heroic sagas assumed their present shape under
certain definite historical and social conditions. Prominent
among these is the personality of the men who composed
or transmitted them. Roughly speaking, these sagas may be
described as a compromise between the views of three classes,
(1) the official bard or story-teller, with his natural love for the
romantic, his natural tendency to retain and magnify that
which gave colour and animation to his story—(2) the official
historian or antiquary, intent upon preserving or inventing
the title-deeds of his clan in tradition, desirous of rationalising the mythic and romantic elements, of assigning a fixed
date, a definite historical action to the vague and shadowy
figures of old-time kings and heroes—and, finally, the compiler, generally a monk, who copied the tales, and may well
have exercised no inconsiderable amount of editorial supervision. The incest form, as it may be called, of Cuchulinn's
birth-story would appeal far less to the first class than either
of the rival versions, involving, as these did, the welcome
machinery of the lords of Faery, and would be profoundly
repugnant to the third class, the Christian compilers and
scribes. To the second class alone would it be welcome
as wearing, apparently, a more historic aspect than either
of the other forms. But at an early stage in the growth of
the Cuchulinn saga a euhemeristic version, which made
him a son of the Ulster chief, Sualtam, became current,
and effectually rivalled any popularity the incest form might
have enjoyed among the learned class. Thus discarded
by the antiquaries, indifferent to the bards, repugnant to
the monks, the incest form had little chance of surviving,

and, as a matter of fact, has barely more than survived. The other two, the abduction and re-incarnation forms, as they may be called, have been more fortunate, though here, as elsewhere in the Cuchulinn saga, the pronounced historic character impressed upon the saga as a whole has tended to obscure or minimise the mythic constituents. Both versions probably enjoyed equal favour, they influenced each other mutually, and at some date we cannot now fix, but which cannot be later than the late tenth century, the fostering strife was added to Version A, which assumed the form represented by the fifteenth century MS., Eg. 1782. Early in the eleventh century a maladroit fusion was made between this Version A and Version B, and the result was copied into the Book of the Dun Cow at the close of the eleventh century.   A purer text of Version B continued to be copied and is now found in Eg. 1782.

These simple facts in the literary history of Cuchulinn's birth-story warrant, I submit, the conclusion that it is no mediæval resetting of a romantic *motif*, but yields the fragmentary, distorted, and obscure remains of a pre-mediæval legend, of at least equal antiquity with the oldest form of the Mongan story.   It is significant to note that the personages are already familiar to us from the Happy Otherworld stories.   Lug, as Lord of Faery, perhaps the earliest ruler of of that domain supplanted later by Manannan, we have already met; whilst Cuchulinn, as we know, went to Faery at the request of Fann, Manannan's Queen.   The attributes of Lug's palace in Version A (for though unnamed there can be no doubt as to his identity) are the same as in other stories: the inexhaustible store of riches and dainties, the property of sudden appearance and equally sudden disappearance, whilst the shape into which

Lug transforms Dechtire and her companions recalls that
assumed by Fann and Liban in Cuchulinn's Sick - Bed.
But Version A only records the love of a supernatural
being for a mortal maiden.   Version B, the really interesting one as far as the present investigation is concerned,
exhibits clearly the re-incarnation process as conceived by
the early Irish story-teller.   It is purely mechanical; the
god lives again as the mortal after duly submitting himself
to the conditions incident to mortal birth.   Whether the
story-teller thought of him as losing his divine identity is
impossible to decide, the fact that Lug figures at a later
stage of the Cuchulinn saga, and remains a prominent
personage throughout Irish mythic romance, having of
course no bearing upon this particular point.   Nor is the
significance of the curious incident of the god's appearance
as the foster-child of his destined mother-wife apparent at
first sight.   So fragmentary is the record that it seems
unsafe to ask from it more than the bare fact of the ancient
Irish belief in the possibility of a god being swallowed as
an animal by a mortal maiden and born in the ordinary
course of nature as a mortal hero.

THE ETAIN BIRTH-STORY.

The personages of the story I now propose citing are also
familiar to us from the first volume. I there quoted (p. 176)
from the *Tochmarc Etaine* (Wooing of Etain) Mider's
ardent appeal to Etain, describing in such vivid colours
the delights of the Happy Otherworld. At the time it
was only necessary to point out that the *Tochmarc Etaine*
involved the conception of re-birth, but to rightly appreciate
the light it throws upon the subject a full summary of at

least a portion of its contents must be given.[1] The drama
of Etain's fortunes comprises three acts, clearly defined not
only by the structure of the legend, but also by the way in
which it has come down to us in the MSS.

(**A**). Etain Echraide, daughter of Ailill, was wife of Mider,
lord of the *sid* (fairy mound) of Bri Leith. He had another
wife, Fuamnach, and she, being jealous of Etain, drove her
rival forth by aid of the magic spells of the druid Bresal
Etarlaim. A foster-son of Mider, Mac Oc [*i.e.* Angus, son
of the Dagda whom we know already as lord of the Happy
Otherworld in its hollow hill form],[2] received the queen and
tended her with loving care. He placed her in a *grianān*
[the usual signification of this word in Irish romance is:
ladies' bower] with glass sides or windows, and he was
wont to carry her about wherever he went. Tidings of
this reached Fuamnach and further inflamed her jealous
hatred. Bethinking her how she might destroy her rival,
she persuaded Mider and Mac Oc, who were at enmity on
Etain's account, to agree to a meeting for the purpose of
making peace. Whilst Mac Oc was thus absent from his
palace, Fuamnach gained access to it and blew 'in the
same way' on (or under) Etain, casting her forth from her
grianān and whirling her hither and thither throughout
Ireland. At last sucked down by the force of the wind
through the chimney of the Ulster chief, Etar of Inber
Cichmaine, Etain fell into the cup of the chief's wife, was
swallowed by her, and in due course was born as a girl.
'It was one thousand and twelve years from the first
begetting of Etain by Ailill to the last begetting by Etar.'

---

[1] Professor Rhys's summary (Arthurian Legend, 25-28) is intended
to illustrate different points in the story, and does not follow the
chronological order.   [2] Vol. i. p. 211.

She retained her name of Etain and was brought up in great state, surrounded by fifty maidens of her own age, daughters of princes, as her companions. One day, as she and her companions were bathing together, they beheld riding towards them a man of the stateliest aspect. When he reached them he sat down on the bank and sang the following lay, alluding to the scenes through which Etain had already passed, and the wars which would be fought on her account : [1]—

1. So is Etain here to-day
   At the Fair Wives' Mound behind Alba.
   Among little children is her lot
   On the banks of Cichmaine's Inver.

2. It is she that healed the monarch's eye
   From the well of Loch dá Líg ;
   It is she was gulped in the drink
   By Etar's wife in a heavy draught.

3. For her sake the king will chase
   The birds away from Tethba,
   And will drown his chargers twain
   In Loch dá Airbrech's waters.

4. Many great battles will chance
   For thy sake to Echaid of Meath ;
   Ruin will fall upon Faery
   And war on myriads of men.[2]

He ended and vanished, no one knew whither.
   But of Mider and Mac Oc it is told how they met and waited a while for Fuamnach. As she did not come, both suspected treachery. Mac Oc hastened home, and, finding

---

[1] Most of the allusions in this poem can be understood no longer, the stories to which they refer having perished.
[2] Professor Rhys's translation, Arthurian Legend, p. 30.

his *grianán* empty, went in search of Fuamnach, surprised
her with the druid Bresal Etarlaim, and struck off her
head, which he carried home.[1]

The second and third acts of the drama may be noted
more briefly.

B. Eochaid Airem was high king of Ireland what time
Conchobor ruled in Ulster, Curoi in Munster, and Ailill in

---

[1] Professor Zimmer conjectures that the effect of the spells which
Bresal Etarlaim laid upon Etain at Fuamnach's request was to transform her into some kind of insect. Such a transformation undoubtedly
does take place at some time in the story, and it seems more natural
to treat it as the result of the druid's spells rather than as due to
Fuamnach's attack upon her in Mac Oc's palace. Note, too, the
statement that Fuamnach blew upon her rival in the *grianán*, 'in the
same way,' presumably as she had done before, which seems to
indicate that Etain, when driven forth from Mider's palace, was
in a shape capable of being blown away. Mac Oc's *grianán*
would thus be a kind of cage, and the statement that he carried her
about with him in all his journey becomes more intelligible. If it be
objected that his loving care of Etain cannot be accounted for on this
hypothesis, it may be answered that the Mac Oc, the wisest and most
cunning of the Tuatha De, knew some means of counteracting the spell
and restoring Etain to her true shape. It frequently happens in folk-
tales of the bespelling type, which are more than commonly frequent
in Celtic folk-lore, that spells are only valid for a given period of years,
or so long as certain circumstances last. Some such idea may underlie
the extremely confused and fragmentary story of Etain's misfortunes.
Professor Rhys treats the whole from a mythological point of view ; he
regards Mac Oc as a Celtic Zeus, Etain as a dawn goddess, and her
dwelling in the glass *grianán*, which the god carries about him, 'seems
to be a sort of picture of the expanse of the heavens lit up by the light
of the sun.' A last faint reflection of mythical conceptions such as
these may quite possibly be contained in our story. But it may also,
without necessary exclusion of the mythological element, be regarded
as embodying scenes and incidents still found in oral folk-tale tradition,
and persisting therein to this day in a form possibly more archaic than

Connaught.[1]   He bade the men of Ireland come feast with him, but they refused, as he had no wife.[2]   So he sent messengers through the length and breadth of Ireland to find a wife worthy of him, and the choice fell upon Etain, daughter of Etar.   Now Ailill Aenguba, Eochaid's brother, fell in love with Etain, and for desire of her he wasted away, and no one could heal him.   Eochaid, having to make a kingly circuit throughout Ireland, left his brother in Etain's charge.   Ailill was thereupon emboldened to confess his love, and Etain said it was pity he had been silent so long, as she would gladly have satisfied his desire.

that of either myth or heroic legend, though these were recorded centuries earlier.   For Fuamnach and Etain suggest inevitable com parison with the rival beauties, heroines of the *Schneewitchen* folk-tale, and Etain, secluded within the glass bower, tended by the wizard lord of the wonderland in the hollow hill, recalls *Schneewitchen* in her glass coffin watched over by the dwarves.   In *Folk-Lore*, vol. iii., I have pointed out that the most archaic extant variant of the *Schneewitchen* story is the Gaelic tale 'Gold Queen and Silver Queen,' and that an allied version underlies and is presupposed by the *lai* of Eliduc, composed by Marie de France in the twelfth century.   At the time I overlooked the Etain parallel, which confirms so decisively the views I expressed. The folk-tale of the two queens, one of whom is persecuted by her jealous rival, may safely be regarded as belonging to the very oldest portion of Celtic romance.

[1] This chronological indication affords a good example of the un-certainty of the traditional chronology.   The death of Eochaid Airem is assigned by the Four Masters to the year 110 before the birth of Christ, yet a legend, probably full as early as any part of the annalistic scheme, ascribed the death of Conchobor, Eochaid's contemporary, to his indignation on hearing of the Crucifixion.   The sixteenth century historian, Keating, gets out of the difficulty by imagining a prophetic druid.

[2] The refusal may be conjectured as due to their fearing excessive use of the '*droit du seigneur*' which belonged to the Irish kings.

As soon as he was well she would fix a meeting-place.
But when the time came Ailill slept, no matter how hard
he tried to keep awake. This happened twice, and meanwhile Etain met each time a man in Ailill's shape who did
nothing but bemoan his weakness. The third time she
asked his name, and he told her he was Mider, her husband,
when she was Etain Echraide, parted from her by the
magic arts of Fuamnach and Bresal Etarlaim. He pressed
her to come with him, but she refused to leave the high
king of Ireland for a man whose family and race were
unknown to her. Would she come, if Eochaid allowed it?
Yes, she answered. When she returned home Ailill was
healed of his love-sickness, which had been caused by
Mider.

C. Mider then waylaid Eochaid and induced him to game
with him. Twice Eochaid won, taking great treasure from
Mider the first time, imposing upon him and his folk great
tasks the second time. But the third time Mider won, and
the stake he claimed was his arms about Etain and the
right of a kiss. A month's delay was asked by the king,
and used in assembling his best warriors. On the last day
of the month the palace doors were closed and the warriors,
arms in hand, surrounded the queen. Of a sudden they
were ware of Mider standing in their midst. He claimed
his stake, reminding Eochaid how *he* had paid when he
lost and Etain of her promise to come with him should the
king permit. Then taking his weapons in his left hand, he
grasped Etain in his right arm and kissed her. Hasty was
the rush of the warriors to avenge the insult done the king,
but Mider and Etain rose through the roof, and all the men
of Ireland saw were two swans winging their way to Sid-
ar-Femain. Eochaid and his host hastened in pursuit,

and long after the king was able to storm Mider's fairy palace and win back his wife. But the enmity of the fairy clan clung to his race, and Eochaid's grandson, Conaire, fell a victim to it.

So far the story. Study of the MS. tradition again yields precious clues as to its age and nature. All three sections are found in a fragmentary form in the Book of the Dun Cow, *i.e.* the story as a whole *must* be as old as the early part of the eleventh century. The first part is only found in this, the oldest profane Irish MS.; parts 2 and 3 are found in later MSS. in two forms, one evidently akin to that found in the Book of the Dun Cow but presenting a better text, and a variant form intended to serve as introduction to the famous heroic tale *Togail Bruidne Dá Derga*, the Destruction of Da Derga's fort, which relates the death at the hand of over-sea pirates of Conaire, the grandson, as we have just seen, of Eochaid Airem. This variant form was the one preserved by the Book of Druim Snechta, a famous MS., now lost, from which many texts in the Book of the Dun Cow and the Book of Leinster are taken, and which cannot have been compiled later than the year 1050. Intended solely to explain the enmity of the fairy clan towards Conaire, this version would naturally omit the first portion of the story, and restrict its narrative to those sections in which Conaire's grandfather, Eochaid, played a part; it is probable that the celebrity of the Book of Druim Snechta, the most famous and important of all the eleventh century collections of national hero tales, caused the omission of the first section in all MSS. of the tale, except, by a lucky chance, the Book of the Dun Cow. But it is evident that, although the first section is preserved by this one MS. alone, it is an essential part of the story, and is presupposed by both of the other sections.[1] The compiler of the MS., copied into the Book of the Dun Cow, was in all probability, as has already been stated, Flann Manistrech, the most learned Irish antiquary and historian of his day. He knew and preserved for us the first section, he knew both versions of the other sections, and, according to his wont, essayed to harmonise them, luckily with less skill than he doubtless prided himself upon possessing, so that it has been easy for Professor Zimmer to disentangle the twisted threads, and lay bare his method of compilation.[2] The chronological remark respecting the difference in time between the two births of Etain is probably due to him. He was, like most Irish scholars of the time, passionately interested in chronological computations—indeed, his chief work is an elaborate series of synchronisms between Irish and classic history. As M. d'Arbois de Jubainville has pointed out, the story itself dates from a period long anterior to the artificial system by which the mythology and heroic romance of early Ireland were recast in a pseudo-historic form modelled upon biblical and classic writers. Etain rejects Mider because she does not know his kin and

---

[1] It is a mere accident that the one MS. which does preserve this section should be the oldest Irish profane MS., or that it should be found in one of the 150 fragmentary folios, which are all that remain to us of the Book of the Dun Cow. Had this portion been copied in the fourteenth or fifteenth century, when the Book of the Dun Cow was far more perfect than now, and had the folio of the original been lost, as folios have been lost within the last five centuries, we should only have a fifteenth century instead of an eleventh century warrant for this portion of the tale. Yet the internal evidence in favour of its early character would be precisely the same as now.

[2] See Zimmer, L.U., pp. 585-594.

race.   But by Flann Manistrech's day, nay long before,
the chiefs of the Tuatha de Danann had their genealogies
properly drawn out and their exact date assigned to them
in the pre-Christian annals.   Etain's remark testifies to a
period when the folk of the goddess Danu still retained
their mythical supernatural nature free from the fetters of
date and human circumstance.

The archaic nature, the early record of our story, are thus,
as in the case of Cuchulinn's Birth-Story, testified to by the
way in which the MSS. have transmitted it to us.   We may
use the extant version, dating back as this does to the early
eleventh century, with full confidence that it represents,
substantially, an original centuries older.

The agreement with the Cuchulinn Birth-Story is marked.
The goddess, equally with the god, has the power of being
re-born in mortal shape, and the same expedient for pro-
ducing conception is adopted in both cases.   There seems
to be no power of sex-change, for Lug is re-born as a
boy, Etain as a girl.   The differences are more interesting
than the resemblances.   Etain is apparently limited to one
manifestation of her personality; at least while she figures
on earth as Etar's daughter we hear nothing of her in
Faery as Mider's wife or Mac Oc's beloved.   She seems to
preserve her identity; it is not a different but the same
Etain that Mider loves, whether as a Tuatha de Danann
or an Ulster princess.   It is not quite easy to be sure if
she loses the sense of her identity, if as a mortal she retains
no recollection of her previous divine existence, but I
think this is most probably the case.   Lug, on the other
hand, though re-born in the same manner as Etain, manifests himself in mortal state whilst retaining his own god
personality; he is, if we take the facts of the story, at once

father and son. In his capacity of son and mortal he puts
off his supernatural attributes—the strength, skill and
valour of Cuchulinn, although extra-human, are not superhuman. These differences may be due to the strong historic
character stamped upon the extant Cuchulinn saga, and to
the consequent obliteration or transformation of features,
originally mythic ; but it may testify to belief in the god's
capacity to express himself in a human avatar without in-
terruption or limitation of his divine personality. In the
points just noted both stories differ from the Mongan-
Finn legend, where the Finn personality disappears, lies
dormant for centuries, and then reappears as Mongan
without losing consciousness of identity.

For the rest, Etain and Mider belong, as do Lug and
Manannan, to that class of the Tuatha De which is especially
associated with the Happy Otherworld, and which owns, as
its chief attribute, the power of assuming all forms at will.[1]

---

[1] On p. 51 I pointed out that the first section of the *Tochmarc
Etaine* yields the earliest recorded post-classic European form of the
folk-tale theme : the jealous wife and persecuted rival, which theme
makes its first appearance in general European literature in Marie de
France's *lai* of Eliduc.   The variant version of sections 2 and 3 (*i.e.*
the version which was known to but not followed by the compiler to
whom we owe the MS. copied into the Book of the Dun Cow) figures,
as already stated, as an introduction to the Destruction of Da Derga's
fort, and is, in part, recapitulated in the opening paragraphs of that
famous hero tale, which, in the estimation of the ancient Irish, ranked
only second to the Tain bo Cuailgne.   Now this tale, as I have noted
(*Folklore*, ii. 87), contains the earliest recorded post-classic European
examples of the following folk-tale themes : The Jealous Stepmother
and Exposed Child (Etain is the stepmother) and the Supernatural
Lover in Bird Shape.   This latter theme makes its earliest appearance
in general European literature in Marie de France's *lai* of Yonec.   I
venture to think the significance of these facts indisputable ; they

The foregoing stories are concerned with the fortunes of kings and heroes : they form part of the web of myth, heroic adventure, fantastic romance, and historic reminiscence that go to the making of heroic saga. Our next tale is purely romantic and unconnected, save loosely and artificially, with the great cycles of heroic legend. It is the story entitled, 'The Begetting of the Two Swineherds,' and it has been edited and translated (into German) by Professor E. Windisch (*Irische Texte*, iii. 1) from the fifteenth century MS. Eg. 1782. A shorter form of the story is preserved by the twelfth century MS. the Book of Leinster. Up to a certain point the two versions agree closely, and give the incidents with great fulness, but after a time the Book of Leinster scribe (or the scribe of the older MSS. copied into the Book of Leinster) seems to have tired of his task, and to have merely jotted down the heads of the story. As no English version is accessible, and as the tale is of the greatest interest to students of romance and folk-lore, I propose to give the narrative part almost entire, availing myself of a translation of the Book of Leinster version (kindly made for me by Professor Kuno Meyer) up to the point where it ceases to give the story in full detail, and rendering the latter portion from Professor Windisch's German translation of the Eg. version.

testify to the Celtic character of Marie's work, which indeed can only be denied by those who are ignorant of the subject ; they also testify to a community of romantic incident between the Celts of Ireland and the Celts of Britain and Brittany, from both of which Celtic districts Marie drew her stories; finally, they demonstrate the great antiquity on Celtic soil of types of romantic fiction to which some scholars wish to assign a modern origin. ,

THE BEGETTING OF THE TWO SWINEHERDS.

Book of Leinster Text

Whence is the Begetting of the Swineherds? Not hard,
viz. the swineherd of Ochall Oichni and the swineherd of
Bodb, the latter king of the síd of Munster, the former of
the síd of Connaught. The síd of Bodb, that is Síd ar
Femun.[1] The síd of Ochall is síd Conachar.[2] There was
friendship between the two. They had two swineherds,
called Friuch and Rucht: Friuch was Bodb's swineherd,
and Rucht Ochall's; and there was also friendship between
them, viz. both possessed the lore of paganism, and used
to shape themselves into any shape, as did Mongan, the
son of Fiachna.

The friendship of the two swineherds was of this sort,
viz. when there was mast in Munster, the swineherd from
the north would come with his lean swine to the south;
and *vice versâ*. People tried to make mischief between
them. The men of Connaught said the power of their
swineherd was greater. The men of Munster said theirs
was greater. One year there was great mast in Munster;
the swineherd from the north came southward with his
swine. His comrade bade him welcome. ' They are
hounding us one against the other. These people say thy
power is greater than mine.' 'It is certainly not less,'
said Ochall's swineherd. 'We can test that,' said Bodb's
swineherd. ' I shall hinder thy swine,[3] though they feed on
the mast, they shall not be fat, whilst mine shall.' And
thus it fell out. Then Ochall's swineherd went home with

[1] In the *Tochmarc Etaine* this síd belongs to Mider.
[2] Cruachan, according to Eg.
[3] ' I shall bespell thy swine.'—Eg.

his lean swine; they hardly reached there what with their wretched state. People laughed at him when he reached home. 'Thou wentest in an evil hour,' said they to him; 'thy comrade's power is greater than thine.' 'That is not good,' said he. 'We shall have mast in our turn, and I shall play the same trick on him.' And so it happened. Bodb's swine dwindled away, so that every one said their power was equal on both sides. Bodb's swineherd returned from the north with his lean swine.

Then Bodb took his swineherd's office from him. The man in the north also had his taken from him. Then they were two full years in the shapes of ravens, one year in the north, in Connaught, on Dún Crúachan, another year on Síd ar Femun. There the men of Munster came together on a certain day. 'What a noise the birds are making!' said they; 'for a whole year have they been slanging each other and never ceasing.' While they were saying this, Fuidell mac Fiadmire, the steward of Ochall, came towards them on the hill. They bid him welcome. 'What a noise the birds are making before your eyes! One would think they were the same two birds which we had in the north last year.' Then they saw the two ravens change into human shape, and recognised them for the two swineherds. They bade them welcome. 'It is not right to welcome us,' said Bodb's swineherd; 'there will be many corpses of friends, and great wailing through us two.' 'What has happened to you?' said Bodb. 'Nothing good,' said he. 'Since we went from you, we have been two years in the shape of birds. You have seen what we have done before your eyes. In that wise we were a whole year in Cruachan, another year on Síd ar Femun, and the men from the north and the south have seen the power of both of us.   We shall now go into the shape of water beasts, and be under seas to the end of two other years.' Thereupon one of them went into the Shannon, the other into the Suir, and they were two years under water.   A whole year they were seen in the Suir devouring each other, another year they were seen in the Shannon.

[Up to this point the Book of Leinster version, save for greater concision of style, corresponds closely with that in Eg. 1782.   But from this onwards only the bare facts of the transformations are given.   I therefore quote the remainder from Professor Windisch's translation of the Eg. version.]

One day the men of Connaught had a great gathering at Ednecha, on the Shannon, and there they saw the two beasts, each as big as a mound or the peak of a hill, and they assailed each other so furiously that fiery swords darted out of their jaws and reached to the sky.   The folk came about them from every side.   They came out of the Shannon, and as they touched the shore, lo! before the eyes of all, two men-shapes, and they were known for the two swineherds.   Ochall bade them welcome.   'What were your wanderings?' said he.   'Truly wearisome wanderings our wanderings!   You have seen what we did in your sight.   Two whole years have we been in this wise in seas and waters.   Now we must take fresh shapes, that each may further test his comrade's might.'   And they went each his own way.   Now for another space of time they were two champions.   One took service with Bodb, king of the síd of Munster, the other with the king of síd Nento-fo-hiusce (that is, Fergna).   Every feat of Bodb's men was by the hand of the champion; 'twas the same with his comrade of *Síd Nento*.   The fame of each soon spread throughout Ireland.   None knew whence either came. Bodb went into Connaught, for the men of Connaught had a great gathering at Loch Riach (I omit a long description of the troop he took with him). Never had come a better warrior host, nor shall there come its like to the end of the world. Seven-score women and the same number of children died beholding them. (Bodb and his followers sit upon the men of Connaught, literally, and crush the life out of the most of them; a parley between the two kings winds up with a challenge from Bodb's champion, Rinn.) Then the three Connaughts spake together, and there was found no man among them to go forth against Rinn. ''Tis a shame,' said Ochall; 'our honour is lost.' Then saw they somewhat, a host from the north (I omit a long description of the brilliant appearance of the strangers). When they came the men of Connaught stood up and made place for them, whence the saying, 'until the day of doom Connaught men under the yoke. The tending of the sons of kings and queens, the tending of hounds, such is their lot for ever.' [1]

---

[1] The indignant scribe has here interpolated the following remark : ' This is entirely untrue, for at that time there were no Connaughtmen in the world. For they are of the seed of Fergus MacRoig, and at that time he was not born. 'Tis the men who aforetimes were in the land that is now Connaught that stood up.' This historical gloss dates back in all probability to the common original of both the Book of Leinster and Eg. 1782. It is just the remark that an eleventh century scribe, familiar with the systematisation of Irish legend that had taken place in the previous hundred years, might be expected to make. The value of an interpolation like this is twofold. It proves how carefully the scribe followed his model, even when it outraged his scholarly convictions, and it proves the lateness of the historical scheme in which he believed so firmly. For, as we shall see, our story in its present form can hardly be carried further back than the ninth or eighth century.

(a) The host sits down and welcome is proffered.
'Welcome to you,' said Ochall.   'We have trust,' said
Fergna.   ''Tis pitiful,' said Mainchenn, a druid from
Britain ; 'from now on and for ever, Fergna, when thou
seest a king, thou and thy seed shall lag in his tracks.
Till now thou wast Fergna the Straight, from henceforth
thou shalt be Fergna the Crooked, and yield tribute for thy
kingship for ever.   Where hast thou left thy horses ?'   'On
the plain.'   'There lay before thee land and dominion, but
another came before thee and has chosen them.'   'Who is
that ?' said Fergna.   'Bodb, king of the síd of Munster,'
said he.   As they saw him in the gathering, a score of men
fell dead before him for horror and deadly terror.   In all
the three Connaughts there was found no man to fight
against Rinn.   Then said Faebar, 'I will go against him.'
'Unwelcome tidings,' said Rinn.   Therewith they shocked
against each other, and fought for three days and three
nights.   They smote each other in such wise that their
lungs were visible.   Then they were separated.   Thereafter
they went astray and became two demons, and a third of
the folk died for fright at them.   The next morning they
lay ill, but Bodb took the field afterwards and carried off
a full victory.

(b) Then came two other hosts to the gathering, one
from Leinster, the other from Meath, three times fifty was
the count of each of them, namely, Breg mac Mide and
Lorc mac Maisten.   Leinster's king went to the king of Connaught, Meath's king went to Bodb.   Two heroes each
had fought with one another on the field, and smote each
other so that their lungs became visible.   The hosts rose
up thereafter one against the other, and a battle was fought
between them, and the four kings fell, namely, Lorc and

Breg, and Ochall and Corpre Cromm, king of Dalriada. It was in *Sid Nento-fo-hi-uscib*. Bodb cleanses the battle-field thereafter, and went to his own land, and takes the two champions with him, namely, Rinn and Faebar.[1]

Thereafter they go into the shape of water beasts, that is, the shape of two worms. One went into the spring of Uarán Garad in Connaught, the other in the river Cruind in Ulster.

Once upon a time Medb went from Cruachan to the spring after she had washed her face, a small bronze vessel in her hand that she might wash her hands. She dipped the vessel in the water, and the beast went swiftly into the vessel, and every colour was to be seen upon him. Long she stood beholding it, and the colour of the beast seemed beautiful to her. The water vanished, and the beast

---

[1] I have quoted these two paragraphs in full, as exemplifying the confused and obscure way in which the story is told, as well as the characteristic inclusion of varying accounts of the same episode. For, as will have been noticed at once by the careful reader, paragraph *b* is a different version of the events recorded in paragraph *a*. In the one Munster and Connaught are alone in presence, in the other, Leinster and Meath likewise join in the fray. In both cases Munster remains victorious. Maistiu is a well-known fairy mound, five miles east of Athy in Kildare. Breg mac Mide recalls Mider of Breg Leith (Etain's husband) whose fairy palace was at Mag Breg. The scribe seems to have muddled his information. Corpre the Crooked, King of Dalriada, (*i.e.* North East Ulster) in the paragraph *b* version seems to correspond to Fergna the Crooked, from the North, in the paragraph *a* version. It should be noted that in the paragraph *a* version Fergna is accompanied by a druid from *Britain* who, as is common in Irish heroic legend, stirs up his masters to action by taunts and foresayings. The historical background of both versions is the same. Munster, aided by Meath, is ranged against the rest of Ireland and comes off victorious.

remained alone in the vessel. 'Pity it is, thou creature,' said the queen, 'that thou dost not speak and tell me somewhat of my fortunes after I have won the sovereignty of Connaught.' 'What wouldst thou soonest ask?' said the beast. 'I would fain know how it is with you in your beast shape?' said she. 'Truly a plagued beast am I, and in every shape have I been.' Then he gave her good counsel. 'Fair as thou art, thou shouldst take to thee a good man to be with thee in thy sway.' 'I have no wish,' said she, 'to take a man of Connaught, to have the upper hand of me.' 'We know a man for thee, Ailill' (here a lengthy eulogium, which I omit). The beast added, 'Food shall come to me from thee every day, to this spring. Crunniuc is my name.' Medb went home, and the beast went back into the spring.

That very day Fiachna mac Dare went to the river Cruinn in Cualgne. As he was washing his hands he saw somewhat, a beast on a stone before him, and no colour but was on it. ''Tis well so, Fiachna,' said the beast. Fiachna was frightened, and stepped back a little. 'Don't run away or be frightened; it will be better for thee to speak with me.' 'What have we to say to each other?' said the king. 'That thou art a lucky man and shalt find a ship full of treasures in thy land.' 'After that,' said Fiachna. 'House me and treat me well,' said the beast. 'How can I treat you well?' 'Give me food.' 'Why should I, you are only a beast?' said Fiachna. 'In reality I am a man, Bodb's swineherd.' 'Thy name?' 'Tummuc.' 'We have heard of thee,' said Fiachna. (The story then tells how Fiachna found his treasure, and how he fed Tummuc with his own hand for a year, Medb doing the same by Crunniuc.)

One day Fiachna went to the river. 'Come and talk with me,' said he to the beast. 'Well it is for thee,' said the beast, 'blessing of corn and milk, of sea and land upon thee, for thou hast been very friendly towards me. Now I am looking forward to a great combat with the beast I told thee of last year, that is in Connaught at this time.' 'How may that be?' asked the king. 'Not hard to say; to-morrow one of thy cows shall drink me, whilst one of Medb's shall drink my comrade. Therefrom shall two bulls be born, and there shall be great war in Ireland on our account. Fare thee well.' All came true, as he said.

The names of these beasts in their divers shapes were these: Rucht and Ruccne[1] as swineherds; Ingen and Ette as ravens; Bled and Blod, two sea-beasts; Rinn and Faebar as champions; Crunniuc and Tummuc, two worms; Finn and Dub, two bulls, Whitehorn and Black of Coolney, the finest bulls ever seen in Ireland, their horns were decked with silver and gold by the provinces of Ireland. In Connaught no bull dared bellow before the bull of the West, nor in Ulster did any dare bellow before the bull of the East. *Finis.*

It may be well to give what corresponds in the Book of Leinster to the foregoing pages translated from Eg. 1782. The language is obscure, and Professor Meyer has had to leave several words unrendered.

Again they were two stags, and either of them would gather the . . . of the other so that he made a . . . of the abode of the other.

They were two champions wounding each other.
They were two spectres, either of them terrifying the other.
They were two dragons, either of them beating (?) snow on

---

[1] It will be noticed that these names differ from those assigned to the swineherds in the opening of the story, another instance of the fusion of variant versions.

the land of the other. They dropped down from the air and were two worms. One of them went into the well of Glass Cruind in Cualgne, where a cow of Dáre mac Fiachnai drunk it up ; and the other went into the well of Garad in Connaught, where a cow of Medb and Ailill's drank it, so that from them sprang the two bulls, The Whitehorn Ai and the Dun of Cualgne.

(Their names were) Rucht (Snout) and Rucne, when they were swineherds.

Ingen (Talon) and Eitte (Wing), when they were birds.

Bled (Whale) and Blod, when they were sea-beasts.

Rind (Point) and Faebar (Edge), when they were champions.

Scáth (Shadow) and Scíath, when they were spectres.

Crunniuc and Tunniuc, when they were worms.

The Whitehorn of Ai and the Dun of Cualgne, when they were cattle.

The unprejudiced reader will certainly agree with Professor Windisch that the Book of Leinster scribe, or his model, had before him a complete version, the same, substantially, as that now found in the fifteenth century MS. Eg. 1782. There are, however, slight differences. Thus the Book of Leinster mentions two transformations, into stags and into dragons, unknown to Eg. 1782, but unknown also to the final recapitulation of the legend which it gives itself. A further proof this, if more were needed, that the story, as it stands, embodies accounts drawn from different sources. The loss of the dragon transformation is particularly regrettable. One remembers the fighting dragons of the Brythonic Merlin story. It is of interest to note that the *Dinnshenchas* has preserved the Two Swineherds legend in forms differing from both the Book of Leinster and the Egerton versions. In the *dinnshenchas* of Ath Luain (*Rev. Celt.*, xv. 464) we learn that 'the two swineherds were incarnate in seven shapes, a full year in each of them. And those were Cronn of Agnoman's two sons, named Rucht and Rucne. Ette and Engan (Wing and Talon) were their two names when they were birds. Cu and Cethen were they when wolves. Bled and Blod were they when trout of the Boyne. Crunniuc and Dubmuc when they were worms.' Another *dinnshenchas*, that of Luimnech (*Rev. Celt.*, xv. 452) represents, again, an entirely different form of the story, and is worth quoting in full. 'There was a set meeting between Munster and Connaught, and the two kings brought with them their champions, the two sons of Smuchaill, son of Bacdub. Rind and Faebur were their names. One of the twain placed himself under the safe-guard of Bodb of Síd Femin, the other under that of Ochall of Síd Cruachan. The champions displayed their swineherd's art. To judge between them every one pressed into the stream. Thereupon came the flood-tide, which they had not perceived, and carried off their cloaks.' These variant forms, all witnessed to by pre-eleventh-century texts, show the popularity and wide spread of the story.

The Begetting of the Two Swineherds, for the most part a folk-tale pure and simple—perhaps the earliest noted folk-tale of post-classic European literature—interests us not alone for the striking way in which it presents the re-birth conception, but also for its allusion to the Mongan story. The shape-shifting power possessed by Mongan, son of Fiachna, is especially signalled out as the chief attribute of the swineherds. Alike then for the history of the re-birth conception in Irish literature and for the history of the Mongan legend, it is necessary to date our story as precisely as may be. The date of the Book of Leinster (about 1140) supplies a *terminus ad quem*, and, the version of this

MS. presupposing, as we have seen, an earlier one, it is safe to date it back to the early twelfth century at the very latest. A *terminus a quo*, for the present form of the story, is supplied by the fact that it is formally numbered among the *remscéla*, or introductions, to the *Táin bó Cuailgne*, the Raid for the Kine of Coolney, the greatest of Irish hero tales. For the last transformation of the two swineherds is into the bulls, the cause of the raid and of the wars that ensued. The story runs thus : Medb, the famous Connaught queen, vaunting her possessions as greater than those of her husband, Ailill, is angered by his remark that her cow, Finnbennach, is inferior to the Black of Coolney. She forms the plan of raiding Ulster and carrying off Finnbennach's rival. Assembling the men of Ireland, and taking advantage of the moment when the Ulster warriors are *en couvade*, she invades the land. But Cuchulinn, exempt from the consequences of the curse that weakens his comrades, single-handed holds at bay the forces of Ireland, and gives Conchobor and his warriors the time to recover. Later, Medb succeeds for a while in carrying off the champion bull, but, when brought into Connaught, he attacks and destroys his rival, and returns home.

Now the present text of this heroic romance goes back, *substantially* (for it was interpolated and worked over in succeeding ages), to the early seventh century. The story goes that it had faded from the memory of the bards of Ireland, and that Fergus, Conchobor's uncle, rose from the dead, at the intercession of the saints of Ireland, to tell it to Senchan Torpeist, the chief bard of the day. A version of this story, without any mention of the saints of Ireland, must be as old as the ninth century, as part of it is imbedded in the oldest portion of Cormac's Glossary. The legend allows of but one interpretation. Senchan Torpeist, a perfectly historical personage, was the author of a redaction of the Tain, which supplanted all earlier versions, and the merits of which were so transcendent as to confer upon it the pre-eminence it has enjoyed throughout the entire range of native Irish literature. It became the fashion to attach other stories, originally independent, to the Tain by way of introduction or continuation.

As early as the first quarter of the eleventh century there was an official list of twelve recognised *remscéla*, or introductions, to the Tain, and among these is our story. The idea was an ingenious one, far more so than is the case with many of the other *remscéla*, some of which have very little connection, apparent to the modern reader, with the Tain. To explain the rivalry of the two bulls, they were made *avatars* of the wizard swineherds, the first occasion of whose dissension thus became the ultimate cause of the great war in which perished so many heroes. But the artificial character of the proceeding is obvious. The *Táin bó Cuailgne*, a glorification of Ulster, is the supreme apotheosis of the chief Ulster brave, Cuchulinn, whilst the Begetting of the Two Swineherds, in so far as it involves historical and racial data, sets forth the rivalry of Munster and Connaught and is, in effect, a long factum on Munster's behalf. Never could such a story have been from the outset an integral portion of the .Tain cycle. Yet it easily lent itself to incorporation in a saga, of which the dominant idea was the failure of Connaught and the triumph of Connaught's foe. Skill and consistency are shown by the adapter; it is the Munster swineherd who finally animates the redoubtable Black of Coolney.

The foregoing conclusions are strengthened by examination of the text. There is a marked difference between what may be called the original story and the Ulster continuation intended to fit it into the Tain cycle. The former is meagre, confused, often incoherent; one feels that the narrator cared for little more than the actual sequence of incidents, and that he was at little pains to give life and animation to the narrative—he was only repeating the story of an alien, an indifferent, if not a hostile tribe. The moment the familiar personages of the Tain cycle come upon the scene, the tone changes, precise, animated and appropriate detail replaces the confused hurry of the older part. The few words placed in Medb's mouth reveal at once the proud ambitious woman, who will have no mistress save herself, whose character is so strongly and consistently marked throughout the Tain cycle—whilst Fiachna, the cautious, timid, avaricious kinglet, is presented with equal dramatic skill.

Thus the Begetting of the Two Swineherds, in its present form, is the working up of an older tale, originally South Irish, to fit it into the great Northern cycle of Conchobor and Cuchulinn. Extant, certainly, in the early part of the eleventh, it cannot well be older than the middle or end of the eighth century. I should be disposed to attribute it to the eighth century, to that period of comparative calm before the outbreak of the Viking storm which we may conjecture to have been the golden age of Irish story-telling, rather than to the Irish renaissance period (950-1050) when the land was recovering from the Viking invasions and reconstituting its ancient mythic and heroic literature.

If these conclusions are valid, there is little weight to be attached to the Mongan reference. It may have been added any time between the composition of the story as we

have it and the period, early eleventh century, to which we
can trace back the existing MS. text. Even if it is due, as is
quite possible, to the eighth century Northern story-teller
who drafted the Munster tale into the Northern cycle, it
simply proves that there were extant in his day stories concerning Mongan the shape-shifter, a conclusion we had
already reached upon other grounds.

Of far more importance are the results for the general
history of Irish romantic literature. The Munster tale of
the Two Swineherds must have enjoyed a favour extending
far beyond the limits of its native province, or it would never
have been deemed worthy of annexation and incorporation
in their great heroic cycle by the Northern story-tellers.
We thus get a glimpse, one of the few vouchsafed to us, of
the considerable mass of romantic narrative that must have
existed in the South before the rise of the Munster Brian
family to supreme power, but which has perished owing to
the fact that the chief collections of heroic and mythic
romance were put together at a time when the Northern
kings of the race of Niall were dominant, and attention was
chiefly paid to the Northern cycles.

We are now in a position to utilise the varying elements
of the tale for the history of the re-birth conception. As
regards the actual incarnation incident (the latest portion
of the extant text), it is of precisely the same nature as in
the Cuchulinn and Etain stories—the *persona incarnanda* has
to actually enter the body of the mother and is subject to
her form and to his own sex. Personality may be assumed
to continue—at least we may say that the story-teller regarded
the enmity of the two bulls as due to more than ordinary
bovine rivalry. The earlier part of the tale is more interesting from the possibilities it suggests, and the circle of per-

sonages it involves. Owing to the concision and incoherence of the extant text it is impossible to have a clear idea of the transformation process. All we can be sure of is that the personality subsists in its entirety whatever be the form under which it manifests itself. But the main point is that the masters of the swineherds belong to the Tuatha de Danann, the same clan of divine beings of which Manannan, Mider, and Lug are members. It is apparently owing to their connection with this mysterious wizard folk that the swineherds possess their superhuman attributes.

The Conchobor Birth-Story.

The tales we have just considered, and which belong respectively to what may be called the Northern mythic, the Northern heroic, and the Southern romantic story groups, have this in common, that the incarnation-transformation incident is the pivot upon which the whole turns. But there are a number of stories into which it enters episodically. Thus, one of the varying accounts of King Conchobor's birth introduces it. For to Conchobor, as to Cuchulinn, different fathers are ascribed in heroic romance. One version makes him a son of Cathbad the druid. It would seem at one time to have been considered derogatory either for a king to be the son of any one else but a king, or for such a famous king to be the son of a druid whom the Christian scribes would naturally regard as a representative *par excellence* of paganism. At all events another version attributes to Ness, Cathbad's wife and Conchobor's mother, an intrigue with the Ulster king, Fachtna Fathach, who was thus the hero-king's father. But this very version contains the following incident. After telling how Cathbad had won Ness to wife—he found her bathing and went between her and her dress, and bared his sword over her head and forced her to do his will [1]—the story proceeds: 'At a certain hour of the night thirst fell upon Cathbad. Ness went through the whole fort to seek a drink, but found none. She went to the river Conchobur and strained the water in the cup through her veil, and then brought it to Cathbad. "Let a light be kindled," said he, "that we may see the water." There were two worms in the water. Cathbad bared his sword over the head of the woman with intent to kill her. "Drink thyself," said he, "what thou wouldst have me drink, or thou wilt be killed." Then she drank twice, a worm at either draught. Thereupon she grew pregnant, and some say it was by the worms that she was pregnant. But Fachtna Fathach was the leman of the maiden, and he caused this pregnancy in violation of (the conjugal rights of) Cathbad, the noble druid.' [2]

We may fairly assume that three different accounts of Conchobor's birth were current in the texts that underlie those that have come down to us. (*a*) He was the son of a druid who mastered a damsel from Faery ; this is sub- stantially the version that has survived, probably because it took the fancy of the story-telling class. (*b*) He was the son of a king and the druid's wife ; this is probably a bit of 'historian' rationalism, and has exercised little influence upon the saga. (*c*) He was the son of a god who incar- nated himself in the same way as did Lug and Etain ; this is probably the oldest form, and it may be owing to the fact

---

[1] This looks very like an attenuated form of the theft of the swan- maid's or mermaid's garments, a widely spread incident in mediæval romance and in current folk literature.

[2] Professor Meyer's translation, R.C. vi. p. 178, from a MS. in the Stowe Collection (A.D. 1300).

that the father's name was unknown that Conchobor is
usually described by the matronymic alone, Conchobor
mac Nessa. As the chief hero of the cycle, Cuchulinn, had
a similar birth-story told of him, this probably led, in
Conchobor's case, to its being passed over in favour of the
rival version.

The Conall Cernach Birth-Story.

Conchobor and Cuchulinn are not the only Ulster heroes
of whom the story is told. Conall Cernach, after Cuchulinn the leading Ulster brave, Cuchulinn's comrade and
avenger, owed his birth to the same cause, as we learn from
the *Côir Anmann* (Fitness of Names), an eleventh to twelfth
century Irish compilation which does for the nicknames of
about three hundred noteworthy Irish persons mentioned in
legend what the *Dinnshenchas* does for the names of noteworthy places. It is, in fact, a mediæval Irish Lemprière. To
account for the name Conall it relates as follows : 'Find-
choem, Cathbad's daughter, Amirgen's wife, suffered from
hesitation of offspring so that she bore no children. But a
certain druid met her and said, " If my fee were good, you
should bear a noble son to Amirgen." " Good shall be thy
fee from me." " Come to the well to-morrow," said the
druid, "and I will go with thee." So on the morrow the
twain fare forth to the well, and the druid sang spells and
prophecies over the spring. And he said, "Wash thyself
therewith and thou wilt bring forth a son, and no child will
be less pious than he to his mother's kin—to wit, the Connaughtmen." Then the damsel drank a draught out of the
well, and with the draught she swallowed a worm, and the
worm was in the hand of the boy as he lay in his mother's
womb, and it pierced the hand and consumed it. When

his mother's brother, Cet mac Magach, heard that his sister would bear a child that should slay more than half the men of Connaught, he continued protecting his sister until she should bring forth her boy. The damsel's time came, and she bore a son. Druids came to baptize the child into heathenism, and they sang the heathen baptism over the little child, and they said, " Never shall be born a boy more impious than this one towards the men of Connaught ; not a night shall he be without a Connaughtman's head on his belt." Then Cet drew the little child towards him, and put it under his heel and bruised its neck, but did not break its spinal marrow. Whereupon its mother exclaims to Cet : "Wolfish (*conda*) is the treachery (*fell*) thou workest, O brother ! " " True," says Cet, "let Conall (*Con-feall*) be his name henceforward." And he gave her son back to her. Whence he is called wry-necked Conall.'[1]

No need to emphasise the traces of antiquity in this intensely savage story, notably the protection afforded the pregnant wife by her brother. It seems implied that the child belongs to the mother's kin, and that such an abnormal case as Conall's enmity to his maternal kinsmen is worthy special note. But it is not quite easy to decide whether the birth incident belongs to a very early stage in the evolution of the conception, before any clear distinction was drawn between human and præterhuman, and no necessity was felt for assigning a semi-divine origin to the event, or whether it be not simply the last worn-down form of a commonplace out of which all true significance has faded. I incline to the latter explanation, but I would not bring forward any definite reason for so doing.

[1] Mr. Whitley Stokes' translation, *Irische Texte* (forthcoming volume, quoted from advance sheets kindly lent me by the translator).

THE TRANSFORMATIONS OF TUAN MAC CAIRILL.

All the tales we have hitherto examined have this in common, that, if not anterior (that is a question I will not prejudge at this stage of the inquiry) to the Christian classic learning which has so profoundly modified much in Irish tradition, they are, at all events, substantially unaffected by it. On the contrary, we have seen that the Christian learned gloss or modification is either in direct contradiction to the text into which it has been foisted, or strongly opposed to it in tendency. We now pass to instances where the antique conception was pressed into the service of the alien learning. The chief creation of the latter was the elaborate system of pre-Christian chronology modelled upon and synchronised with that of Biblical and classical antiquity. The mythology, the heroic legends, the genuine historical traditions of the race, were thrown into one melting-pot and transformed into a series of annals reaching back to the Deluge. The main feature of the annalistic scheme is furnished by the so-called invasions of, or immigrations into, Ireland. Much ingenuity has been spent in finding an historic basis for the traditions presented in this form, and this much may be conceded, that memories of the various races that have undoubtedly inhabited Ireland in historic times, and of the various immigrations that have without doubt taken place, may be dimly reflected therein, but when it is remembered that one of these pre-Christian races is that of the Tuatha de Danann, the representatives of an early Gaelic Olympus, it would seem a thankless task to extract *definite* historic record from what is told of them. Now a peculiarity of this highly artificial annalistic scheme is, that each successive race is supposed to have died out or vanished from mortal ken. The question naturally arose, by what means was the knowledge of past races handed down? The answer is supplied by the legend of Tuan mac Cairill, the oldest text of which is preserved by the Book of the Dun Cow (going back therefore to the beginning of the eleventh century at the latest) as a species of preface to the *Lebor Gabála*, or Book of Invasions. I summarise the story from M. d'Arbois de Jubainville's French version (*Cycle Mythologique*, 47 *et seq.*).[1]

St. Finnen is one of the chief saints of sixth-century Ireland. He it was who had the celebrated dispute about a copy of the gospels with Columba, the consequences of which were the battle of Cooldrumma, Columba's exile to Iona and evangelisation of Scottish Pictland, and the ensuing Gaelic settlement in Western Scotland. One day Finnen came to the fort of a pagan warrior, who at first refused him entrance. Finnen had recourse to a practice widely spread in ancient Ireland, and still living in modern Brahminic India; he fasted upon the denier of hospitality. The latter yielded, and Finnen and he became great friends.[2] His name was Tuan, son of Cairell, a man of Ulster. Once he was known as Tuan, son of Starn, the brother of Partholon, the first man who came to Ireland. Finnen is as fond of a tale as Patrick in the Ossianic cycle of legends, and demands immediately the story of all that has passed in Ireland since those days. Tuan pleads for a delay, to be

[1] An edition and translation by Professor Kuno Meyer, of the oldest version of this story, will be found in Appendix A. It will be noticed that it differs in several respects from M. d'Arbois de Jubainville's translation.

[2] As will be seen from Professor Meyer's translation, Tuan is not the same as the warrior who denied the saint hospitality.

employed in studying the new faith of which Finnen has told him, but the saint grants him permission to relate the history of the past, an example which may be commended to modern missionaries. So Tuan relates as follows :—

There had been five immigrations into Ireland up to the present time. Before the Deluge no one came thither, nor after the Deluge until three hundred and twelve years had passed. Then came Partholon and twenty-four companions ; they multiplied until they were five thousand, and then all perished of the plague save Tuan alone. For twenty-two years he was the sole inhabitant of Ireland. Then came Nemed, and by that time Tuan was grey, decrepit, naked, long-haired and clawed. One evening he slept, and awoke on the morrow as a stag, full of youth and vigour. He sang Nemed's coming and his transformation. Now Nemed had come with but eight companions ; they multiplied until they were four hundred and thirty thousand of either sex, and then all perished. By this time Tuan had again reached the extreme limit of age ; again he changed his form for that of a boar, and he sang as follows : ' To-day I am a boar, a king, a mighty one, looking forward to triumph. Once I was in the assembly which gave the judgment of Partholon ; it was sung, and all praised the melody. Full of pleasantness was the chant of my judgment—pleasant to the young women, the very fair ones. My voice was grave and sweet, my step in the battle was swift and firm, my face was full of charm. . . . To-day I am a black boar.' Years passed, and age again overtook Tuan. He returned to his Ulster home, where the change always took place. Meanwhile Semion, son of Stariat, from whom descended the Firbolg and the Galiuin, had occupied Ireland. So Tuan minded him of the forms he had formerly

had. He fasted three days, as was his wont before each
change, and he became a great eagle of the sea. He sang
a song, and proclaimed his trust in the true God. Then
came Beothach, son of Iarbonel, and from him are sprung
the Tuatha de Danann, gods and false gods; they came
probably from the sky, hence their skill and knowledge.
Whilst Tuan was in the shape of an eagle came the last of
the invasions into Ireland, that of Mil and his sons. Then
after a nine days' fast Tuan changed into a salmon, and,
thanks to the protection of God, he escaped all dangers—
the net of the fisherman, the talon of the bird of prey, the
spear of the huntsman. One day, however, he was caught
in a net and brought to the wife of Cairell. He recollected
well how he was roasted on the gridiron, and how Cairell's
wife ate him, so that he passed into her womb, and whilst
there he heard and recollected the talk of the household
concerning the deeds that were done in Ireland at the time.
He grew up and became a prophet, and, after a while, when
Patrick came to Ireland, he was baptized and believed in
God, Creator of all things.

One of the MSS. which have preserved this legend tells us
that Tuan was a hundred years in man's shape, eighty years
as a stag, twenty as a boar, a hundred as an eagle, twenty
as a salmon, so that until his second birth as a man there
elapsed a period of three hundred and twenty years.[1]

---

[1] Dr. Jevons calls my attention to the coincidence between the facts
of this tale and Egyptian transmigration belief as recorded by
Herodotus. I quote B.R.'s racy version : 'The same people were
they that first helde the opinion that the soule of man was immortall,
passing from one body into another by a continuall course, as every
one tooke hys beginning and generation of another, and when it had
passed through all bodyes that have their beeyng eyther in the lande,

To apprehend the full significance of this remarkable tale, and to appreciate at its proper value the evidence it supplies toward reconstituting the history of the re-incarnation conception in Ireland, we must have a definite idea of its nature. I look upon it as a Christian learned utilisation of the incident we have found in a pagan heroic form in the Cuchulinn and Etain cycles, in a pagan romantic form in the story of the Two Swineherds. In other words, it presupposes themes and incidents such as meet us in these tales. If we can date it with any accuracy, we obtain a fresh *terminus ad quem* for dating the earlier stories upon which it is modelled. Now certain Irish antiquaries, not content with tracing the story of their country up to within three hundred and twenty years of the Deluge, must needs bring a daughter of Noah, the Lady Cessair, to Ireland before the Deluge. She had the ingenious idea that, as the world was to be drowned for its sins, could she reach a land, sinless because uninhabited, she might escape. But in this she was mistaken, save as regards one of her companions, Fintan, who was miraculously preserved until the coming of Patrick. This is evidently an extension of the idea contained in the Tuan mac Cairill story, with further insistence upon the biblical and further elimination of the pagan (the transformation) element. As Cessair is mentioned by Eochaid hua Flainn, who died in 984, the legend of which she is the heroine cannot be much younger than the middle of the tenth century, and the Tuan story must be older. In

---

sea, or aire, then consequentlie to returne into the body of man agayne, which course it finished within the course of 3000 yeares.' Dr. Jevons suggests a possibility of influence upon the Irish story. I do not think this likely, quite apart from any question of the knowledge of Herodotus, or a Latin account based upon Herodotus, in Ireland.

its designation of Partholon as the first invader of Ireland it agrees with Nennius, who noted a brief account of the early history of Ireland, certainly derived from Irish sources, in his *Historia Brittonum*, compiled in the early part of the ninth century. It would be unsafe, however, to carry the Tuan legend so far back, especially as the name of his father, Starn, is decidedly Norse, which would seem to indicate that the legend only took shape after the Viking invasions. It is probably a production of the late ninth or early tenth century, and may be regarded as the first attempt to give a rational answer to questions raised by the annalistic scheme; the incident, familiar from heroic legend and the current romantic fiction of the day, of an individual passing through several phases of existence, offered a convenient machinery which was utilised with no little skill. It is possible, indeed, that a pagan story has been taken over bodily, and that only the annalistic framework and Christian details are due to the ninth-tenth century adapter. But I incline rather to look upon it as a new composition upon old lines than as the amplification of an old composition.

In either case, witness is borne to the popularity of the theme in Ireland. Nor do we fail to notice that, however pious be the intent of the narrator, however grave the show of historical learning, the actual machinery of the re-birth is as crude and archaic as in purely pagan stories. It seems, moreover, to be implied that, having once quitted human for animal shape, birth according to the ordinary course of nature was necessary before Tuan could re-assume humanity. The phenomenon of motherhood cannot be overlooked; that of fatherhood may easily escape notice at a certain stage of development. Hence, as may be seen by the

countless examples brought together by Mr. Hartland in
the first volume of his Legend of Perseus, the widespread
occurrence of belief in conception without male intervention. In this respect other Irish stories show the characteristic marks of a very early stage of thought.

In view of the prominence of the re-birth incident in the
Ulster cycles of Conchobor and Cuchulinn, and of Mongan,
the Ulster origin of Tuan and the presence of the story in
the great Ulster MS., the Book of the Dun Cow, are noteworthy. Noteworthy, too, the association of antique legend
with Finnen, Columba's teacher, recalling as it does a like
association of Columba and Mongan.   We are brought
back in this, as in other cases, to the sixth century as the
formative and transformative period when, quickened by
contact with the higher culture of Christianity, Irish heroic
and mythic romance manifested itself in definite literary
form ; we are also brought back to a small group of northern
saints as intermediaries and conciliators between the pagan
lore they loved and the Christian faith they adored.[1]

THE BIRTH-STORY OF AED SLANE.

The next story also has Finnen as one of its chief actors.
It is the well-known birth-story of Aed Slane, high king
of Ireland from 594 to 600. It runs as follows : Once upon
a time there was a great gathering of the Gael in Tailtin.
Diarmaid the king, son of Fergus Cerrbel, was there with
his two wives, Mairend the Bald and Mugain of Munster.
Mugain was jealous of Mairend, and egged on a satirist to

[1] In this connection the likeness of name between Forgoll the poet,
who figures in the Mongan stories, and Dallan Forgaill, Columba's
disciple and panegyrist, may be noted.

make her rival remove the golden crown wherewith the bald one hid her shame. So the satirist craved a boon of the queen, and, being gainsaid, tore the crown from her head. 'God and Ciaran be my aid,' cried the queen, and lo! before a glance could be cast at her, the long, fine wavy golden locks were over the ford of her shoulders, such was the marvellous might of Ciaran. Then, turning to her rival, Mairend said, 'Mayest thou suffer shame for this in the presence of the men of Ireland.' Thereafter Mugain became barren, and she was sad because the king was minded to put her away, and because all the other wives of Diarmaid were fruitful. So she sought help of Finnen, and the cleric blessed water and gave her to drink; and she conceived. But first a lamb made its appearance, then a silver trout, and only at the third trial was Aed Slane born.

This story, preserved by the Book of the Dun Cow, has come down to us in two forms: (*a*) a prose text, abridged above; (*b*) a poem of Flann Manistrech, which omits the rivalry between the queen and merely gives the birth-story. Neither text can be carried back linguistically beyond the early eleventh century; but the date of the form, it must again be stated, does not decide the date of the substance.

If we compare the account of Aed Slane's birth with that of Conall Cernach (*supra*, pp. 74, 75) we find them exactly similar. In either case a barren queen applies to a wizard for offspring. True, in the one case it is a pagan druid, in the other a Christian saint; but both act in the same way. The one sings spells over the water, the other blesses it; the queen drinks and conceives. The chief difference would seem to lie in the superior skill of the pagan over the Christian wizard. I think my readers will agree that the one tale is simply a Christianised version of the other, the details of which have somewhat suffered in the transforming process, or by the contamination of two originally independent stories—that of the jealous queen and that of the miraculous birth. It is possible that in the former the curse of the beshamed queen actually caused her rival to bring forth animals instead of human children, and that this has influenced the other incident. Possible, again, that of Aed Slane, as of his contemporary, Mongan, stories were afloat concerning previous existences of his which, as with Tuan mac Cairill, were passed in animal shape. The story as it stands, wrested to the purposes of Christian symbolism, has departed too widely from its basis to allow of perfectly sure reconstruction.

THE TALIESSIN LEGEND.

I have recited nearly every important instance of the re-birth incident in Irish legend, but before discussing the import of the evidence we have collected it may be well to turn once more to Welsh romance, which has already supplied us with such valuable material for comparison. The story of Taliessin is one of the best-known Welsh tales. Its existing form cannot be traced farther back than the end of the sixteenth or beginning of the seventeenth century ; but its component elements are of immeasurably greater antiquity, as I hope to show beyond possibility of doubt.

There was a man named Tegid Voel, whose dwelling was in the midst of the lake Tegid, and his wife was called Caridwen. Their daughter was the fairest of the world's maidens, but one of their sons, Avagddu, the most ill-favoured man of the world. His mother was grieved at this and resolved, according to the books of Vergil, to boil

a caldron of inspiration and science for him that his reception might be honourable because of his knowledge of the
mysteries of the future state of the world.   A whole year
and a day the caldron was to boil, and Gwion Bach was
set to stir the caldron, and a blind man, Mordu, to kindle
the fire beneath it.   It chanced that one day towards the
end of the year three drops of the charmed liquor flew out
of the caldron and fell on Gwion Bach's finger, which he
put to his mouth and straightway foresaw everything that
was to come, and perceived that his chief care must be to
guard against the wiles of Caridwen.   So he fled in great
fear.   But the caldron burst in two, and when Caridwen,
hastening towards it, saw all her labour lost, she pursued
Gwion.   He saw her, changed into a hare, and fled.   But
she changed herself into a greyhound.   Then he ran to the
river and became a fish ; she, as an otter, chased him until
he was fain to turn himself into a beast of the air.   She, as
a hawk, followed him until, in fear of death, he espied a
heap of winnowed wheat upon the floor and, dropping
among it, turned himself into one of the grains.   She transformed herself into a high-crested black hen and went to
the wheat and scratched it with her feet and found him out
and swallowed him.   And, as the story says, she bore him
nine months, and when she was delivered of him she could
not find it in her heart to kill him by reason of his beauty.
So she exposed him on the sea ; he was rescued by Elphin,
and became Taliessin, prince of the bards.   His after-
adventures do not interest us at present.[1]

The story, as I have said, cannot be traced back beyond
the end of the sixteenth century.   But the transformation-
fight incidents are presupposed by several poems in the

[1] Summarised from Lady Charlotte Guest's translation.

so-called Book of Taliessin, a MS. of the thirteenth century, containing a number of poems, for the most part ascribed to the sixth-century Welsh bard Taliessin, but concerning the real date and nature of which we know very little. It is a collection of pieces of the most diverse character, of which some may go back to the ninth or eighth centuries, whilst others are probably little older than the date at which they were incorporated in the MS. The poems which refer to incidents of the prose tale are those brought together by Mr. Skene in his translation (*Four Ancient Books of Wales*, i. 523 *et seq.*). The chief passage is as follows :—

> ' A second time was I formed,
> I have been a blue salmon ;
> I have been a dog ; I have been a stag ;
> I have been a roebuck on the mountain.
>
> .   .   .   .
>
> I have been a grain discovered
> Which grew upon a hill.
>
> .   .   .   .
>
> A hen received me
> With muddy claws and parting comb,
> I rested nine nights.
> In her womb a child.'

This fact alone should have been sufficient to deter the rash persons who have described the prose story of Taliessin as an eighteenth-century imitation of the Second Calendar in the Arabian Nights. It is obvious that prose and verse relate to the same tradition, obvious also that the verse presupposes a story, the incidents of which were familiar to the poet's hearers. It is to my mind equally evident that the story presupposed by the verse differed in details from the prose one preserved in a solitary late MS. The unprejudiced reader fresh from the consideration of tales such as those of Tuan mac Cairill, and the Two Swineherds cannot fail to recognise in the *Hanes Taliessin* a kindred story involving the same elements, though undoubtedly far younger in actual redaction. This may have taken place at the end of the sixteenth century, the traditional date of Hopkin ap Philip, to whom it is ascribed. But if so, one can only say that Hopkin was a skilful archaiciser. I should be far more inclined to place its composition in the late fourteenth century; it would then correspond in Welsh literature to tales like the Adventures of Teigue mac Cein in Irish literature.

As for the substance of the tale, we may either look upon it as a Welsh adaptation, fitted into the national history, of an Irish romance, in which case it is not likely to be younger . than the twelfth century, after which date Irish literature does not seem to have affected Wales, or treat it as going back to the hypothetical Goidels of Britain ; or, again, as belonging to a fund of mythic romance common to both Goidels and Brythons. There is much that speaks in favour of the second hypothesis—indeed of all the products of Welsh romance the *Hanes Taliessin* is the one that testifies most strongly to community of mythic tradition between the race to which it is due and the Goidels of Ireland. In the first place, Professor Rhys has equated *Telyessin* (a probably more archaic form of the name) son of Gwion with *Ossin* son of Finn. To fully appreciate the force of the parallel we must note that, whilst there is no story which makes Ossin a re-birth of Finn, yet we have a story to the effect that he was born whilst his mother was in animal shape, and we recall that Finn was re-born as Mongan. Thus the philological equation is sustained by some likeness of circumstance between the Irish and Welsh father and son. This likeness is, however, limited to the central conception ; the details are so different that it is entirely out of the question to regard the Taliessin birth-story as a possible loan from the Finn cycle, which, as it has come down to us, contains nothing that could suggest the incidents of the Welsh tale. The equation must therefore date back to a time when elements, which have disappeared from the Finn saga, or have survived casually like Finn's re-birth as Mongan, or Ossin's animal parentage, were far more prominent. As I pointed out fifteen years ago,[1] Finn is the chief Gaelic representative of the Aryan hero whose fortunes have been summed up by J. G. von Hahn as the Aryan Expulsion and Return formula. In this cycle, of which we find examples among every Aryan-speaking race (even among the Romans, who are so un-accountably deficient in other types of mythical narrative), the hero's birth may be mythical as in the case of Perseus, Cuchulinn, or Romulus and Remus, or historical as in the case of Cyrus, Siegfried, Finn, and, in the extant form of the legend, Arthur, though here the mythical incident has survived in an attenuated form. Now Taliessin's birth-story is as marked an example of the mythical form of the incident as can be found within the entire range of the cycle. His after-adventures do not correspond at all to the formula type, whereas those of Finn present it in a singularly complete form. Taliessin, the miraculously con-ceived re-birth of a Welsh equivalent of Finn and of a goddess dwelling beneath the waves (Caridwen's husband lived in the midst of Lake Tegid), that is, of one form of

[1] In my study upon the Aryan Expulsion and Return formula among the Celts, *Folklore Record*, vol. iv.

the Celtic Otherworld, thus takes us back to a stage of the
Finn legend which must have been extremely rich in
mythical incident.   Let us pursue the parallel further.   In
Irish legend Finn's re-birth Mongan, is son of Manannan,
lord of the Happy Otherworld lying beyond the western
waves, and is himself closely connected with that land.
In Welsh legend Finn's (Gwion's) re-birth Taliessin, son of
the Otherworld goddess, Caridwen, is likewise connected
with that mysterious realm.   Thus a remarkable poem,
No. xiv. of the Book of Taliessin,[1] makes the bard utter
the following description of a land we can at once identify
with the domain of Manannan, Lug, or Mider :—

> ' Perfect is my chair in Caer Sidi ;
> Plague and age hurt him not who 's in it,
> They know Manawyddan and Pryderi ;[2]
> Three organs round a fire sing before it,
> And about its points are ocean's streams
> And the abundant well above it—
> Sweeter than white wine the drink in it. '

Another very interesting poem in the same collection
describes an expedition to Annwfn or Hades, made by
Arthur, in which the poet took part.   Mention is made of
a wonderful caldron, the chief treasure of the land :

> ' The head of Hades' caldron—what is it like ?
> A rim it has, with pearls round its border ;
> It boils not a coward's food ; it would not be perjured ;'[3]

---

[1] Skene, ii. p. 274.   I use Professor Rhys's translation, Arthurian
Legend, 301.
[2] *i.e.* Manannan and his son, if I am right in my surmise, *supra*, p. 17.
[3] Professor Rhys's translation in the preface to Messrs. Dent's edition
of the Morte d'Arthur.   *Cf.* Skene, ii. 264.

which recalls the magic goblets of Angus and of Manannan.
The facts I have cited amply warrant the conclusion that
the legends connected with the name of Taliessin, late as
may be the date of their transcription, are substantially
as old as anything extant in Welsh literature, and may be
used with the same confidence with which we use the
parallel Irish legends.[1]

In addition to these poems in the Book of Taliessin, in
which the bard recalls a series of metamorphoses through
which he has passed evidently akin to that by means of
which the flying Gwion seeks to elude the pursuit of the
wrathful goddess of the caldron, there exist others which
claim for him a capacity of metamorphosis more general in
its character.   Thus, in the remarkable poem called *Kat
Godeu*, the Battle of Godeu, Skene, i. 276, the poet sings :

> ' I have been in a multitude of shapes,
> Before I assumed a consistent form.'

[1] In weighing the evidence furnished by Welsh poetry, ascribed to
Taliessin and other early bards, which treats of the same group of
traditions as the Mabinogion, we must bear in mind the essentially
different nature and purpose of the two classes of literature.   The
prose texts are intended to condense the tradition, so that it can be
conveniently memorised by the bard ; the poems are examples of the
use to which he puts this learning.   The more obscure, the more far-
fetched, the more artificially allusive his handling of the traditions, the
greater would seem to have been its merit in the eyes of his contemporaries.   An interesting parallel is furnished by the Skaldic poems,
resting upon and continually presupposing a basis of mythico-heroic tradition, and Snorre's Edda, intended as a handbook to that tradition for
the use of apprentice Skalds.   In the one case as in the other the prose is
a masterpiece of direct story-telling, the verse a masterpiece of perverted
ingenuity.   In either case the simple prose presupposes the artificial
verse, which again presupposes a current oral tradition which cannot
have differed substantially from the far later prose version.

He then enumerates them : a sword, a tear in the air, the dullest of stars, a word among letters, a book, the light of lanterns, an eagle, a coracle in the sea, a drop in a shower, a sword in the grasp of the hand, a shield in battle, a string in a harp, sponge in the fire, wood in the covert. Continuing, the poet alludes in an incomprehensibly obscure style to a number of adventures through which he has passed, and which seem to indicate some such story as that of Tuan mac Cairill, a life prolonged indefinitely, manifesting itself in various shapes and witnessing the passing of various races. Towards the end is a more intelligible passage :—

> ' I have been a speckled snake on the hill,
> I have been a viper in the Llyn.
> I have been a bill-hook crooked that cuts,
> I have been a ferocious spear.'

In face of such a self-identification, not only with forms of life, but with forces and properties of nature, with products of art and craft, the word pantheism naturally suggests itself. Let us glance at an Irish parallel.

When the sons of Mil invaded Ireland, they were led by Mil's son, the poet Amairgen. Setting foot upon the land he was about to conquer, Amairgen burst into song :—

> ' I am the wind which blows o'er the sea ;
> I am the wave of the deep ;
> I am the bull of seven battles ;
> I am the eagle on the rock ;
> I am a tear of the sun ;
> I am the fairest of plants ;
> I am a boar for courage ;
> I am a salmon in the water ;
> I am a lake in the plain ;
> I am the word of knowledge ;

I am the head of the battle-dealing spear ;
I am the god who fashions fire in the head ;[1]
Who spreads light in the gathering on the mountain ?[2]
Who foretells the ages of the moon ?[3]
Who teaches the spot where the sun rests ?'[4]

Amairgen, chief poet of the race which is to conquer the Tuatha de Danann, the lords of Faery, and Taliessin, chief of the Welsh poets, son of the enemy of the goddess of the cauldron, the Welsh counterpart of the Irish Tuatha De, may be regarded as varying forms of one mythic original. Their pretensions are the same, and have the same basis. Foes of the wizard gods who shift their shape, who are invisible at will, who manifest themselves under different forms, they, too, by might of the magic all-compelling chanted spell, have acquired like powers. It has been pointed out by M. d'Arbois de Jubainville, and Professor Rhys agrees with him,[5] that the Irish version has retained a more archaic form of the conception underlying both poems. Amairgen says 'I am,' Taliessin 'I have been.' But what is claimed for the poet is not so much the memory of past existences as the capacity to assume all shapes at will ; this it is which puts him on a level with and enables him to overcome his superhuman adversaries.[6]

[1] Fire = thought.   Of man is understood.
[2] Gloss : Who clears up each question but I ?
[3] Gloss : Who tells you the ages of the moon but I ?
[4] Gloss : Unless it be the poet?
[5] *Cycle Myth.* 246.   *Hibbert Lectures*, 549.
[6] In regard to the date of the poems ascribed to Amairgen it must be noted that they occur in those MSS. of the Lebor Gabála, or Book of Invasions, which give what may be called the second edition of that work, that which makes Cessair the first immigrant into Ireland. The poems are, however, heavily glossed, and it is almost certain that

We have examined all the chief examples of the re-birth theme in Celtic literature which can be decidedly, or quasi-decidedly, assigned to a period earlier than the eleventh century. The most marked characteristic of the theme is its almost invariable association with the Tuatha de Danann, that is, with the gods of ancient Ireland. Lug re-born as Cuchulinn, Etain re-born as Etain, are members of the god clan. Mongan, re-birth of Finn, by one account, is son of Manannan, another member of the god clan, according to another account. Taliessin, re-birth of a Welsh counterpart of Finn, is son of a Welsh goddess akin to the Tuatha De. The Two Swineherds are trusted servants of two kings of the same clan. A feature common to so many forms must be regarded as an essential element of the conception. If this be admitted, we must probably treat certain stories as secondary because they do not contain this feature. Such are the birth-stories of Conall Cernach,[1] of Conchobor,[2] of Aed Slane, the story of Tuan mac Cairill. As regards this latter, the secondary nature of the extant version is obvious—it is a case of a current popular conception being used for a special didactic purpose. As regards the other stories, it is harder to decide; once the Ulster saga cycle had been thoroughly systematised, one might reasonably presume that the special circumstances

they formed part of the original edition of the Lebor Gabála, which, known as it was to the early ninth century Nennius, must be a product of the eighth century at the latest. It is quite possible that the poems are as old substantially as the first coming of the Goidelic Celts to Ireland. For other questions raised by these poems see *infra*.

[1] Though, as already hinted, this may in reality testify to an even earlier stage of the conception.

[2] Though here as surmised *supra*, there may even have been a form of the incident involving god re-birth.

attending the birth of the chief personage of the cycle, Cuchulinn, would be imitated, so that we may have here an instance of a feature common to all mythico-heroic cycles, transference of characteristics from the chief to secondary personages; on the other hand, the greater simplicity of the incident might warrant the surmise of greater age. I believe the former to be the correct explanation. The Aed Slane legend also betrays its secondary nature; it is the annexation, to the profit of a Christian saint, of an originally pagan idea.

Now, the distinguishing trait of the Tuatha de Danann throughout Irish romance, from the most archaic sagas down to tales still current among the peasantry, is their supremacy in magic. It is this which enables them to overcome in their strife with the earlier races that disputed with them the possession of Ireland; if they yield to the sons of Mil it is because these in the person of their poet leader have mastered the all-compelling spell and fight on an equality with their wizard adversaries. Hence the capacity for transformation, for self-manifestation in divers forms, the supreme test of the wizard's art, is assigned to Amairgen; hence Taliessin, in whose complex legend some of the individuality of this ancient arch poet-wizard seems to be represented, has at once like pretensions and is a re-birth. These stories are secondary in this sense, that their heroes would not be characterised as they are had there not previously existed in the Tuatha de Danann an ideal type of achievement to which they must conform; they are primary in so far as the retreat of the divine clan, which can only be effected by their being beaten at their own game, is an integral portion of the mythology.

If association, whether directly or by way of transference

or by contrast, with the Tuatha de Danann be the salient mark of the re-birth conception in Irish mythic legend, that which characterises the forms under which it has been preserved to us is incoherence, lack of precise intelligible presentment. We have to wrest the incident from the sagas of Cuchulinn and Etain and Conchobor; not only too are its outlines blurred, its lines confused, but we note in the literary tradition a tendency to put it on one side, to replace it by other legendary *motifs*; we discern dimly a certain embarrassment in dealing with the theme. By far the clearest and most straightforward handling is that in the Two Swineherds, to be accounted for, if I am right in my surmise, by the fact that it was from the outset a simpler, more popular version of the theme, and that the adaptation necessary to fit it into the Ulster heroic cycle only involved animal and not human re-birth.

A conception, thus, very old in itself, having its roots deep down in an early mythology, a conception which, as it comes before us in Irish romance, is in the act of fading, of replacing significant by insignificant traits, of yielding the field to other conceptions—such, to judge it from the evidence set forth in the preceding pages, is the old Irish conception of re-birth.

If, apart from the dominant element of the conception and the history of the forms in which it is embodied, we consider the machinery by means of which it is expressed, we note the crude materialism of the legends. In commenting upon the story of the Two Swineherds, Professor Windisch says: 'Wenn in der Mongansage Cailte von Mongan sagt dass dieser der wiedergekommene Finn sei, so könnte dies an die buddhistischen Jatakas erinnern, allein die indische Seelenwanderungslehre ist doch wesentlich anders, denn sie ist der systematisierte Causalnexus und umfasst alle Wesen, während in der irischen Sage nur einzelnen Personen, die mythischen Ursprungs sind oder derer sich der Mythus bemächtigt hat, verschiedene Existenzen zugeschrieben werden, und zwar ohne dass dabei die Idee der Vergeltung scharf hervortrete.' This statement, the correctness of which, as far as it goes, I have endeavoured to prove in the foregoing pages, is however not sufficiently precise or restrictive. It is not enough to say that the idea of retribution is not insisted upon in the Irish stories; it is in fact entirely absent from them. It is not enough to point out that the Indian doctrine of soul-transmigration applies to all beings instead of to a favoured few in Ireland; it should be noted that the Irish doctrine, if doctrine it may be called, has no apparent connection with any belief in a soul as distinct from the body, or in a life led by the soul after the death of the body. With the exception of the poems connected with Amairgen and Taliessin, all the forms of the re-birth conception are innocent of metaphysical colouring. In respect of this, as in respect to the Irish Vision of a Happy Otherworld, the impression left on our minds by a pre-liminary survey of the entire mass of mythic romance is that it is the outcome of no religious or philosophical impulse.

Before passing on to inquire if we must regard this belief as belonging to the pagan stratum of Irish thought, or if it must be explained as a loan from Christian classic culture, I must note one chance and casual reference which would seem to indicate how widely it was spread and what profound influence it exercised:

Cuchulinn had reached manhood and was still unmarried.   The warriors of Ulster were doubly uneasy about this.   In the first place, they feared for their wives so long as the irresistible young hero was free, and in the second, they desired that his supreme martial virtues should be perpetuated—they urged the hero to wed because they knew ' that his re-birth would be of himself.'[1]

[1] 'The Wooing of Emer,' Prof. Meyer's translation, *Arch. Review*, i. 70.

CHAPTER XV

The possible influence of Christianity upon the Irish re-birth legends; must be discarded ; the Conall Cernach and Aed Slane birth-stories—The alleged Irish origin of Erigena's pantheism ; must be rejected—The classical statements respecting the Pythagoreanism of the Celts ; their import, value, the historic conditions under which they took shape, the legitimate deductions to be drawn from them—Necessity for studying the Greek conceptions out of which Pythagoras formed his doctrine.

THE leading examples of the re-birth theme in early Irish mythico-romantic literature have now been laid before the reader, and the conclusions which may fairly be drawn from them have been set forth. Searching for analogies for a possible origin, we naturally turn in the first place to Christianity and its doctrines. The central incident of the Christian scheme, the Incarnation, weighty with consequences of such incalculable import, in itself striking, picturesque, and presented, even in the canonical gospels, with sufficient realism to enable its apprehension by the minds of a race in the culture stage of the early Irish, might well be expected to have exercised a profound and far-reaching influence upon their imaginations. There are good reasons, as will presently be seen, not only for dispensing with, but for decisively discarding Christian agency in the formation of these Irish legends. Before adducing them, the problem may profitably be discussed on general

98

grounds. Is it then, or is it not, *likely* that Christian literature should be the source of the stories set forth in the preceding chapters? I italicise the word likely, as likelihood is all we can attain in such an investigation, and whether or not we are held to have attained it depends less upon technical knowledge of Irish or Christian literature than upon considerations of a general common-sense character.

Lest I be taxed with understating the case for Christian influence, I would point out that the canonical writings are of far less importance in this connection than the apocryphal and hagiological literature produced in such profusion during the first six centuries of Christianity. Take the very incident of the Incarnation; the restraint, the dignity, the grace of the Gospel narrative are far from being followed in writings representing the more popular side of Christian teaching. From these, indeed, instances might be cited representing a level of feeling and fancy scarce higher than that of the Irish sagas. The question raised above would probably be met by most investigators with an uncompromising negative if comparison were restricted to the New Testament. The first chapter of St. Matthew is hardly likely to have originated the birth-story of Cuchulinn. But hesitation is legitimate in the face of so many popular Christian texts, all vouched for at a far earlier date than the Irish legends, and for the most part, probably, if not certainly, known in Christian Ireland. Nevertheless, a candid and dispassionate survey of the extant Irish texts, together with due consideration of the way in which they have come down to us, must, I believe, apart from other evidence, lead to the conclusion that the influence of Christianity, if exercised at all, was of the slightest character. In considering the Christian texts we must bear in mind the conclusions forced upon us by study of the Happy Otherworld conception. There, too, we noted scant kinship between the Irish and the canonical Christian account, whereas the points of contact between Ireland and popular Christian literature were many and marked. But this arose, as we saw, from the assimilation by Christianity of older material. The same possibility in the case of the re-birth conception must at least be admitted. It is, however, upon the occurrence of the theme as a whole in Irish legend that I lay stress in arguing against Christian influence. In no case is it found associated with a personage of the national mythology who might be set up as a possible rival to Christ ; there is no hint here, as in certain portions of the Scandinavian mythology—*e.g.* the Balder myth—of a possible loan from the armoury of the alien faith, made with the intent of more effectually combating it. Nor, indeed, does the history of Ireland record any such persistent and conscious struggle between the old and new, the native and foreign faiths, as is known to have been waged in the North. And yet, seeing that association with the members of the pagan Irish pantheon, the Tuatha de Danann, is characteristic of the re-birth theme, opportunity was afforded, had such been desired, for trumping the Christian ace by the elaboration of an Irish divine virgin-born being, who could be successfully opposed to the foreign deity. The entire absence of even the faintest attempt in this direction is to my mind proof conclusive that pagan Ireland did not borrow directly and deliberately from the incoming creed. Again, the confused, fragmentary nature of the traditions themselves, the evident effort revealed by the texts to rationalise or discard

the features of the re-birth theme, point in the same direction.   It is only what might fairly be expected from our
knowledge of the introduction of Christianity into Ireland,
a task achieved with far greater tenderness than elsewhere
for the existing native beliefs, with far greater accommoda-
tion to the social organisation of the race to be converted.
Whether the shamrock incident actually occurred or not,
the story certainly yields a glimpse of the methods by
which Christian dogma was recommended to the native
theologian.   Is it too much to assert that the first Christian
missionaries would probably appeal to the existence of
birth-stories, such as those told of Cuchulinn or Conall, as
evidence for the miraculous birth of Christ?   Later, when
the faith was firmly established, a different feeling would
undoubtedly form itself; stories in any way parallel with
the great mystery of Christianity would come to wear an
uncanny aspect; unconsciously they would tend to be
minimised, to be replaced by other versions.   The orthodox
Irish monk-antiquary of the tenth-eleventh centuries would
doubtless regard such stories much in the same way as does
the orthodox believer of to-day stories of virgin-birth in
the sacred records of other than the Christian religion ; his
attitude would be the same—the least said the soonest
mended.   To this unconscious glossing, rationalising,
eliminating attitude on the part of the class to which,
materially, we owe the preservation of Irish mythic romance,
I attribute the features characterising the texts in which
the re-birth theme is embodied.

In one instance we can test directly the strength of these
general considerations.   The birth-stories of Aed Slane
and of Conall Cernach are beyond doubt variants of one
incident, differentiated solely by the fact that the miracle is

ascribed in the one case to Christian, in the other to pagan agency. The Christian story is probably the older of the two in so far as its present form is concerned ; it was certainly written down, as we have it, not later than the early eleventh century, whereas the other story is part of a compilation probably fifty, possibly a hundred years later. The age of this particular bit of the compilation can only be guessed at, nor is it even known if it was derived from written or oral sources. Thus all the outward conditions are favourable to the thesis of Christian priority. But see to what conclusions this leads. We must imagine a mediæval story-teller, at a period when Ireland had been Christian for centuries, gifted with sufficient critical and historical imagination to adapt a Christian story to a pagan hero by careful elimination of every Christian feature, whilst, as may be seen by a reference to the tale itself, printed *supra*, p. 75, 'to give verisimilitude to a bald and unconvincing narrative,' he artfully inserted casual remarks about pagan baptism. The veriest tiro in mediæval literature knows that this could never have happened, and no candid student who reads the two stories together but will admit the one to be simply a Christian adaptation (the Christian veneer being thin in the extreme) of an incident preserved by the other in a pre-Christian form.

THE PANTHEISM OF ERIGENA.

Before quitting the ground of *a priori* argument, and citing the facts which effectually prove the contention I have been urging, I would glance for a moment at an alleged point of contact between Irish pre-Christian and Christian doctrine. At first blush the point may seem remote from the purpose of this work ; it will be found, however, to stand in unexpected but intimate connection with it.

The ninth century is a decisive turning-point in the history of Western religious thought; it witnessed marked elaboration of dogma, and, in especial, the birth of that philosophy of the schools which was to furnish the intellectual sustenance of Christendom for ages. The chief mover in these great changes, the intellectual giant who dominates the century, was John the Irishman, known as Erigena. In his own age he was vehemently accused of heresy; at a later period he fell under the condemnation of the Church, and works of his were doomed to the public fire. And still the controversy rages whether this condemnation was justified or not, whether Erigena is to be reckoned among the great doctors or the great false teachers. Both sides fortify themselves with citations from his works, nor is it difficult by judicious selection to triumphantly demonstrate either his orthodoxy or his heterodoxy. The reason is apparent when his work is carefully considered. A logician, as acute and subtle as any of the schoolmen, he accepted for his scheme of the universe, a metaphysical basis irreconcilable in reality with the fundamental postulates of Christianity. He strove perpetually to bring the superstructure reared upon this basis into accord with those elements of the faith which, logically, he should have excluded, but to which emotionally and morally he was attached. Hence, at the decisive point of the argument, a frequent stopping short, or the interposition of a supersubtle gloss, by which its essential unorthodoxy may be concealed. In using the latter word I impute no wilful double-dealing. Erigena was clever enough, had he wished it, to convey an impression really clear though apparently obscure. His position, however, though apparently clear, is in reality ambiguous, by reason of his equal allegiance to two mutually exclusive doctrinal schemes. A layman like myself, without dogmatic pre-possessions, can have little doubt that Erigena's opponents were in the right, and that the logical consequences of his philosophy are fatal to the orthodox Christian scheme. His great achievement was to make current in the West the mystic philosophy of the pseudo-Dionysius the Areo-pagite, and his leading Greek commentator, Maximus the Confessor, developing and elaborating the whole into a comprehensive scheme of the universe. But the pseudo-Dionysian writings are in the main Neo-Platonic specula-tions arbitrarily and fancifully interpreted in a Christian sense. The basis of these speculations is pantheistic ; the resulting philosophy of Erigena is likewise pantheistic, strive as he did to evade the consequences of his own reasoning, strive as his apologists may to deny it by insist-ing upon his evasions. Now, as we saw in the last chapter, there exists, both in Irish and Welsh, a body of utterances, ascribed in either case to a magician bard, which certainly wear a pantheistic aspect. M. d'Arbois de Jubainville quotes in his *Cycle Mythologique Irlandais* certain passages from Erigena, and continues :—' Telle est, au neuvième siècle, la doctrine enseignée en France par l'Irlandais Jean Scot. C'est la doctrine que l'épopée mythologique irlandaise met dans la bouche d'Amairgen, quand elle lui fait dire, " Je suis le dieu qui met dans la tête (de l'homme) le feu (de la pensée), je suis la vague de l'océan, je suis le murmure des flots, etc." Le *file*, le savant chez lequel la science, c'est à dire l'idée divine, s'est manifestée, et qui devient ainsi la personification de cette idée, peut, sans orgueil, se proclamer identique à l'être unique et universel dont tous les êtres secondaires ne sont que les apparences ou les manifestations.   Sa propre existence se confond avec celle de ces êtres secondaires.'[1]

Such a conclusion seems to me unwarranted.   There is no necessity for seeking the origin of Erigena's pantheism elsewhere than in his Greek sources.   As a simple matter of fact, the very passages upon which M. d'Arbois relies are definitely connected with the teaching of the Areopagite by his Irish expounder.   Where a cause suffices it is not advisable to cast about for another.   Moreover, I feel by no means sure that M. d'Arbois does not read into the sayings attributed to the spell-mighty soothsayer of the Tuatha De more than they mean.   The question whether they do really embody even the crudest form of a doctrine properly to be styled pantheism is fraught with difficulties. For the present I do not propose to attempt an answer. Again, it is evident that M. d'Arbois begs the question of the age and origin of the Irish-Welsh texts.   So far from being a possible source of Erigena's teaching, they might be claimed as offshoots.   It is possible that M. d'Arbois did not think it worth while to state, much less to refute, a theory which is, indeed, inadmissible, and which I only mention to reject.   Not for one moment can it be admitted that speculations such as Erigena's, cast in an abstract but definitely Christian mould, could originate the sayings ascribed to Amairgen, found in the *Lebor Gabála*, compiled in the eighth, and revised in the late tenth century, or to Taliessin in the Book of Taliessin, many portions of which, so far as their redaction is concerned, must go back to the eleventh century.   It is inconceivable, even if the dates

[1] *Cycle Mythologique*, p. 249.

were more favourable, that the one species of literature could have given rise to the other.[1]

If, then, both hypotheses are to be rejected, that which derives Erigena's pantheism from pre-Christian Irish doctrine, and that which detects in his writings the source of the quasi-pantheistic utterances found in certain Irish and Welsh texts of the early Middle Ages, what remains? Little more, I think, than this: Erigena may possibly have inherited a tendency towards pantheism, or derived it from early hearing of old tales and poems fancifully interpreted by his logical and mystical intellect, and this may have facilitated his reception and advocacy of the pseudo-Dionysian writings.   To speak of an identity of doctrine is to go far beyond what the evidence allows.

But if direct connection be set aside, an indirect connection of an extremely suggestive kind may be hinted at. Erigena founded himself upon a Christian interpretation of the Neo-Platonists, who in their turn worked into their reconstruction of the Platonic scheme many additional elements from those Orphic-Pythagorean doctrines of which Plato himself had made such far-reaching use.   In especial the pantheism associated vaguely and crudely with these doctrines seems to have attracted the Neo-Platonists.

Thus at an early stage of our investigation into the re-birth theme we are brought face to face with that body of Greek belief, half-magical, half-philosophical, at once mystic and realistic, the importance of which came out so prominently in the first section of this essay.   For, as will

[1] A popular account of Erigena by Mr. W. Larminie may be found in the *Contemporary Review*, March 1897.   Mr. Larminie accepts too readily, in my opinion, M. d'Arbois' reference of Erigena's pantheism to Celtic sources.

be recollected, it was through the medium of these doctrines and of the mysteries in which they were embodied that Greek eschatology assumed a shape which Christianity took over with little alteration.

THE CLASSICAL EVIDENCE RESPECTING CELTIC DOCTRINE.

I now proceed to cite the facts which render the hypothesis of Christian origin to account for the re-birth theme in archaic Irish literature unnecessary, nay, which compel us to put it aside as certainly false.

We learn as a rule very little concerning the beliefs of the Celtic races from the Greeks and Latins with whom they came so often and so much in contact. But in regard to this very point we have a comparatively extensive body of testimony to the existence of a belief which reminded the ancients of the Pythagorean doctrine of metempsychosis, or transmigration of souls.

The texts follow in chronological order as far as can be ascertained.[1]

(1) Between 82 and 60 B.C. Alexander Polyhistor wrote a work entitled Pythagoric Symbols. A passage of this lost treatise quoted by Clement of Alexandria [2] is to the effect that Pythagoras was a disciple of the Galatians (the Celts settled in Asia Minor) and the Brahmins.

[1] These texts have been previously discussed by, *inter alios*, Jules Leflocq, *Etudes de Mythologie Celtique*, M. Henri Gaidoz, *Mythologie Gauloise*, and M. d'Arbois de Jubainville, alike in his *Introduction à l'étude de la Littérature Celtique*, and in his *Cycle Mythologique*.

[2] Printed, Mullach, *Frag. Hist. Graec.*, iii. 239.

(2) About 50 B.C. Julius Cæsar wrote as follows about the druids, a name first used by him of the sacerdotal class among the Celtic races inhabiting the present France. After stating that the druids were exempt from military service, that their doctrines were supposed to be derived from Britain, that their instruction was purely oral and lasted in some cases for upwards of twenty years, he continues: 'In primis hoc volunt persuadere, non interire animas, sed ab aliis post mortem transire ad alios, atque hoc maxime ad virtutem excitari putant, metu mortis neglecto. Multa praeterea de sideribus atque de eorum motu, de mundi et terrarum magnitudine, de rerum natura, de deorum immortalium vi ac potestate disputant et juventuti tradunt.'[1]

(3) About 40 B.C. Diodorus of Sicily wrote as follows of the druids: 'Among them the doctrine of Pythagoras had force, namely, that the souls of men are undying, and that after achieving their term of existence they pass into another body. Accordingly, at the burial of the dead, some cast letters, addressed to their departed relatives, upon the funeral pile, under the belief that the dead will read them in the next world.'[2]

(4) The Greek historian Timagenes wrote his History of Gaul during the reign of Augustus, probably about 20 B.C. The original has perished, but Ammianus Marcellinus quotes him to the following effect in a passage describing the origin of Gauls, and the organisation of their learned men in three classes, bards, euhages, and druids: 'Inter eos druides

---

[1] De Bello Gallico, lib. vi. c. xiv.   [2] Book v. ch. 28.

ingeniis celsiores, ut auctoritas Pythagorae decrevit, sodaliciis adstricti consortiis, quaestionibus occult- arum rerum altarumque erecti sunt, et despectantes humana, pronuntiarunt animas immortales.' [1]

(5) Strabo, writing about the year 19 A.D., mentions the studies of the druids both in natural science and in moral philosophy. Popular belief, he says, urged liberality towards them as ensuring abundant har- vests. He adds, that they, like other people, taught the immortality of souls and of the world, but held that fire and water would one day prevail over all things. [2]

(6) Valerius Maximus, writing about the year 20 A.D., thus alludes to the druids: 'Persuasum habuerunt animas hominum immortales esse. Dicerem stultos nisi idem bracati sensissent quod palliatus Pythagoras credidit' (VI. vi. 10). 'They would fain have us believe that the souls of men are immortal. I should be tempted to call these breeches-wearing gentry fools, were not their doctrine the same as that of the mantle-clad Pythagoras.' In the preceding sentence Valerius alludes to a belief likewise noted by Mela: 'Money loans are given to be repaid in the next world, because they hold men's souls to be immortal.'

(7) Pomponius Mela wrote a treatise on geography, which he finished about the year 44 A.D. He speaks as follows of the Gauls and their druids: 'Gentes superbae superstitiosae, aliquando, etiam immanes adeo ut hominem optimam et gratissimam diis

---

[1] Amm. Marc. xv. 9 (Gardthausen's edition, i. p. 69. Gardthausen reads drasidae instead of druides) ; and cf. Mullach, Frag. Hist. Graec. iii. 323.   [2] Strabo, book iv. ch. 4. p. 197.

victimam crederent . . . Habent tamen magistros
sapientiae druidas.   Hi terrae mundique magni-
tudinem et formam, motus coeli ac siderum, et,
quid dii velint, scire profitentur.   Docent multa
nobilissimos gentis clam et diu, vicenis annis, aut
in specu aut in abditis saltibus.   Unum ex his
quae praecipiunt in vulgus effluxit, videlicet ut
forent ad bella meliores, aeternas esse animas,
vitamque alteram ad Manes.'[1]

Mela likewise alludes to the Gaulish custom of
burning the dead, and confirms Valerius Maximus
in regard to the funereal beliefs and practices of the
Celts of his day :—' Business accounts and pay-
ments of debts were passed on to the next world,
and there were some who of their own free-will cast
themselves upon the funeral piles of their relatives,
expecting to live along with them.'[2]   Both Valerius
and Mela are describing the practice and feeling of
a people far more *civilised* than when, one hundred
to one hundred and fifty years previously, it had
attracted the notice of classical observers.

(8) Lucan in the Pharsalia, written about 60-70 A.D., has a

---

[1] Book iii. ch. ii.   At first sight Mela seems to be simply repeating
the statements of Cæsar ; he adds, however, to the latter's account the
fact that in his day the druids had to carry on their teaching secretly.
This is in accordance with historic fact, as we know that from the
time of Tiberius onwards severe laws were passed by the Roman em-
perors against the exercise by the druids of their religion.   If Mela
were simply transcribing Cæsar, we should hardly find this insistence
upon the secret and retired character of druidic teaching.

[2] Itaque cum mortuis cremant ac defodiunt apta viventibus.   Olim
negotiorum ratio etiam et exactio crediti deferebatur ad inferos,
erantque qui in rogos suorum velut una victuri libenter inmitterent.

famous and often quoted passage about the druids,
which Mr. Matthew Arnold has thus rendered: ' To
you only is given knowledge or ignorance, whichever it be, of the gods and the powers of heaven.
From you we learn that the bourne of man's ghost
is not the senseless grave, not the pale realm of the
monarch below; in another world his spirit survives
still; death, if your lore be true, is but the passage
to enduring life.' (*Celtic Literature*, p. 42.)

This version by no means gives the full force of
the Latin.   Lucan says:

> .   .   .   regit idem spiritus artus,
> Orbe alio.   .   .   .   (Pharsalia, i. 455-56)

i.e. the same spirit animates a body in another
world.   It is thus not merely a question of the
spirit's surviving, but of the renewed linking of its
fate with a body.   Thus, as the passage continues:

> longae, canitis si cognita, vitae
> Mors media est,   .   .   .

death is the centre, not the finish, of the round of
life.   The continuation of the passage accounts for
the doctrine in the same way as Cæsar and
Pomponius Mela:

> Certe populi quos despicit Arctos
> Felices errore suo, quos ille timorum
> Maximus haud urget leti metus.   Inde ruendi
> In ferrum mens prona viris, animaèque capaces
> Mortis, et ignavum rediturae parcere vitae.

' Happy the folk upon whom the Bear looks down,
happy in this error, whom of fears the greatest moves

not, the dread of death.   Hence their warrior's
heart hurls them against the steel, hence their ready
welcome of death, for who were coward enough to
grudge a life sure of its return.'

The precise weight to be attached to this evidence re-
quires most careful determination.   In the first place, it
should be noted that two distinct conceptions of what
happens to man, or rather to a special element of the
complex entity man, after death are indicated.   Certain
passages merely note that the belief, familiar to the classic
observers in their own religions, as well as from observation
of barbarous nations other than the Celts, in the existence
of another world in which men lived a life not too dissimilar from the earthly one, was held by the Celts with
peculiar vividness.   Other passages again, in especial that
of Cæsar, definitely formulate a belief in metempsychosis ;
the soul of man, instead of taking up its abode in another
world, remains in this world, but inhabits another body.
These passages, explicit as they seem, can undoubtedly be
explained away ; although they reach us from various
sources, they are in reality, it may be urged, echoes of one
original, due, probably, to the Greek Posidonius, who
travelled in southern Gaul at the beginning of the first
century B.C. ; the guild organisation of the druids (a touch
preserved by Timagenes, who almost certainly used
Posidonius), recalled to him the Pythagorean confrater-
nities, and association of ideas led him to impart a Pythagorean colouring to the druidic beliefs concerning the
other life.   Or again, it may be said that Cæsar's assertion
concerning the druids, 'hoc *volunt* persuadere,' 'they try to
convince men of this,' proves that the doctrine he ascribes

to them does not belong to the Celts at large, but solely to the Druid class. Give their due weight to these considerations, yet I hold that enough remains to show that some form of a belief in metempsychosis and re-birth was current among Celtic races of the Continent in pre-Christian times. Where belief existed, myth may safely be postulated. That the insular Celts shared, to some extent at all events, the beliefs and practices of their continental kinsmen is likely, *a priori*, and is positively asserted by Cæsar.[1] And if we bear in mind the inherent difficulties which beset any attempt to explain the Irish mythic legends by reference to Christian literature, we are forced to the conclusion that they have their roots in a mental state akin to that of the continental Celts as described by classical writers of the century before Christ. If the classical evidence proves nothing else, it surely proves the possibility of Celtic pre-Christian re-birth legends. Whether it does or does not prove more must now be examined.

The more important of the classical texts just cited belong to the hundred years preceding the birth of Christ. Their evidence may be considered from two points of view: that of the Celtic tribes, probably inhabitants of southern Gaul and northern Italy, which formed the subject of Græco-Roman observation, and that of the Græco-Roman beliefs, which were used as a standard by which to roughly characterise the barbarian creed. As regards the first point there is no *prima facie* justification for carrying back the features of Celtic belief disclosed by the texts much beyond the

[1] Cæsar's statement that the druidic doctrine was believed to have been *discovered* in Britain, and thence brought into Gaul (vi. c. xiii.)—Disciplina in Britannia reperta atque in Galliam translata esse existimatur—will be discussed later.

first century B.C.; the classical observers would probably have been incapable of judging, had they even cared to inquire, whether the beliefs they noted were old or recent. As regards the second point, the classical statements must be taken as representing average well-educated Græco-Roman opinion of from 150 to 50 B.C. Now the three most important testimonies, those of Alexander Polyhistor, Diodorus, and Cæsar, indicate, the two first explicitly, the third implicitly, a comparison with the doctrine of Pythagoras. The testimony of Valerius Maximus is partly to the same effect, whilst the reference to Pythagoras by Timagenes may possibly convey the same implication. It thus becomes necessary, in order to appreciate the full force of the classical evidence, not indeed to discuss at this stage the origin and real nature of the Pythagorean system, but to set forth the current opinion concerning it prevalent in well-informed circles of Græco-Roman society during the first and second centuries before Christ.[1]

The Pythagorean doctrine may be briefly described as follows : The soul exists prior to and independent of the body with which it is associated in life. Such association has a penal character; the body is a prison in which the Deity has confined the soul and from which it may not free itself voluntarily. Virtue in this life, and by virtue must be understood the exact following of the rules of conduct laid down by the philosopher, enables the soul, when freed from the body by death, to lead an incorporeal existence in the upper air; vice, on the contrary, leads to further imprisonment in the flesh by re-birth in human or even in

---

[1] In what follows I rely mainly upon Zeller's exposition : *Griechische Philosophie*, i.

animal form, or to the pains of Tartarus. Life as a whole thus wears a probationary aspect, the outcome of which— release from the chains of the flesh, renewed bondage, or damnation to hell—is dependent upon acceptance of a philosophical doctrine and conformity to an ethico-ritualistic rule.

Apart from the more strictly philosophico-religious side of the doctrine, stories were afloat as early as the fourth century B.C. if we accept Diogenes Laertius' ascription of them to Heraclides of Pontus, that Pythagoras proclaimed himself a son of Hermes in a previous existence, and professed to have derived from his divine father the memory of the various forms through which he had passed. The fable that Pythagoras had been present at the siege of Troy in the shape of Euphorbos seems to be older than the time of Heraclides of Pontus, by whom it was amplified into a long series of re-births. Stories such as these were universally popular, and would perhaps occur more readily to the mind of the average man of the world, in thinking of Pythagoras, than the ethical basis of the re-birth doctrine.

Connected with the Pythagorean theory of souls was the doctrine of δαίμονες, beings living partly under the earth, partly occupying the spaces of the air, appearing at times to mankind, conceived of generally as bodiless souls, but also as elemental spirits, and from whom was derived the knowledge of soothsaying and of lustral rites. Heroes would seem to have been counted among the δαίμονες.

Must we accept the classical statements *au pied de la lettre*, and postulate upon their basis a close and far-reaching kinship between the two systems of doctrine—the Pythagorean and that of the southern Gauls? Before doing so we must try and put ourselves back into the mental altitude of the first century Græco-Roman observers, a far from easy task. The Roman mind, quickened by Greek culture, had come into contact with races in a much lower stage of civilisation, occupying widely spread regions. Two modern analogies present themselves, but both are deceptive. In the sixteenth century the peoples of western Europe were brought into new and extensive contact with races far lower in the culture scale; during the last hundred years the careful study of lower by higher races has been pursued with unremitting zeal. But the sixteenth century European, as a rule far less removed, intellectually and artistically, from the native of America or Asia, than was the Greek or Roman from the Celt or German, was hampered with a religion which forbade his taking interest in one side of barbarian life, or wellnigh forced him to take a false view of it. Whilst in our own days a new faculty, practically unknown in classical times, that of critical comparative analysis, has been developed.[1] Thus neither in the full, but prejudiced and uncritical, accounts of sixteenth-century travellers, nor in the critical studies of modern investigators, seeking as they do to indicate differences as well as resemblances, to describe native life from the native instead of from our point of view, can we hope to find parallels to the mode of observing natural to a Posidonius or a Cæsar. They observed *grosso modo* and superficially; they were interested in themselves far more than in the barbarians whose peculiarities they might note,

---

[1] This statement, perhaps too rigid, must be taken as applying more especially to the Græco-*Roman* world. Had Cæsar been accompanied by an Aristotle, our knowledge of our Celtic and Teutonic forefathers would certainly be more precise and detailed.

but they were not likely to be prejudiced by religious or scientific prepossessions.   In so far as they cared to see at all they probably saw accurately and set down concisely.

The classical references to the Pythagoreanism of the Celtic races may thus be looked upon as the traveller's rough indication to his stay-at-home countrymen of a religious phenomenon, the exact particulars of which the one would not have cared to know if the other had cared to note, rather than as the outcome of close and searching study, and they must be interpreted as much in the light of the current anecdotes respecting the Samian sage as by the formal doctrine of the schools.   We must remember, too, that if the attitude of civilised man towards barbarian belief differed in antiquity from that of our times, so equally did the attitude of the barbarian towards the civilised creed. He had neither persecution nor patronage to dread, nor were his crude fancies scrutinised and tested.   It was far easier on both sides to imagine a kinship of belief, and by so imagining to effect a fusion, than it is nowadays.

These considerations may help us in determining the value to be attached to the classical testimonies.   Two extreme cases may be put; the southern Celts simply possessed mythico-romantic legends of much the same character as those found at a later date among the Irish, and classical travellers read into them the features of the philosophical system to which they presented some affinity; or, again, they possessed not alone a mythology, but also an ethico-philosophic system of doctrine really comparable with the Pythagorean.   The truth probàbly lies between these two extremes, but inclining rather towards the latter. Cæsar's testimony demonstrates to my mind the existence of a doctrine of metempsychosis, applicable to men generally, the subject of quasi-religious teaching and possessing an ethical basis. These traits would probably appear to the classical observer a sufficient warrant for the identifying the druidic and Pythagorean systems.[1]

Having admitted some basis of fact in justification of the classical view, we must ask if it is to be accounted for by historical influence of the one system upon the other. This is Maass' view (Orpheus 160[59]). Commenting upon Cæsar's statement he says, 'The astronomical studies (of the druids), as well as their doctrine of metempsychosis, are probably to be laid to the account of the Greek population of Massilia and the neighbouring coast land.' This is an easy way of settling the question. Let us note, however, that if the southern Celts did borrow metempsychosis from Greek believers in Pythagoreanism, they forthwith and utterly transformed the ethical spirit of the doctrine. The Greek philosopher and his disciples said—Be virtuous that you may not be born again; the Gaulish druid said—Be brave (and bravery was probably the chief element in his

---

[1] It matters little in this connection whether Cæsar's remark is the result of personal observation or whether he is simply repeating statements of Posidonius, as has recently been conjectured by an ingenious German afflicted with the current mania for asserting that everything is merely copied from something else. Posidonius, a Greek, a naturalist and a schoolman, was more likely to observe accurately a point of this kind than Cæsar. I have already alluded (*supra*, p. 112) to the possibility, to which my friend Professor Jevons has called my attention, that Posidonius was led into exaggerating the Pythagoreanism of the druidic doctrine because he was struck by certain similarities between Pythagorean and druidic organisation. Had he lived when the quasi-monastic communities of the Pythagorean congregations was a novel and a striking phenomenon in the Hellenic world, I should give more weight to the possibility. In the first century B.C. it strikes me as unlikely in the extreme.

ideal of virtue), because you will be born again.   If the point of view was so entirely different, the reason for borrowing is not apparent.

None the less is it probable that the druids, the learned priestly class, of the southern Celts were considerably influenced by contact with Greek culture, and that the development of features in their own teaching bearing any affinity with that of their Greek neighbours would be conditioned by this influence.   But there must have been germs susceptible of development.   Had the southern Celts, when they became acquainted with Greek learning, lacked a mythology, lacked a theory of the relation of this to the other life, they would hardly, I believe, have borrowed precisely the Pythagorean doctrine of metempsychosis, or, having borrowed, have transformed it in the sense indicated by Cæsar.   Something there must have been, common to both races, which the druids could proudly point to in token of a kinship with the wiser, more learned, more powerful Greek, something which the Greek could note with a half-amused superficial interest as akin to his own speculations.   The points of likeness would be exaggerated, the differences minimised, on the one side from vainglory, on the other from good-humoured indifference, on both from want of the true critical spirit.

I have dwelt upon this aspect of the question at some length, because if it be once admitted that the classical testimonies simply describe the result of a century's contact between southern Celt and Massilian Greek, it would be easy to claim the Irish legends as a further outcome of this influence of the higher Greek upon the lower Celtic culture. They, indeed, would represent its effects, not at first-hand, as in the case of the southern Celts described by Cæsar and by others, but at third, tenth, or possibly twentieth hand. Would not, it may be asked, the higher and more spiritual elements of the original doctrine be gradually but inevitably sloughed off, and the naturalistic elements be rudely and grossly transformed? Here we have, it may be said, a parallel case of development to that which we can observe in the series of pre-Roman British coins, the design of which, originally borrowed from the Macedonian Stater, was gradually rudened and simplified out of recognition.

In deciding how far this analogy is true and valid, we must note the points of difference between the Irish mythico-romantic legends and the doctrines described by Cæsar and others as current throughout southern Gaul in the first century B.C. The former *say* nothing of a theory of souls, nor do they so much as hint at an ethical system deriving its sanction from this theory. They vouch for a belief in the capacity of certain supernatural beings (probably regarded as gods in the ages prior to that in which the stories were written down), to enter into human shape, and either assume a new individuality or reshape their own. Beings partly or wholly human (though the second feature cannot be definitely asserted), can also assume different shapes, or pass through different stages of existence. If the Irish belief, recoverable solely from the legends, lacks the positive doctrinal and ethical features we may fairly ascribe to southern Celtic belief, it is, on the other hand, partly associated with a crude pantheism (in the Amairgen and Taliessin poems), of which the classical observers of southern Celtic belief say no word, and which is conspicuously absent (however prominent it may have been in the Orphicism out of which Pythagoras developed his system), from Pythagoreanism itself. If, then, we assume that the insular Celts were influenced by the latter at second-hand through their continental kinsfolk, we must further assume that they threw back the conception into a mythological stage by eliminating the metaphysical, social, and ethical elements, which gave it character and vitality, and, possibly, that they substituted a fresh metaphysical element, which should be styled panwizardism rather than pantheism—a belief, not in the immanence of deity, so that all shapes are but manifestations of one essence, but in the all-might of the soothsayer and spellwright, who is superior to, can control and overrule the forms in which life, animate or inanimate, manifests itself.

Such a series of assumptions, not very probable in themselves, takes no account of the fact that pre-Christian Irish belief, in all matters concerning the relation of this to the other life, cannot be fairly judged solely on the evidence of the mythico-romantic legends. Early Irish religion must have possessed some ritual, and what, in default of an apter term, must be styled philosophical as well as mythological elements. Practically, the latter alone have come down to us, and that in a romantic rather than in a strictly mythical form. Could we judge Greek religion aright if fragments of Apollodorus or the *Metamorphoses* were all that survived of the literature it inspired?

Considerations such as these suggest several possibilities in connection with the Irish re-birth legends. They may be the mythic expression of a creed which on its ritual and metaphysical side was akin to that of Cæsar's Gauls, or they may be the romantic outcome of contact with an alien higher culture, or, again, they may represent a stage of mythic fancy and thought out of which the southern Celts had partly passed owing to Greek influence, but in which they, and perhaps the Greeks also, must at one time have sojourned.   The validity of these various explanations may be tested in two ways.   Archaic Irish culture must be examined for indications of belief other than those yielded by the romantic legends.   Archaic Greek culture must be examined for possible phases of belief and fancy more closely comparable with those of the Irish sagas than the points of contact noted in classic times between Pythagoreanism and the druidism of the southern Celts.   Should these be found to exist, it will be difficult to resist the conviction that the last of the three explanations suggested above is the correct one.

I propose taking the second way first.   Pythagoreanism is no isolated and underived element of Greek religious growth.   It has its roots in the past of the Hellenic race ; it is a synthesis of far older manifestations of religious fancy.   These must now be investigated.   Should they reveal, as I hope to show, striking points of kinship with the Irish sagas, points in which both differ from the formal Pythagorean doctrine, the task before us will be singularly facilitated.   For if we can reasonably assign the Irish myths to a stage of religious thought and expression known to have existed in archaic Greece, we are entitled to interpret the scanty and obscure hints respecting the non-romantic sides of Irish mythology and religion in the light of the far more abundant evidence preserved by the literary and material monuments of Hellas.

It may be well to briefly recapitulate the steps of the investigation.   The Irish re-birth legends are probably the common property of the Goidels of both Britain and Ireland ; they are certainly pre-Christian in contents and spirit ; they are probably akin to mythical tales which ᴧave existed among the southern Celts, representing, ᴧver, an earlier stage of mythic fancy, unaffected by ᴧtact with late Greek culture; they show traces of a ᴧude pantheism lacking in southern Celtic belief as described by classical writers, and in the Pythagorean system with which that belief was compared.

CHAPTER XVI

AGRICULTURAL RITUAL IN GREECE AND IRELAND

Pythagoras and Orpheus—Orphicism in the Hellenic world—Philosophic
Orphicism insufficient to account for Celtic belief—Ritual Orphicism;
the myth of Zagreus; points of contact between ritual Orphicism and
Celtic belief—Orphic pantheism and Celtic panwizardism—The
origins of Orphicism—Rohde's exposition of the Dionysus cult—
Orgiastic mania the common root of Orphic and Celtic transformation
and reincarnation beliefs—The agricultural origin of the Dionysus
ritual—The existence of agricultural and ritual sacrifice among the
Celts: (a) on the Continent; the priestesses of the Namnites; (b) in
Ireland; the worship at Mag Slecht—The Greek origin of the
Dionysus cult—Both Greeks and Celts have passed through a stage of
agricultural ritual sacrifice, in which the Greek Dionysus and the Irish
Tuatha de Danann mythologies have their root.

It would be foreign to my object to enter into an elaborate
discussion of the relation between the doctrines of Pythagoras and those of his forerunners and contemporaries. I
content myself with citing what Professor Erwin Rohde says
in this connection: 'The teaching of Pythagoras, whilst it
enabled him to weld his followers into a congregation at
once wider and stricter in its organisation than any Orphic
sect, must have coincided in all essential points with
the practical religious side of Orphic theology' (*Psyche*,
452), supported in the main as is this statement by the
authority of Zeller, and exceeded as it is by the contentions
of E. Maass, who, in his *Orpheus: Untersuchungen zur
griechischen römischen altchristlichen Jenseitsdichtung und*

124

Religion (1895), represents the high-water mark of scholarly critical appreciation of the Orphic doctrines. Indeed the brief summary of the Pythagorean system given above might be applied with scarce a change to the Orphic beliefs recognised by the most competent scholars as existing in the middle of the sixth century B.C. at the latest. Orphicism represented the soul as in bondage to the body, a prisoner in its dungeon from which it may not free itself, and from which death itself affords no certain release; for when the soul has quitted the body, wandering free in the upper air, it is breathed again into a new body, and thus, subjected to the 'round of necessity,' to the 'wheel of birth,' it divides its existence between unfettered bodilessness and bondage in human and animal form. From this fate there is but one means of deliverance; participation in the Orphic Dionysiac mysteries enables the initiate 'to step out of the round,' 'to have a respite from woe.' Not his own strength, but the grace of the 'releasing gods' has man to thank for his deliverance. But this grace insists upon the observation of rules, principally ascetic ones. Animal flesh as food is to be shunned; the soul imprisoned in the body in 'expiation' of its 'imperfection,' or rather in 'satisfaction of its debt,'[1] may be kept pure from the contaminating influence of its prison-house by adherence to elaborate rules for the preservation of ritual purity. The Orphic initiates are alone 'the pure ones'; when they die they have little to fear from the dread judgment of Hades; not for them the terrors of Tartarus or the foul horrors of the filth-swamp in

---

[1] The fault or debt on account of which the soul suffers imprisonment is nowhere pointed out. As Rohde remarks (*Psyche*), the effect of this doctrine is to treat life in the flesh as contrary to the true and natural destination of the soul.

which wallow the impure, the uninitiated, but sojourn in the
'fair meadows that lie along deep-flowing Acheron.' Nay,
so great is the power of initiation that, thanks to it, children
may intercede successfully for the 'miserable souls' of their
parents or ancestors, and procure for them cleansing and
remission.

Such are certain features of the doctrine widely spread
throughout the Grecian world in the sixth century B.C., which
appealed to the strong ethical instinct of Pythagoras, and
were definitely systematised by him. The pivot upon which
the doctrine turns is, as the reader will doubtless have noticed,
twofold : dread of the punishments of Hades duplicates the
desire to be released from the chains of carnal existence,
and is in reality inconsistent with it. Older Orphicism
would seem (for definite evidence is lacking) to have
resolved the inconsistency, by regarding the stay in Hades
as purgatorial only, and, possibly, by a quasi-pantheistic
doctrine concerning the ultimate fate of the regenerated
soul, which, released from its 'body-grave' ($\sigma\hat{\omega}\mu\alpha$-$\sigma\hat{\eta}\mu\alpha$),
was to be reabsorbed into the all-embracing Godhead.
Pythagoras, on the other hand, seems to have laid greater
stress upon the metempsychosis side of the doctrine; certain
it is that late antiquity associated his name with it.

Concerning the after-fate of this body of doctrine, which
we must call the Orphic-Pythagorean, denoting thereby at
once the priority of the Orphic and the indissoluble fusion
of both elements, it is sufficient to quote the words of
Maass, 'Platonic philosophy bestowed upon Orphic teaching concerning immortality, new life, fresh spirit, and
complete expression' (*Orpheus*, 171). Plato synthesised,
developed, and transformed the beliefs and fancies of his
predecessors ; since his time they have become an integral

and imperishable portion of man's intellectual and moral patrimony.

Vital, however, as may be the interest and import of Orphicism for the religious and philosophical evolution of humanity, there is little in the foregoing considerations to enlighten us concerning the special points we are investigating. For the side of Orphic doctrine upon which I have dwelt differs so little from the fully-developed Pythagorean system as to yield no clue concerning the possible influence of Greek upon Celtic culture in the three centuries preceding the birth of Christ, or concerning a possible prehistoric community of Greek and Celtic belief. Let us take the first point and ask a question which has not presented itself, so far as I have been able to ascertain, to any of the scholars who have asserted, more or less definitely, the dependence of Celtic upon Greek culture. Why should the Celts, who came into contact with the Græco-Roman world of the western Mediterranean towards the close of the third century B.C., have borrowed precisely the doctrine of metempsychosis? They borrowed much else, it may be answered, if we interpret Cæsar's words in accordance with the probabilities of the case. But even if we admit that all the subjects of druidic study enumerated by Cæsar are loans from Greek culture, still the fact remains that metempsychosis was especially signalled out by classical observers as a characteristic Celtic doctrine. If the Celts borrowed it, they did so on such a large scale that the nature of the borrowed conception remained practically unchanged. Why, I again repeat, should they have borrowed this particular doctrine instead of the many others concerning the nature and destiny of the soul elaborated by Greek philosophy? We must recollect that important as have been the consequences of the Orphic-Pythagorean systems, their direct effect upon Hellenic life was slight, their *direct* effect upon Hellenic thought before 150-100 B.C. but little slighter. Of the great lyric poets, Pindar alone is markedly affected by Orphic doctrine; of the great dramatists, Æschylus and Sophocles are almost entirely uninfluenced; and although Euripides shows decided leaning to Orphicism in many passages, the import of this fact is greatly lessened when the insatiable intellectual and moral curiosity which led him to welcome every form of emotional thought is borne in mind. Even contemporaries of Plato, like the orators, betray in their references to a future life and the destiny of the soul how little the average Greek citizen was affected by the mystic theosophy of the Orphic-Pythagorean sects. After Plato, it is true, the personality and immortality of the soul are integral elements of philosophic speculation, but the schools by no means retained the spiritualist conclusions of Plato.

In regard to all questions connected with the nature and destiny of the soul, post-Platonic speculation is, comparatively, agnostic. It is certainly not impossible for the Celts to have picked up Orphic-Pythagorean doctrines from the Greeks of southern Gaul in the second and first centuries B.C. But it is equally certain that these doctrines had fallen into disrepute at this time among the philosophers, whilst the average man, in so far as his creed was not a mere echoed smattering of the fashionable philosophy of the day, contented himself, in all probability, with obeying the ritual dictates of the traditional religion which the Orphic-Pythagorean movement was designed to supplement and supplant, even if it be not regarded as a definite protest against it.

If the features of Orphicism noted in the foregoing pages neither reveal any *prima facie* reason why the Celts should have borrowed metempsychosis from the Greeks, nor why, if the fact of borrowing be admitted, they should have transformed the ethical basis of the conception, still less do they throw any light upon the Irish re-birth legends. There is as great a gulf fixed between these and the half-religious, half-philosophical doctrine of the Orphic sects, as there is between the elaborate eschatology of Orphicism and the simple sensuous pictures of the Irish land of women and everlasting youth. There is, however, in Orphicism another element, ignored by Pythagoras. As this comes before us in its earliest manifestations, it may be described as a naturalistic pantheism set forth by myths and ritual symbols of a rude character. This Orphic pantheism may possibly have contributed towards and influenced those Stoic doctrines of pantheism which were such a marked feature of the Stoic system throughout the centuries immediately preceding the rise of Christianity, though, as a matter of fact, the completed outcome of Stoic speculation differed *toto cælo* from Orphic imaginings. It certainly entered very largely into the tangled web of Neo-Pythagorean and Neo-Platonist mysticism ; here the old naturalistic doctrine, interpreted in the most diverse ways, and in a spirit equally arbitrary and fanciful, was sublimated into a confused mass of occult mystical theosophies. The larger portion of the professed Orphic texts, as well as of the comments upon the doctrine, belong to the later stage in the evolution of Orphicism which lasted far down into the Christian period. The investigator into the creed and history of the Orphic sects is therefore much in the position of a student of Christianity who had to rely mainly upon the writings of Swedenborg,

Blake, and Madame Blavatsky. Yet enough has survived of early, *i.e.* pre-Platonic, Orphicism to enable a fairly clear idea of its nature.

The elements in the Orphic system now to be examined were expressed in purely mythological terms instead of forming the material of a philosophic ethical doctrine. Fruitful comparison with the Celtic legends is thus possible. For evidently if Celtdom *was* influenced by Greece in historic times, such influence is likely to have been exercised by a ritualistic mythology rather than by an abstract ethical philosophy. Again the Irish re-birth legends are, as we have seen, strongly mythological by virtue of their association with the Tuatha de Danann, the representatives of a pre-Christian Irish Olympus; and if prehistoric contact can be established between these legends and early Greek belief, it must be on mythological ground.

Participation in the Dionysiac mysteries was the chief ritual act of the Orphic sectary. The mystery therein set forth is the story of Dionysus Zagreus. The general remarks made above concerning the nature of Orphic tradition are strongly exemplified in this special instance. Our most detailed authority is the Greek poet Nonnus[1] who wrote in the fifth century of the Christian era; yet there is substantially no doubt but that he and other authorities, almost as late, reproduce faithfully the outlines of a myth known to Onomacritos in the sixth century before Christ.[2] The story runs thus:

The Zagreus Myth.

Zeus had committed the care of this world to Zagreus,

---

[1] In his *Dionysiaca*; cf. Book vi. v. 170 *et seq.*

[2] Rohde, *Psyche*, 411 *b.*

his and Persephone's son. But the wicked Titans, urged
on by the jealous Hera, won the child's confidence by
many gifts, especially by that of a mirror, and were thus
able to fall upon, and, as they thought, to slay him. But
though his limbs, pierced by the Titans' swords, ceased to
beat with life, the end of one existence was for him but the
beginning of another; he reappeared in a new form in
diverse shapes. Now he was a young man, the son of
Kronos, the bolt-wielder; now old Kronos himself, heavy
kneed, bestower of rain. A thousand were his transformations, from childhood to manhood, from a roaring lion to
a neighing long-maned steed, from a horned dragon to a
spotted tiger. Lastly he assumed bull shape and warred
against the Titans with his sharp horns, fighting for his life.
Then Hera, the cruel stepmother, took part in the fray; to
his bellowings answered the bellowings of the air, and all
the steeps of Olympus shook to the roaring tempest. The
bull succumbed, and Zagreus in his bull form was rent into
pieces by the knives of his foes. Nay, they went further,
and the torn, quivering fragments of the god-bull were
devoured by his foes. The heart alone was rescued by
Athene and by her given to Zeus. According to one
account he himself ate, according to another he gave it
mixed with drink to Semele. Whichever account was
followed, the son of Zeus and Semele, Dionysus, was looked
upon as Zagreus re-born.[1]

To fully appreciate the import of this myth, it should be
noted that Zeus was also represented as begetting Zagreus
upon his own daughter Persephone in serpent form, she
having assumed that shape to evade his amorous pursuit,[2]

[1] Roscher, *Lexikon*, 1056.
[2] *Ibid.*, 1058; cf. the worm form common in the Irish re-birth legends.

and that in his intercourse with Semele he displays the same capacity for shape-shifting as is attributed to Zagreus-Dionysus: 'now fitting a bull's head to human limbs Zeus imitated the bellowings of Dionysus the bull; now a heavy-maned lion, anon a leopard, or again a coiled and creeping dragon.'[1] Finally, metamorphosis is more often met with in the fully developed Dionysus legend than in that of any other god, saving, of course, Zeus, to whom the supreme attribute of godhead, shape-shifting, is always pre-eminently assigned.

RITUAL ORPHICISM AND CELTIC BELIEF.

That this group of mythical conceptions affords a far more fruitful ground of comparison with Irish legend than the fully-developed Orphic metempsychosis doctrine is self-evident. Comparison can be instituted moreover without in any way prejudging the question whether the obvious parallelism of the two mythologies is due to prehistoric community or to historic contact. Either cause is possible. Orphic mysteries were spread throughout the Greek-speaking world, and retained their popularity until a far later date than that of the historic contact of Celt and Greek in the third and second centuries before Christ. The objection to the possibility of Greek influence, valid, so long as the sole mode under which the latter could be manifested seemed to be that of a highly-advanced ethico-philosophic doctrine, now loses its force. For although the third or second century Greek might interpret his Orphic mysteries in the light of philosophic speculation, whether due to

[1] Nonnus, *Dionysiaca*, vii. 319.

Pythagoras, Plato, or the later Stoics, yet the actual ritual and the explanatory myths retained their primitive form, and would be passed on to the ruder Celt unsophisticated by religious or philosophic gloss. I freely admit therefore that the ritual and mythological sides of Orphicism afford a possible origin for the Irish mythic sagas set forth in the preceding chapters. Zeus, the shape-shifting father of the shape-shifting wonder-child Dionysus, may have supplied the model upon which the sagas of Manannan and Mongan, of Lug and Cuchulinn, of Ceridwen and Taliessin were framed. The re-birth of Dionysus, due to material incorporation with father and mother, in the latter case through the medium of a draught, is on the same level of savage archaic fancy as the birth-stories of Cuchulinn, of Conall Cernach, of Etain ; the essence of the myth may well have passed unchanged from the one race to the other.

But possibility must always be carefully distinguished from probability. The course of investigation has brought us to the same stage in regard to the re-birth conception as it did in regard to the presentment of the Happy Otherworld. Irish mythic legend shows in both cases the closest affinity with what is apparently the most archaic, most primitive stratum of Greek myth. Although the two conceptions have been studied separately, nevertheless the result of either study is, *mutatis mutandis*, valid for the other. Let us note then that whilst, owing to the presentment in ritual form thanks to which its archaic features were retained, the Greek re-birth myths were preserved down to the period of ascertained historic contact between the Hellenic and Celtic worlds, in such a form as to make their influence upon Celtic belief and fancy possible, this was not the case with the Elysium myths. The older Greek

Elysium, which presents such marked analogy with the Irish Happy Otherworld, had been replaced, save as a literary survival, by the Orphic-Pythagorean heaven, a conception which, as we saw every reason to believe, could no more have originated the Irish mythic legends than could the still later form it assumed after assimilation and modification by Christianity.   The strong likelihood that the affinity between the Greek and Celtic Elysium myths is due to prehistoric community rather than to historic contact justifies a similar presumption in the case of the re-birth myths.   If the latter stood entirely by themselves, it would, I think, be safer, having found a possible origin for the Irish legends in the Orphic ritual-myths not to seek any further.   But the close connection of Elysium and re-birth conceptions, and the more than probable prehistoric nature of the former in Ireland, make it necessary to pursue investigation in the case of the latter.

ORPHIC PANTHEISM.

To clear away at once the more advanced phases of Orphicism, it should be noted that the crude pantheism involved in the ritual myths had, even at the earliest period at which we meet the doctrine, been strongly developed in a dogmatic and philosophic sense.   The Orphic dictum vouched for by Plato, Ζεὺς κεφαλὴ, Ζεὺς μέσσα, Διὸς δ' ἐκ πάντα τέτυκται, is sufficient to prove this, although, as Zeller has pointed out, the greater part of Orphic pantheistic texts belong to a far later stage of Orphic literature, a stage in which the original ritual myth had been duplicated in that of Phanes, the mysterious being in whom were combined at once the primal creative power and created substance, who was swallowed by Zeus

and re-born as the existing creation, which is thus a manifestation in its totality of Zeus' active essence.   It is the
first philosophical stage of Orphic pantheism which affected
the later schools, in especial Stoicism, and which in all probability furnished the philosophic interpretation put upon
the Orphic myths by the Greeks of the third and second
centuries B.C.   This interpretation, although differing, we
must believe, from still later explanations such as we find in
Plutarch,[1] must have differed even more from that special
form of pantheism, or rather, as I have called it, panwizardism, recoverable from the Amairgen and Taliessin poems.
The fact that Celtic mythic belief presents the more archaic
form of the pantheistic doctrine, just as it presents the more
archaic picture of Elysium, gives a hint, slight but significant,
that the affinity of Celtic mythology with Orphicism must
be older than the contact of Greek and Celt in the third
and second centuries B.C.

Thus, just as reference to the Pythagoreanism of the
period immediately preceding the Christian era was found
insufficient to account for the Irish re-birth, so reference to
the older Orphicism of the sixth century B.C., out of which
the Pythagorean system was largely developed, leaves us

[1] 'What the poets have fabled concerning the dismembering of
Dionysus, and the Titans' assault upon him, together with their punishment, and how they were destroyed by lightning, sets forth in hidden
meaning the doctrine of resurrection ; that element of our nature which
is brutish, devoid of reason, devilish, and not divine, was styled by our
forefathers, the Titans ; that element in us, it is, which suffers punishment, and on which justice is wrought.'—Plutarch 'On the eating of
human flesh.'
The Zagreus myth was brought into connection with the deluge ;
Zeus to revenge the slaying of Zagreus would burn the world by withholding rain—he relents, and the excessive downpour causes the deluge.

also at fault.   But it is noteworthy that the further back we get the more numerous and more important are the points of contact.   The similarity between Pythagoreanism and the South Celtic belief which so impressed the classical observers is found to be due to the wholesale borrowing by Pythagoras of older Orphic doctrines.   As elaborated by Pythagoras they were incapable of exercising any real influence upon Celtdom ; even in their earlier form, presented in terms of an archaic ritualism, they are found associated with a pantheism, which, crude though it be in comparison with Stoic speculation, is yet far more highly developed than that preserved in the Irish texts.   It is of course possible, as I have already said, for Celtdom to have absorbed the archaic whilst remaining unaffected by the more advanced features of the system.   But it is equally possible for the kinship of Hellenic and Celtic mythic fancy to antedate that first development of Orphicism in a philosophical direction, which, through the medium of Pythagoras, of Plato, of the Platonising Christian Fathers, was ultimately to furnish such a large element in the philosophic scheme of the ninth century Christian Pantheist, John Erigena, the Irishman.   To test this possibility we cannot afford to stop at the oldest literary manifestations of Orphicism in the sixth century B.C.   We must track it further back and examine its place in the entirety of Greek religion, belief, and fancy.   Before doing so, I would again emphasise the fact that we are not absolutely compelled to do so, if we are concerned solely with the origin of the Irish mythic stories set forth in the preceding pages ; rigorously speaking, the Orphic-mythic system, as we know it from the sixth century onwards, may be accepted as their sole source. But we shall see, when we come to discuss these stories in connection with such other features of Irish mythology as have survived, that an explanation valid for them alone will not account for the wider group of facts. I am, however, somewhat anticipating the course of the argument in insisting upon the need of pushing the investigation further.

THE DIONYSUS CULT.

Orphicism centres, as we have seen, round the Dionysiac mysteries. As a body of doctrine, as a ritual organisation, we cannot, positively, carry it beyond the sixth century B.C., or, probably, a century or two further back. It is otherwise, however, with the worship of Dionysus, alluded to as this is in a well-known Homeric passage, familiar as it is to Hesiod, and attested as it is by a mass of varied archæological evidence which compels us to assume its existence in Greece in the ninth or eighth century B.C. at the latest. Let us then consider the Dionysiac cult apart from any special connection with fully developed Orphicism. I cannot do better than summarise Professor Rohde's brilliant sketch in *Psyche* (pp. 319 *et seq.*). Although, as will be shown later, I draw somewhat different conclusions from part of the material he has adduced, although we may see reason to supplement or rectify his argument, still the bird's-eye view he affords will be found singularly vivid and illuminating. Moreover, by setting forth certain facts and suggestions in the words of a scholar whose exposition is based upon other principles and has other objects in view than those of the present investigation, I avoid the reproach I might otherwise incur of selecting such facts and conclusions as suit my thesis. The reader may be startled by seeing how aptly Greek myth and ritual illustrate Irish romance, and will certainly view the process with less suspicion if he realise its independence of the facts I have adduced and the inferences I have drawn from them. The following paragraphs thus render in brief Professor Rohde's exposition. My comment thereon is reserved for a later stage of the inquiry.

Belief in the immortality of the soul involves acceptance of its affinity to the divine nature, for immortality is the especial attribute of godhood. The Homeric presentment of Hades, and of the bloodless, phantom-like existence of its dwellers, was incapable of originating and nourishing such a belief; the roots of this we must seek in the Dionysian cult.

In mankind at large in an early stage of development the state of ecstasy, mania, has always had special weight and import. In it the patient, freed from the chains of sense, passes into a world wherein the capacities of will and desire seem commensurate, wherein the bonds of individuality are loosened, wherein the fixed and settled outlines of nature by which man is controlled and confined shift and transform themselves and accommodate themselves to his directed energy. Life viewed from this ecstatic standpoint is not a series of individual manifestations rigidly confined within irremovable limits, but is a plastic essence the infinite potentialities of which are accessible to whoso knows the means of attaining and mastering them. The state of ecstasy may be reached in many ways, chief among them the rapid motion prolonged to exhaustion, the music maddening to the senses, the sudden change from the blackness of night to the fierce flare of torch and bonfire, in short all the accompaniments of the frenzied midnight worship we know to have characterised the cult of Dionysus amid the mountains of Thrace. Doubtless more artificial means were not lacking; hemp and other narcotics may have aided in provoking the god-possessed frenzy in which Maenad and Bassarid, with senses exacerbated to insensibility, rent asunder the living victim and devoured his quivering flesh. The god, the very god enters into them, the bull-horned devotee is at once symbol and manifestation of the bull-god he worships. As such he shares the divine energies, the divine privileges. ' 'Tis when they are full of the god that the Bacchæ draw milk and honey from the stream, not when they have come to themselves,' says Plato ; 'wine and honey gush forth from the earth, they are amidst the sweet smells of Syria,' says Euripides, in the play from which more than from any other source we may gain some idea of the divine frenzy of the Dionysus worshipper. The contrast between the fierce energies, the fierce joys of ecstasy and the condition of ordinary life easily led to a dualistic conception of life. The very word ἔκστασις involves the idea that soul, or spirit, call it what one may, is capable of leaving the body, of being elsewhere. To free the spirit, to enable it to transcend bodily conditions, to bring it into communion with the god, such are the objects aimed at by the devotee. Such men and women as displayed a greater capacity for entering the 'possessed' state, and in whom the god manifested himself with the strongest energy, would naturally excel their fellows ; somewhat of their power would abide with them in their ordinary life ; a caste of soothsayers, of wizards would constitute itself. And in very deed the soothsaying power of the Thracians was far-famed.

This yearning for the powers and joys of the ecstatic state, the feeling of communion with mightier, freer beings, which it, and it alone, afforded, are, as already said, almost world-wide.   And they are always accompanied by intense belief in the life and power of the spirit apart from the body.   So too with the Thracian worshippers of Dionysus. Herodotus tells of the Thracian Getæ, whose belief 'made men immortal.'[1]   After this life they passed away to an endless one with Zalmoxis their god, who ever sits in the hollowed hill.   Again we learn from Pomponius Mela, 'that they deemed the souls of the departed would return.'[2] Such a conception is implied too in the assumption, widely prevalent in antiquity, of a kinship between the Thracian and Pythagorean doctrine concerning the soul, and justifying the ascription to the Thracians of a belief that the soul entered into a new body in which it continued its earthly existence, and in so far was 'immortal.'   It is significant that in the *Hecuba* of Euripides it is the Thracian Polymestor who tells the queen, in answer to her question concerning her fate after death, that she shall become a dog.

If the spirit can attain to and recruit itself with the divine essence in the state of ecstasy, must not its own essence be divine, and if divine, immortal, and may not death as a permanent separation of body and spirit be the portal of immortality for the latter?   And, if so, who would not yearn for death as admitting the spirit to a realm it can only attain here in rare moments of 'possession' by communion with the god?   Thus, as Herodotus reports, the Thracian greeted the new-born child with cry and lament, whilst the dead were buried with joyful clamour, for that they henceforth lived in perfect bliss.[3]   Hence the Thracian readiness for death, which astounded the ancients; to these barbarians it seemed, as Galen notes, 'a fair thing to die.'

---

[1] Herodotus, iv. 94.
[2] Pomponius Mela, ii. 18.   [3] Herodotus, v. 4.

The cult of Dionysus had penetrated the Hellenic world before the period in which the Homeric poems took shape, but in Homer's days it was as yet a minor and local worship ; Dionysus has no place among Homer's Olympians. At a later period, perchance during the storm and stress of the Dorian invasion, the Thracian god made rapid conquests throughout the Grecian world in spite of the fundamental opposition between the spirit of his cult and the genius of the Hellenic race. Greek religion was profoundly modified in consequence, but so also was the Thracian cult ; it became humanised, Hellenised. Yet it ever retained its primal animating principle, and even in such a comparatively late manifestation of Dionysus' power as the origination of comedy we can detect the link which unites the comedian's art, the art of transformation, of manifestation in diverse personalities, with the midnight orgy in which the frenzied devotee sought from the god the power of loosening himself from the chains of sense, of entering into the ecstatic state.

Among the Olympians it is with the most typical of Hellenic deities, with Apollo, that Dionysus became most closely associated ; and the mutual action and reaction upon each other of these worships, so diverse in their original spirit, form an important chapter in the history of Greek religion.[1] The Dionysus worship was not only softened, it was regularised ; the frame of mind in which ecstasy was yearned and striven for yielded the elements of an elaborate system of purificatory and ascetic rites. For as the object aimed at is the release of the spirit from the bonds of the flesh, the more permanent mode of accom-

---

[1] Rohde does not explain this association, a natural and inevitable one, in my opinion. See *infra, passim.*

plishing this by means of ascetic mortification came to rival, and with minds of a higher cast, to supplant the temporary excitement of the orgiastic frenzy.   Again, the influence of a sacerdotal hierarchy, such as that associated with the cult of Apollo, would make for the substitution of a symbolic ritual, performed, and only to be performed by itself, rather than for the perpetuation of an actual ritual shared in by all the worshippers.

But the evolution of the religious idea did not stop here. If ecstasy, release for a time, shorter or longer as orgiastic frenzy or ascetic mortification is the mode adopted, from the bonds of carnal sense, be the consummation to be achieved, then subjection to these bonds must be regarded as the highest evil, and it must be the devotee's aim to escape therefrom, not only in this life, but in possible manifestations of the spirit, after this life ; the necessary existence of such manifestations being an inevitable deduction from the phenomena of ecstasy.   Thus are reached the half-religious, half-metaphysical conceptions of the soul prisoner of the body, and the purely religious corollary therefrom, that the task of the devotee is to minimise the effects of this bondage in this life, and to escape from it altogether after death.

So far Professor Rohde, whose entire exposition, with its buttressing apparatus of citation from Greek literature, should be read.   But the summary I have just given is sufficient to focus upon the phenomena of Irish mythic romance a light under which they assumed ordered and reasoned significance.   For we see that a body of myth in which shape-shifting, the capacity for self-manifestation under diverse forms, are prominent features is most naturally explained by the existence of a body of religious belief in the attainment of ecstasy through the medium of orgiastic frenzy.   And by carrying the analysis of the Dionysus cult beyond the stage reached by Professor Rohde we shall find the wherewithal to account for the other features of Celtic belief, besides its pseudo - Pythagoreanism noted by the ancients, and to make it more than probable that similar beliefs existed among the insular Celts.

DIONYSUS AND ELYSIUM.

Before entering upon this task the two pregnant citations from Plato and Euripides demand more than passing notice.   They supply a psychological reason for that association of Elysium and metamorphosis which persists so strongly in the Irish mythic romances, and which might otherwise seem inexplicable.   The one belief as the other is seen to be rooted in the phenomena of ecstasy.   The devotee who seeks to escape from the fetters imposed upon him by bodily conditions also seeks to escape to a realm in which his ideal of felicity, dependent, however, at first wholly upon bodily conditions, may be realised.   Fancy links together the two conceptions, and even though in the course of evolution they develop independently, still the connection remains apparent, inexplicable as its cause may seem.   The hint afforded by Plato and Euripides must be borne in mind when the history of the twin conceptions among the Aryan-speaking races is investigated, and it is sought to determine whether or no they are derived, mediately or immediately, from the older cultures of the East.

To return to the Dionysus cult, Professor Rohde's analysis, brilliant and suggestive as it is, brings into prominence elements which are mainly secondary, at least in the stage in which he considers them, and omits to duly emphasise others which are primary. This is easily explicable when his object—the discussion of Hellenic spirit-belief—is remembered. But the conceptions which he passes by are of first-rate importance for us.

THE TRUE NATURE OF THE DIONYSUS CULT.[1]

There can be little, indeed we say no doubt, that we must regard the ritual involved in the oldest forms of Dionysus worship as akin to a great mass of symbolic rites prevalent throughout large areas of both the Old and New World, the purport of which is to strengthen the life of the vegetation upon which that of man depends, by infusing into it the vital energy of a specially selected victim. The greater the potentialities of life and vigour possessed by the victim, the greater the benefit ensuing from his sacrifice. Hence, at an early stage of thought, the conclusion that if the mysterious being or power, the god, of whom growth and life, both animal and vegetable, may be regarded as an attribute or manifestation, can be sacrificed, the greatest amount of advantage can be counted upon. In practice this resolves itself into treating the victim as a manifestation or a symbol of the god, with the natural consequence of intensifying the conception of his metamorphic nature. He is ever being sacrificed but to remanifest himself in new

---

[1] In this paragraph I am practically summarising and restating the views of Mannhardt and Mr. Frazer. I refer to the latter's *Golden Bough*, and to Mr. Hartland's *Legend of Perseus*, for a full exposition and justification of the theory. Cf. also Robertson Smith's article, 'Sacrifice,' in the ninth edition of the *Encyclopædia Britannica*, and his *Religion of the Semites*, and Voigt's article, ' Dionysus,' in Roscher's *Lexikon*.

forms, and with added potencies. Nor must another advantage be overlooked. If the life and energy of the sacrificed god can be made to pass indirectly into man through the vegetation upon which he subsists, so it can pass directly Thus a twofold aspect of the sacrifice. The vital essence of the victim, existing in the blood, in the heaving, quivering, quick flesh, is distributed, partly to mother-earth that she may nourish and in due season bring forth the fruit of her womb, the god-son by whom she is impregnated, and whom she bears ; partly, to the devotee. And the latter is straightway justified, for does he not acquire by participation in the rite access to that state of ecstasy in which for the time being he seems to pass out of the mortal into the immortal, out of the confined into the unconfined, to leave behind him human limitations, and ascend into the sphere of the superhuman, the divine?

Take such a series of assumptions and conceptions as the basis of a creed expressing itself in ritual form, and it may put on the most diverse aspects according to the genius and social organisation of the race. Among an essentially warlike people, exercising sway over subject populations, dependent for its power and influence and wealth upon its martial valour and consequent prestige, what may be called the agricultural side of the creed would tend to be minimised ; the powers, the energies which the ruling warrior caste, and its priestly representatives, would seek to attain, would be less the quickening of bud and fruit, than the heightening and intensifying of human individuality as directed to combat and domination. Sacrifice would tend to lose its fixed calendarial character determined by the unchanging round of natural processes, and to form a fund, so to say, of reserve energy, upon which the race could draw when and as needed. In such a way those usages of human sacrifice attested to by classical observers of the second and first centuries B.C., as existing among their Celtic neighbours, might establish themselves. They should be regarded as renewing the vital energies of the race, as seizing upon and utilising for the conqueror the stock of life existing among the conquered.[1]

The strong stress laid by classical observers upon the psychological basis of the Celtic doctrine, which they compared with the Pythagorean metempsychosis, is in consonance with this interpretation. Death had no terror for the Celt, for had not his priest power to furnish him with a fresh stock of life, and whence could this power be derived save through the medium of sacrifice? It was after all a logical deduction from the original conception. If sacrifice, ritually performed (and in course of time ritual creates inevitably a priestly class), could renew and recreate the sources of life manifested in nature, why not in man?

The theory thus adumbrated accounts reasonably for two features of Celtic religion which more than any other impressed classical observers: human sacrifice, on a scale and with circumstances of horror which startled even the cruel and callous Roman, and a doctrine of life in which they detected an analogy to the Pythagorean system. But a hypothesis cannot be regarded as satisfactory simply because it satisfactorily accounts for facts, it must also in some measure rest upon independent evidence. Tacitly, I have postulated among the Celts such a ritual of sacrifice,

---

[1] C. Caesar's explanation of Celtic sacrifice: 'They think that unless a man's life is rendered up for a man's life, the will of the immortal God cannot be satisfied, and they have sacrifices of this kind as a national institution.'

originally agricultural, as we find among the Thracians and as developed with the Greeks into the Dionysus worship of historic times. This ritual I assume to have departed from its agricultural type, and to have developed so as to suit the needs of a community essentially warlike in spirit and organisation. But traces of the original form and significance of the ritual must have persisted. Do such exist?

RITUAL SACRIFICE IN THE CELTIC WORLD.

One of the few facts concerning Celtic ritual in the period before Christ which has come down to us is due to the Greek traveller Posidonius. Strabo and Dionysius Periegetes have preserved his account of the priestesses of the Namnites, who celebrated their rites in an island at the mouth of the Loire. No man durst set foot on this island, which was solely devoted to the use of these priestesses, but at times they visited men on the mainland. These women 'possessed of Dionysus,' in a state of frenzy, accomplished once a year the following rite: the temple of the god they worshipped was roofed, but annually the priestesses unroofed it; it had, however, to be roofed again before sunset. So each of the women came to the work bringing upon her shoulders a burden of the requisite materials, and in case any one allowed her burden to fall to the ground she was instantly torn to pieces by her companions, who carried her mangled remains round the temple until the flame of their fury burned itself out. Each succeeding year saw the horrid scenes repeated (Rhys, *Hibb. Lect.* 197, quoting Strabo, iv. 4).

With this account of the Namnites priestesses must be compared that given some hundred and fifty years later by Pomponius Mela of the priestesses of the island Sena, probably the modern Seine, and, if so, not far distant from the unnamed isle of Posidonius. I quote Professor Rhys' version (*Hibb. Lect.* 196): 'Sena, in the Britannic Sea, opposite the coast of the Osismi, is famous for the oracle of a Gaulish god, whose priestesses, living in the holiness of perpetual virginity, are said to be nine in number. They call them Gallizenae, and they believe them to be endowed with extraordinary gifts : to rouse the sea and wind by their incantations, to turn themselves into whatsoever animal form they may chose, to cure diseases which among others are incurable, to know what is to come, and to foretell it. They are, however, devoted to the service of voyagers only who have set out on no other errand than to consult them' (Mela, iii. 6).

Before discussing these accounts I may be allowed to note the essential kinship between the historic island of women devoted to the worship of a god, in which men durst not set foot, but whose dwellers sallied forth to seek temporary mates on the mainland, and the isle of women in Irish legend, whose goddess dwellers come to Ireland to seek out heroes whose love they may win.

To return to the classical accounts. That they apply, if not to the very same, at least to closely allied institutions, is evident, also that they at once mutually complement each other and reveal a development which we know from other sources to have taken place. The bloody and ferocious rite mentioned by the earlier traveller has disappeared by the time of Mela, in consequence, it cannot be doubted, of the stringent enactments made by the Roman power against the Druidic practice of human sacrifice. The object of the cult has suffered some change in consequence, a different aim has been assigned to the might of the priestess, and she is on the way of tranformation into the mediæval witch with her power over wind and tide. Yet Mela has preserved a trait unnoted by the older traveller ; the priestesses of the old god, giver of life, manifester of life, lord of form and shape, whose flesh and blood supply the plastic essence out of which Nature is ever fashioning, and into which she is ever refashioning herself, possess and retain the might and attribute of their master ; like the swineherd servants of the Tuatha De kings in Irish legend, they can 'turn themselves into whatsoever animal form they may choose.'

That the nature of the ritual described by Posidonius is originally agricultural may be proved, I think, by its periodicity. The god of vegetable growth, unlike him of war or of the windy sea, must be strengthened and placated at fixed seasons. The sacrifice of the priestess of Sena may be looked upon as akin to the Meriah sacrifice among the Khonds of Bengal.

RITUAL SACRIFICE IN IRELAND.

As we shall see later, survivals of the practice have persisted in Britain which, when compared with more perfectly preserved examples elsewhere, put its real nature beyond doubt. But at this stage I do not wish to appeal to inferential and analogical, but solely to direct, evidence. Fortunately among the very few statements respecting the ritual side of old Irish religion we possess, one there is, conclusive on the point under investigation. The *dinnshenchas* of Mag Slecht runs as follows : ' ''Tis there was the King idol of Erin, namely the Crom Croich, and around him twelve idols made of stones ; but he was of gold. Until Patrick's advent he was the god of every folk that colonised

Ireland. To him they used to offer the firstlings of every issue and the chief scions of every clan. 'Tis to him that Erin's king, Tigernmas, son of Follach, repaired on Hallowtide, together with the men and women of Ireland, in order to adore him. And they all prostrated themselves before him, so that the tops of their foreheads and the gristle of their noses, and the caps of their knees and the ends of their elbows broke, and three-fourths of the men of Erin perished at these prostrations; whence *Mag Slecht*, "Plain of Prostration"' (Stokes, *Rennes Dindsenchas*, R.C. xvi. 35-36).[1]

As previously stated (*supra*, i. 196), many of the prose *dinnshenchas* are also found in a verse form in the Book of Leinster version; this is the case with the Mag Slecht *dinnsenchas*, and the verse adds the information that the object of the men of Ireland in offering one-third of their progeny was to obtain corn and milk; whence, as Mr. Whitley Stokes comments, 'we may infer that the Irish Celts, like other races, held that the Earth-gods could be propitiated by human sacrifices' (l.c. 36). Although the *Dinnshenchas* is, as previously stated, a comparatively late compilation (it was put together in the eleventh and twelfth centuries out of material, some of which, *e.g.* the verse found in the Book of Leinster may have been redacted a couple of centuries before) this particular tradition, like the majority of those contained in it, must be of pre-Christian origin. It would have been quite impossible for a Christian monk to have invented such a story, and we may accept it as a perfectly genuine bit of

---

[1] In Appendix B. Professor Kuno Meyer has edited and translated the metrical version of this *dinnshenchas* found in the Book of Leinster. This is probably the oldest form, from which the prose versions are abridged.

information respecting the ritual side of insular Celtic religion.

The insular Celts, then, as also the Continental, practised what may be called agricultural sacrifice; in the case of the Continental Celts the circumstances of the ritual, the sex of the officiating priests, the fierce frenzy which accompanied it, were such as to suggest to the Greek observer the Dionysus cult of his own land. The parallel he thus implied was truer than he knew; Dionysus too, son of Zeus and Semele, comrade of Apollo, lord of the ecstasy of wine, of the drama's glamour, had indeed been aforetime such a one as the priestesses of Seine worshipped when they rent and devoured their stumbling comrade.

COMPARISON OF GREEK AND CELTIC AGRICULTURAL SACRIFICIAL CULTS.

Thus we find among the Celts traces of a form of religion closely akin to that out of which the historical Greek Dionysus cult was evolved; the social and historic conditions of either race, Celt and Greek, differing greatly as they did, the development of this religion differed likewise. Bloody and ferocious as it was at the outset, its savage characteristics were intensified among the Celts by divorce from the agricultural, by association with the warlike interests of the race, nor had it to suffer rebuke and competition from the cult of milder gods. In Greece, on the other hand, the agricultural side of Dionysus persisted, but humanised and refined; whilst association with deities of a more *civilised* character (I give the word its etymological value) conferred upon the god an infinitely wider and more varied range of attributes and interests. But differ, as came to do the two cults, they retained an essential kinship due to common origin; the root conception of both is the capacity of renewing, transmitting, transforming the life inherent in the god, his ministers, or his devotees; the sanction of this conception is in both cases the same; the participant in the rites attains a state in which this capacity manifests itself beyond all doubt, in which, too, the highest ideal of felicity may be grasped by him. The romantic fiction which was the outcome of this religion is necessarily dominated and animated by the mutually related conception of escape from the bonds which confine man to one manifestation of his being, of escape from an earth which, at its happiest, makes but a sorry show by side of the Elysium he pictures in his frenzy.

The close parallel between the fifth century Greek account of the Thracians and the first century Græco-Roman account of the Celts may be noted *en passant*. The same things strike Herodotus about the one set of barbarians as strike Posidonius about the other, the tenacity of belief in another life, the contempt of death, the existence of conceptions which reminded both observers of Pythagoreanism. I note the parallel but disclaim any idea of suggesting racial affinity between Thracians and Celts. To argue this would be, I believe, to misunderstand the history of the Aryan-speaking races in Europe. Both Thracians and Celts are Aryan-speaking peoples, and in the dark backward of time to which we are carried by the necessity of dating the Thracian Dionysus worship before the Greek phase of it, revealed by the Homeric mention, say from 1500 to 1000 B.C., I hold that there would be singularly little difference in religious conceptions and social organisation between the various less-advanced members of the Aryan group who occupied Central and Northern Europe. The historic causes which were to differentiate Celt and Teuton and Slav had not yet begun to operate, and it is quite indifferent to our thesis to which branch of the Aryan family the Thracian Aryans are to be affiliated. All that need be noted is that Greece, coming in contact at four centuries of distance with Aryan barbarians of substantially the same social and religious culture, was struck by the same phenomena.

GREEK ORIGIN AND NATURE OF THE DIONYSUS CULT.

Of more importance than the exact racial affinities of the prehistoric Thracians is the question whether the Dionysus cult is Greek in origin and development, or an alien intrusive element in Greek religion. The Greeks of the fifth and following centuries were of the latter opinion for the most part, and it has been widely held by modern scholars. A series of myths, similar in outline and import, were, until recently, interpreted as traces of the opposition which the alien cult encountered in the Hellenic world. Stories went how this or that king, fearing the frenzied worship paid to the new god, strove against him, and how Dionysus sent madness upon his very family so that they knew him not, and when he would have spied upon or interfered with their midnight rites tore him to pieces—a striking symbol of the fierce conflict which this un-Hellenic cult had to pass through before it could effect a lodgment in the Hellenic world ! But of late these myths have been interpreted in an entirely different sense : they are regarded as attempts to explain a ritual, the true significance of which had been lost. The ritual comprised, as we have, seen, the sacrifice of the god to the god—of his representative, that is, in animal or human form. Now the human representative might be invested with special powers and attributes and sanctities, such as made him for the time the chief man of his tribe or family, attributes and sanctities which assimilated him to the god and ensured corresponding advantage from his sacrifice. Thus, the story of the king or chief torn in pieces by the women of his own household and kin might well be no fiction, but an echo of what had actually taken place at one time. But as the race outgrew the stage of agricultural sacrifice, the ferocious slaughter of the king-victim would assume an aspect utterly inexplicable. His death, instead of being the chief act in the worship of the god, came to be regarded as punishment for opposition to him, and in this way such stories as those of Pentheus and Lycurgus would arise.

Now if this interpretation be correct, not only does it afford no warrant for the alien origin of the Dionysus cult, it conclusively disproves the theory of *recent* alien origin. Had the cult been introduced into Greece in historic times with the full-blown ritual of sacrifice in its original form, a phenomenon so strange, so repugnant to Greek feeling must needs have justified its existence in such a way that misapprehension of its significance would be impossible. If we admit what may be called the anthropological interpretation, we must needs hold that the Greeks were dealing with a survival, with a rite that maintained itself, as rites will, long after the animating conception had fallen away from the popular mind. But this is a process involving a lengthened period of time. Moreover, as Professor Jevons has acutely observed (*Folklore* ii.), the most famous of these legends, that in which King Lycurgus is the victim, is no witness to the Thracian origin of the cult, as Lycurgus is represented as a Thracian king. It is singular that Professor Rohde, whilst admitting the anthropological explanation of the

Lycurgus and alien myths, yet argues for the comparatively late introduction of the cult into Greece, which that explanation disproves. Another German scholar, Professor Maass, has in his *Orpheus* felt the difficulty and essayed to clear it up. His work is, as already noted, an argument in favour of the early and genuinely Hellenic character of the Orphic doctrine. He is thus led to distinguish two distinct myths of the sacrificed and eaten god; one, purely Hellenic, in which Orpheus is the victim-deity whose essence by the act of sacrifice is diffused throughout the creation; one, of Thracian origin, in which Dionysus-Zagreus plays a similar part. Fusion of the two cults took place in Thrace in the sixth century, and the Thracian god supplanted the original Greek protagonist of the myth. Orphicism received in consequence an accession of primitive, barbaric energy which enabled it, under the shadow thrown upon the Greek world by the advancing menace of Persian invasion, to successfully appeal to large sections of the Hellenic race (*Orpheus*, pp. 169 *et seq*).

Maass himself admits the paradoxical character of certain among his conclusions, notably the replacing of Orpheus by a Thracian supplanter as late as the sixth-century. It seems hardly necessary to argue against a theory which runs counter to all we know of sixth-century Orphicism; it is sufficient to point out that the complicated hypothesis is unnecessary. It is far simpler to treat the *ensemble* of Dionysiac-Orphic conception as being Greek from the beginning, as falling into disuse and disrepute, thanks to a combination of historic conditions which turned the Greek mind in other directions, and impressed upon it, as a whole, a stamp alien to these conceptions. Yet, they nevertheless persisted, as elements connected with religion will persist;

they still formed a portion of the emotional and intellectual store of the Greek mind, and were subject to the phases of the development through which that mind passed. That development not only led the Greeks away from the fierce and unbridled frenzy in which the Dionysian creed found its most characteristic manifestations, it was equally hostile to the ascetic doctrine into which that frenzy ultimately transformed itself. The Greek soon outgrew the primitive stage of the cult, and by the time it reached the ascetic stage, he had grown away from that likewise. Thus the Pythagoreanism which was the last outcome of the Dionysian cult (and truly Pythagoras himself never imagined a stranger metamorphosis) exercised so little influence upon Hellas, whilst the corresponding ascetic doctrine of Buddha revolutionised India. On the other hand, the Greek turned Dionysus to an account equally consonant with the nature of the god and the genius of the race, making him the patron of the most varied and living of all forms of literary art, of the drama.

To claim the Dionysus cult as belonging to Greece from the earliest time to which we can hark back is by no means to deny its Thracian character likewise. It is simply to assume that the Greeks and their northern neighbours had once possessed similar rites, that the former outgrew and transformed, whilst the latter retained them in their primitive aspect. It is quite possible that such traces of primitive barbarism as lingered in Greek usages should be reinforced during times of closer contact between the more and less advanced peoples. Such a time of contact may well have been, as Rohde conjectures, the period of the Dorian invasion, and thus may be explained the wilder, savager nature of the Dionysus ritual in Sparta. Nor is it wonderful that under these circumstances the later Greeks should be tempted to assign a worship, features of which had become strange if not actually repugnant to them, wholly to alien influence.

A remark of Professor Maass might be further adduced in support of the original Greek character of the Dionysus worship: he would explain the Orphic-Pythagorean metempsychosis doctrine by the instinctive fondness of the Greek race for a mythology based upon the conception of metamorphosis, combining with it the various theories which it had gradually elaborated concerning the nature and fate of the soul. This may be admitted if we recollect that a mythology such as the German scholar alludes to is in itself an outcome of and a witness to religious conceptions and ritual practices, of which the original Dionysus cult is the most characteristic and famous example.

We may take it then that the Aryan-Greek like the Aryan-Celt passed at one stage of his development through a phase of religion which may be styled the agricultural-sacrificial, and that in the one case as in the other the resultant mythology outlived the official recognition and practice of the ritual. Unofficially we shall see reason for believing that the latter also did persist. In both cases, too, this phase of religion gave rise to a philosophy, as far subtler and more complex in the one case than the other as the Greek outstripped the Celt in every form of culture. But with the Greek an ethical system as well as a philosophy came into being. And here the reader will doubtless have detected an apparent fault in the argument. The Orphic sectary of the sixth century, whose highest lure is that he can release man from the cycle of birth, from possibility of entering into another form after death's release from the present one, is the lineal heir of the votary who sought in frenzy the means of attaining the power of transformation. How has the change come about? Professor Rohde, it will be recollected, has essayed to answer this question (*supra*, p. 142). The steps according to him are: desire to throw off the bonds of sense; disgust with the body which in this life frustrates the effort; dread of similar bondage after the present life is closed by death; consequent desire to escape re-birth which can only be conceived of as an association of spirit and body. It may seem unlikely that such a subtle chain of reasoning should result in convictions which deeply moved no inconsiderable section of the Hellenic race as did the Orphic doctrines. If the sanction of Orphicism was really escape from re-birth, one would naturally seek for a less far-fetched cause. But the question need not be examined here. A similar phenomenon confronts us in India; there too, and in the sixth century likewise, the moral revolution of Buddhism rests upon the passionate longing to have done with life, to be released from the horror of possible re-birth. The nature and cause of these strangely similar phenomena should be inquired into at the same time.

The discussion of these points, secondary though they be, is not useless for our argument. It is of moment to show that Greek and Celt share certain fundamental conceptions: it is well to remember that Asia as well as Europe has its share in the Aryan problem, for, so rapidly has the pendulum swung, one is in danger of forgetting nowadays that the men who sang the hymns of the Rig Veda or told the stories of the Jatakas spoke an Aryan tongue equally with the men who listened to the lays of Homer or pictured Cuchulinn holding the warriors of Ireland single-handed at bay.

We must now return to Ireland. Comparison with Greek myth and ritual has revealed the sources of that body of mythic romance of which the Voyage of Bran is but one, and not the most striking example. We can assert with some confidence that this body of romance drew life and inspiration from such a conception of nature, animate and inanimate, as in Greece produced alike the cult of Dionysus and the rich store of metamorphosis myth associated with his name. To verify this hypothesis we must essay to determine with greater precision than has hitherto been attained the real nature of the mysterious beings who play so large a part in the Voyage of Bran and allied legends. If the surmise to which we have been led be correct, some traces of the nature we assign hypothetically to the Tuatha De Danann must be recoverable from the stories told of them. And in investigating the character and attributes of this mysterious race, let us remember that we are also attacking the problem of the origin and nature of Irish fairy-belief; for what the Irish peasant of to-day fables and believes of the *good people*, his ancestors of a thousand years ago fabled and believed of the Folk of the Goddess.

Lest I be misunderstood, I would say that whilst I claim already to have found an immediate source for certain features of Celtic and Greek mythic romance and worship in cults akin to that of Dionysus, I prejudge nothing as to the ultimate origin of these cults themselves. These may be due to the influence of the East upon Aryan Europe, or they may be the result of a contact wholly European between Aryan and non-Aryan. Before essaying to solve this final problem we have still to supply many details in our sketch of the purely Aryan, and in especial of the purely Irish, development of this phase of religion.

CHAPTER XVII

THE TUATHA DE DANNAN

The *dinnshenchas* of Mag Slecht and the mythic reign of Tighernmas ; the Annalistic account ; apparent discrepancy with the Dinnshenchas— The true nature of the Tighernmas tradition ; consequences for Irish mythology—Classification of Irish mythical literature concerning the Tuatha de Danann—The Annalistic account ; the romantic account of Battle of Moytura ; the Rabelaisian element in Irish mythology ; comparison of Annalistic and romantic accounts ; necessary deduction as to agricultural origin of the Tuatha de Danann ; Dinnshenchas mentions of the Tuatha de Danann and discussion of the traditions concerning the fairs of Carman and Tailtinn—The heroic saga mentions of the Tuatha de Danann ; validity of this evidence ; comparison between the mythic literature of Greece and Ireland ; true import of heroic saga evidence — Development of the Tuatha de Danann mythology.

THE ANNALISTIC ACCOUNT OF TIGHERNMAS.

A CONVENIENT starting-point for our investigation into the origin and nature of the mysterious folk of the goddess Danu is afforded by the *dinnshenchas* of Mag Slecht, quoted in the last chapter. From it we learn that at Hallowtide—at the close, that is, of the autumn and beginning of the winter season—the ancient Irish worshipped the image or symbol of a god with human sacrifice. Now the Irish annals have somewhat to say about the cult practised at Mag Slecht. In the Annals of the Four Masters we read, A.M. 3656 (*i.e.* according to the chronology of the Four

160

Masters, 1538 years before the birth of Christ), as follows concerning Tighernmas, king of Ireland at the time: 'It was by Tighearnmas also that gold was first smelted in Ireland. . . . It was by him that goblets and brooches were first covered with gold and silver in Ireland. It was by him that cloths were dyed purple and blue and green. It was in his reign that the three black rivers of Ireland burst forth. . . . At the end of the year he died with three-fourths of the men of Ireland about him, at the meeting of Mag Slecht, in Breifne, at the worshipping of Crom Cruach, which was the chief idol of adoration in Ireland. This happened in the night of Samhain (All Hallows) precisely. It was from the genuflections that the men of Ireland made about Tighearnmas here that the plain was named.'

Keating, a contemporary of the Four Masters, adds many details in his summary of the older annals. He dates Tighernmas, A.M. 2186 (1219 years before Christ in his system of chronology). Nine lakes burst over the land in his time; ornaments, fringes, and brooches were first used by the Irish upon their dress; he first established it as a custom in Ireland that there should be one colour in the dress of a slave, two in that of a peasant, and so on to the nine colours in the dress of a king or queen; he first began to offer idolatrous worship to Crom Cruaich in Ireland, about a hundred years after the arrival of the Gaels (p. 223).

NATURE AND IMPORT OF ANNALISTIC ACCOUNT.

In dealing with the statements of these seventeenth century compilers we must remember that they confined themselves to extracting from the older historical writers what they deemed most worthy of preservation, to comparing the varying accounts of the same personage or event, noting that which they considered the best, and to arranging chronologically the facts they recorded.   Keating was, luckily for us, a man of liberal faith, and admitted many stories which the Four Masters evidently rejected as fabulous.   He was also far less precise in his chronology.   But in the main, the principle and the practice of both compilers are the same; the traditional history is accepted as genuine, even though it be necessary here and there to correct its statements.   Now, this traditional history was put together, in the form under which it is reproduced by the seventeenth century writers, from the eighth to the eleventh century.   We can detect two drafts—the first belonging to the eighth century, the second to the renaissance period (950-1150) of Ireland's recovery from the Viking invasions.   Of the first draft only one considerable fragment has survived imbedded in the *Historia Brittonum* of the eighth-ninth century Welsh chronicler, Nennius.   But it is probable that many of the traditions preserved in the Dinnshenchas go back to this draft even where they do not represent the scattered, independent local traditions upon which it was based.   The second draft is represented by a number of poems, assigned to antiquary historians of the tenth and eleventh centuries,[1] in which the history of the country was memorised for teaching purposes, and by annalistic works compiled by the same class of men or founded upon their writings.   The most learned and critical of the eleventh century Irish chroniclers, Tighernach, judged the traditional history, prior to the third century B.C., to be

---

[1] Thus the statement that Tighernmas first smelted gold in Ireland is found in a poem by Gilla Coemain (who died 1072), preserved in *The Book of Leinster*, p. 16.   The passage is quoted by M. d'Arbois, *Cycle Myth.*, p. 200.

'*incerta*.'[1]   The statements concerning Tighernmas which have just been quoted from compilations of the seventeenth century, but which go back to the eleventh century at the latest, would thus have come under Tighernach's condemnation.   But traditions may have interest and value even if they are not history in the sense of being an actual record of fact, and it would be unwise to disregard these traditions because an eleventh century Irish chronicler had sufficient critical insight to discern their unhistorical character.

DISCREPANCY BETWEEN ANNALS AND DINNSHENCHAS.

If we examine the statement concerning the cult of Crom Cruaich found, on the one side, in the Dinnshenchas, on the other, in the Annals, we notice an apparent discrepancy. The Dinnshenchas says that the idol was the god of every folk that colonised Ireland.   The Annalists, on the contrary, first mention the cult in connection with Tighernmas, a king of the last race—the Milesian—that invaded Ireland ; and one of them, Keating, definitely ascribes its establishment to him.   It seems natural at first blush to treat this discrepancy as due to difference in age between the two sources of tradition ; the Dinnshenchas, the older of the two, has, it may be thought, retained a trait, the pre-Milesian (*i.e.* pre-Goidelic, pre-Aryan) origin of the worship, which the Annals, representing the tradition of Milesian, *i.e.* Goidelic bards, have forgotten or slurred over.   Or, again, it may be held to testify to a change in the nature of the cult consequent upon the settlement of the Goidels in Ireland.   Such a change has been assumed by me to have

[1] Tighernach's *Annals* are being edited and translated by Dr. Whitley Stokes, in vol. xvii. of the *Revue Celtique*.

taken place among the continental Celts, sacrifices which were at the outset purely agricultural in character suffering considerable modification at the hands of a warlike aristocracy; here, it may be said, in evidence of a similar evolution among the insular Celts. But a tacit implication underlies both of these explanations—namely, that the legends recorded in the Annals have a genuine historic basis; that the succession of the various races, said to have colonised Ireland, represents a genuine succession of races, or, at all events, of stages of culture. Such an implication is, in my opinion, baseless, and a careful examination of the tradition proves that the real solution of the problem must be sought for in another direction, and has consequences of a far wider import.

THE REAL NATURE OF THE TIGHERNMAS TRADITIONS.

What have the Annals to say about Tighernmas? His reign wears an aspect obviously fabulous. Not only is it marked by great natural convulsions, but within its limits the arts and crafts, the rules and appliances, of social life are stated to have originated. We cannot fail to recognise a variant of a myth found at the beginning of history in the case of nearly all early races which have attained to the conception of history at all; the civilisation which early man sees around him—material, social, religious—must have had a cause, a beginning. This cause, this beginning, are sought in the activity, in the rule, of some greatly gifted king. The idea of slow evolution is either incomprehensible to man at a certain stage of mental development, or else is expressed wholly in mythic terms; his tendency is to synthesise long periods of growth, and to express this synthesis under the concrete symbol of a wonder-working reign. Although this interpretation of the traditions about Tighernmas is put forward for the first time,[1] I do not think it will fail to command the assent of all who have studied early traditional history, and I venture to regard it as established.

It is but natural that religious worship should be among the institutions the origin of which is assigned to Tighernmas's reign. The practices in question were intimately connected with the whole fabric of civilisation known to the framers of these traditions, and it would have gravely discredited my interpretation if reference to them had been lacking.

We can now appreciate the significance of the fact that Tighernmas's reign, the starting-point of Goidelic civilisation as the Goidel bards and wizards imagined it, is not assigned to the first arrival of the sons of Mil in Ireland, but to a period dated by different Annalists a hundred to one hundred and fifty years later. Milesian history prior to Tighernmas, including the account of the Milesian invasion and struggle against the Tuatha de Danann, is as purely mythological as is the history of the Tuatha De themselves. I do not imply by this that the traditions concerning Tighernmas are historic, in the sense of being a record of fact, in contradistinction to earlier mythical traditions; in a sense they, too, are mythical, but they are myths of a different character from those euhemerised in the annalistic account of the Tuatha de Danann. In the one case we have a mass of fiction based upon the personification of natural phenomena, or arising out of a ritual worship of natural

---

[1] M. d'Arbois, it is true, equates the reign of Tighernmas with the 'golden age,' when Kronos was Master of the Universe, in Greek mythology (*Cycle Mythologique*, p. 200), but his opinion of the texts differs considerably from mine.

energies and manifestations; in the other we have a synthesis of genuine historic processes expressed in a concrete symbol. The traditions about Tighernmas thus furnish us with a fixed point in the confused welter of prehistoric Irish mythic romance. The Goidels believed at one time that with this king started their civilisation, a vital element of which was their religion. Before him then their history is, in reality, occupied with beings, the object of religion—gods, that is; in other words, it is a mythology in the usual acceptation of the term.

This is a consequence of considerable moment for the criticism of the Irish pre-Christian records, reached solely by an unforced exegesis of the texts. A still more momentous consequence follows, for the reconstruction of Irish pre-Christian belief; the origin of this belief was by the Irish Celts themselves associated with the practice of ritual sacrifice, thus confirming amply both the statements of classical observers respecting the importance of this element in the religion of other branches of the Celtic race, and the inferences concerning it deduced from the classical account of Celtic metempsychosis in the foregoing chapter. The results, drawn from two wholly disconnected series of facts and observations, confirm each other, without, I trust, either result being due to a strained interpretation of the evidence. In this connection we cannot fail to be struck by the annalistic statements that Tighernmas perished whilst adoring Crom Cruaich, recalling as it does the fact that the ritual sacrifice of the king-priest, the representative and incarnation of the god, is the supreme act of worship in similar cults among other races.

If, in the light of this theory, we turn back to the double stream of tradition from whose apparent discrepancy concerning the Crom Cruaich cult we started, we plainly discern that it is apparent only. The Dinnshenchas statement may be regarded as testifying to a stage of tradition in which the mythic and heroic history of the race have already begun to be symbolised as successive colonisations of the island, without attaining the degree of precision and detailed fullness found in the Annals; it simply notes the immemorial antiquity of the worship in Ireland. The Annals belong to a more advanced stage; the mythology has been thoroughly euhemerised, with the consequence that the mythical reign, the fount and origin of civilisation, instead of being placed in the very beginning of the Annalistic record, is inserted in a long series of shadowy reigns, and its true character is thus disguised.

The theory I have just expounded by no means excludes the possibility that the Annalistic records may likewise reveal changes and developments in the ritual, following the arrival of the Goidels in Ireland. It is not necessary to assume at this stage that the cult we postulate belonged to this or that race exclusively. Our interpretation of the records is consistent either with the hypothesis of its purely Goidelic character, or with the supposition that it was taken over by the Goidels from a conquered pre-Aryan population. A myth concerning the origin of the cult would naturally attract to itself, influence, and be influenced by, any traditions concerning later modifications of the cult.

The mythical nature of the Tuatha de Danann has indeed been taken for granted throughout the course of this investigation. I could not do otherwise than agree with all previous writers on the subject whose knowledge and critical capacity qualified them to form a judgment. It was well, however, to clearly establish the fact, not on the strength of the romantic fiction devoted to this mysterious race of beings, but on the far more cogent, because unde-signed, evidence afforded by the form under which the traditions have come down to us, and the method adopted for turning them into pseudo-history. All doubt on the subject being, as I venture to think, finally removed, we may now proceed to consider the general mass of legendary fiction connected with the Tuatha de Danann.

CLASSIFICATION OF IRISH MYTHICAL LITERATURE.

Extant evidence may be divided into several classes. (1) We have in the Dinnshenchas a considerable mass of undated fragmentary tradition. It is *a priori* likely that the eleventh to twelfth century compilers of this collection took their matter indiscriminately from all kinds of sources, and the hastiest perusal confirms this surmise. Much of the matter contained in it may go back to the earliest stage of Irish story-telling, but each special item has to be tested upon its own merits. (2) In the Annals we find the fortunes of the Tuatha De euhemerised—*i.e.* these beings, originally gods, figure as mortal kings and heroes with well-assigned dates. This process of euhemerisation must have begun not very long after the Irish became acquainted with Christianity and Christian-classic culture; it offered the simplest means of saving the legends to which literary class and people alike were attached. As the tradition has come down to us it belongs, in the main, not to the pre-Viking period of formation (to the sixth-eighth centuries, that is), but to the great anti-quaries of the tenth-eleventh centuries who reconstructed Irish history and Irish legend after the stress of the Viking invasions had died away. The possibility of new elements having been introduced during the Viking period (roughly speaking, 800-950) must always be kept in view. In both these classes of tradition we find matters concerning the Tuatha De grouped together and forming more or less compact wholes. (3) But our next class of evidence is furnished by the incidental references to the Tuatha De scattered throughout the heroic legends, and of which so many examples have been quoted throughout this essay. I have cited sufficient to bear out the assertion that the tellers of these heroic legends did *not* regard the Tuatha De in the same light as the Annalists. Far from treating them as men who had once lived and were now dead, the Tuatha De figure in the legends as supernatural beings— immortal, or at all events unassigned to any definite period. (4) A further class of evidence is constituted by tales presenting substantially the same sequence and mass of incidents as the Tuatha de Danann sections in the Annals, but conceived and related in a romantic spirit. The question has not yet been even raised, let alone settled, whether these tales represent the material upon which the Annalist worked, or are romantic amplifications of the Annalistic statement.[1] (5) There is, finally, another class of evidence : the belief of the Irish peasantry of this and the previous century in the fairies who have succeeded to the attributes of the Tuatha de Danann ; our estimate of the value of this evidence must, of course, largely depend upon the results disclosed by our examination of the earlier classes.

THE ANNALISTIC ACCOUNT OF THE TUATHA DE DANANN.

It will be convenient to note precisely what the Annals have to record. The Four Masters and Keating give, be-

---

[1] M. d'Arbois, in his *Cycle Mythologique*, assumes their priority to the Annalistic account, but does not discuss the question in any detail.

tween them, the gist of what may be called the pseudo-historic or euhemeristic version—a version the outlines of which had begun to assume shape in all probability as early as the seventh century, but to which, even as late as the eleventh century, a distinguished Irish chronicler, Tighernach, refused historic credibility.

According to the Four Masters the Firbolgs took possession of Ireland, *anno mundi* 3266 (*i.e.* 1928 years before Christ), and ruled until they were vanquished by the Tuatha de Danann in the year 3303 at the battle of Moytura. In this battle Nuada, king of the Tuatha de Danann, lost his hand, and (it being a rule among the ancient Irish that no one with a personal defect or blemish could rule) Bress, son of Elatham, reigned in his stead. After seven years, Bress resigned the kingship to Nuada, who had had a hand of silver made for him by Dian-Cecht and Creidne the artificers. After a twenty years' reign Nuada was attacked by the Fomorians, led by Balor of the mighty blows. In the ensuing, the second battle of Moytura, Nuada was slain by Balor. He was succeeded by Lugh, the long-handed, who reigned for forty years, and was in his turn succeeded by Eochaidh Ollathair, named the Daghda. Suffice to say, that the rule of the Tuatha de Danann lasted until the year 3500, when the sons of Mil invaded Ireland, and in the battle of Tailtinn totally defeated the Tuatha De, after which two of the Milesian chieftains divided Ireland between them.

Such is the bald narrative of the Four Masters, which represents the supreme effort of the antiquary-historian class to rationalise Irish mythology, and to present it as a sober record of fact. If we turn to Keating, we note a far more liberal acceptance of the mythical, romantic element found in the older writers from which he and the Four Masters drew. Thus, we learn from him that the Tuatha De Danann were expert in magic art. An example of this is quoted from their history before they came to Ireland. They inhabited the present Greece, and, when the Athenians were assailed by the Syrians, aided them most effectually, 'for they used to send demons into the bodies of the slain Athenians, quickening them by means of their heathen lore' (p. 136). Thus the first glimpse we obtain of them is in that capacity of masters over the essence and manifestation of life which they retain throughout Irish legend. Afterwards they went to the north of Europe, where they dwelt a while in the four cities of Falias, Gorias, Finias, and Murias, whence they sailed for North Britain and Ireland, bringing with them four talismans : the Lia Fail, which possessed the property of roaring under every king of Ireland on his election [1] ; the sword of Lugh the long-handed ; the spear that the same Lugh used ; and the caldron of the Daghda. When they reach Ireland, they surround themselves with a magical mist, under cover of which they land unperceived. The account of the two battles of Moytura is substantially the same as in the Four Masters, but the supernatural character of the race is, more or less, definitely asserted in many of the passages quoted from older writers. It is, however, in his account of the Milesian invasion that Keating reproduces the largest amount of fable ; much of this is of no interest, being simple monkish fabrication with a view to connecting the Goidels with the peoples of antiquity, and in especial with the Hebrews, but some

---

[1] Cf. vol. i. p. 187. The earliest preserved mention of the talisman is in a poem of Eochaid ua Flainn's, preserved in the Book of Leinster.

interesting facts may be noted.   Thus, Mil himself is made
a contemporary of Pharaoh Nectanebus, a perfectly accept-
able date if we regard the Milesian invasion as a romantic
account of the Goidelic settlement in Ireland ; it is true
that this settlement conflicts utterly with Keating's later
chronology, which places the arrival of the sons of Mil in
Ireland about 1300 B.C., but this is only one proof among
many of the way in which independent and mutually
inconsistent traditions were forced into one Procrustean
bed by the Irish antiquaries.   When the sons of Mil
approached the coast, the Tuatha de Danann defended
themselves by their old expedient of a magical mist, and by
raising a magical storm, but in the end they were defeated.

Such is the pseudo-historical account.   Even in Keating,
with his love for a romantic tale, the rationalising process
has been thoroughly carried out, and, save for a few chance
references, little remains to attest the mythical character of
the Folk of the goddess Danu.   It is significant that one
of them should commemorate this capacity to restore the
dead to life, whilst another ascribes to them the power
attributed by classical writers to the priestesses of Sein,
namely, of raising and quelling storms by art magic.

The Battle of Moytura.

We may now compare a text belonging to the fourth
class of evidence discriminated above—that of romantic
tales which relate substantially the same events as those
found in the Annals.   The text in question is known as the
Battle of Moytura, and has been edited and translated by
Mr. Whitley Stokes in the twelfth volume of the *Revue
Celtique.*   It has only survived in a recent MS. (of the
fifteenth century), and its linguistic features do not allow its

ascription, *in its present form*, to an earlier period than the eleventh century. But I must again repeat, the date of the redaction, which has fortuitously come down to us, yields no certain clue to the date of the story itself. As the *Revue Celtique* is not accessible to the general reader, a somewhat full summary of the tale may be of interest.

The opening finds the Tuatha de Danann 'in the northern isles of the world, learning lore and magic, and druidism and wizardry and cunning.' The tradition is substantially the same as in Keating, but the latter can hardly have known our story, or he would not have missed its picturesque details. Thus, of the talismans it is told: 'the spear of Lugh, no battle was ever won against it or him who held it in his hand; the sword of Nuada, when it was drawn from its deadly sheath, no one ever escaped from it; the Dagdae's caldron, no company ever went from it unthankful.' We then learn that the Tuatha De made an alliance with the Fomorians: Balor, grandson of Net, giving his daughter Ethne to Cian, son of Dian-Cecht, 'and she brought forward the gifted child, Lug.' The Tuatha De then invaded Ireland, and here comes in a naïve bit of rationalism, which betrays the composite nature of our text, and the lateness of its final redaction: 'they burnt their barques at once on reaching Connemara, so that they should not think of retreating to them, and the smoke and mist that came from the vessels filled the neighbouring land and air; therefore it was conceived that they had arrived in a mist.' The first battle of Moytura follows, between the Tuatha de Danann and the Firbolgs; the latter are defeated, and seek refuge with the Fomorians. Nuada, being wounded, is ineligible for kingship, and the choice falls upon Bres, whose father, Elatha, is king of the

Fomorians. 'Now the conception of Bres came to pass in this wise. Eri, Delbaeth's daughter, a woman of the Tuatha De, was one day looking at the sea and the land, and she beheld the sea in perfect calm as it were a level board. And as she was there she saw somewhat. A vessel of silver was revealed to her on the sea. . . . Then she saw that in it was a man of fairest form. Golden yellow hair was on him as far as his two shoulders. A mantle with bands of golden thread was around him. His shirt had trimmings of golden thread. On his breast was a brooch of gold, with the sheen of a precious stone therein.' He woos expeditiously, and the maiden is not coy. When he would leave her she wept. 'Severing from thee I lament; the fair youth of the Tuatha Dea Danonn have been intreating me in vain, and my desire is for thee as thou hast possessed me.' He leaves her a gold ring, charging her not to part with it save to one whose finger it should fit. He also tells his name. 'Elotha, son of Delbaeth,[1] King of the Fomorians, hath come to thee. Thou shalt bear a boy, Eochaid Bres, that is, Eochaid the beautiful.' When the boy was born he had a fortnight's growth after a week, and at seven had reached a growth of fourteen years. Now when he was made king, the Fomorians 'bound their tribute upon Ireland, so that there was not a smoke from a roof in Ireland that was not under tribute to them.' The Tuatha de Danann champions were also reduced to menial service; Ogma had to carry a bundle of firewood, the Dagdae to build raths. The story is then told of Dian-Cecht's making a hand of silver for Nuada, and of his slaying his son who approved himself a better leech than

[1] Bres is thus apparently a son of brother and sister, as is Siegfried in German legend.

his father. Meanwhile, the chiefs of the Tuatha De murmured greatly against Bres: 'their knives were not greased by him, and however often they visited him their breaths did not smell of ale.' For this niggardliness he was made the subject of the first satire known in Ireland, and he was only allowed to remain king on promise of remitting the rent and tribute. But in his heart he purposed gathering together the champions of the Fairy-Mound, even the Fomorians, to overmaster the tribes. He got the recognition ring from his mother, and together they went to the land of the Fomorians. Recognised by his father, the latter refused to help him because his cause was not just, but sent him to Balor, King of the Isles, and to Indech, son of Dea Domnand, King of the Fomorians, 'and these assembled all their forces westwards unto Ireland, so that they made one bridge of vessels from the Foreigner's Isles to Erin.' [1]

Nuada was in sovranty over the Tuatha De. Once a great feast was being held at Tara, and the doorkeeper beheld a strange company coming towards him. 'A young warrior, fair and shapely, with a king's trappings, was in the forefront of the band.' On being asked his name, he answered that he was 'Lug, son of Cian, son of Dian-Cecht and of Ethne, daughter of Balor.' He was then asked his craft, 'for no one without an art entered Tara.' 'A wright,' said he. They needed no wright. 'A smith.' They needed no smith. 'A champion.' No! 'A harper.' No! 'A hero.' No! 'A poet and historian.' No! 'A sorcerer.' No! 'A leech.' No! 'A cupbearer.' No! 'A brazier.' No! Then he said, 'Ask the king if he has

---

[1] All this part of the story is undoubtedly coloured by events of the Viking period.

a single man who possesses all these arts, and if he has, I will not enter Tara.' The king then ordered the chess-boards [1] in Tara to be sent out to him, and he won all the stakes; and when *that* was told to Nuada, 'Let him into the garth,' said the king, 'for never before has a man like him entered this fortress.' Lug approved himself equally skilful as warrior and as harpist; and when Nuada beheld his many powers, he considered if here were not a champion able to put away the bondage under which they suffered from the Fomorians; and he changed seats with Lug until thirteen days were ended.[2] Thereafter Lug met with the Dagdae, Ogma, Goibniu, and Dian-Cecht, and they held secret converse for a year, and they summoned to them the wizards of Ireland, and their leeches and charioteers and smiths and farmers and brehons. But the king first sought to learn what

---

[1] Here occurs in the original one of the interesting examples of scribal interpolation which are not uncommon in Irish texts. 'But if chess was invented at the time of the Trojan war, it had not reached Ireland then, for the battle of Moytura and the destruction of Troy occurred at the same time.' The interest of such an interpolation is manifold; it shows the class of men to whom is due the final redaction of these stories, thoroughly well educated—nay, learned for their time, and gifted with critical power as well as with learning. Familiar with the Annalistic chronology as it had been developed by a succession of learned antiquaries, the scribe could not but note what seemed to him a gross historical blunder. Nevertheless, he made no change in the text he was reproducing, but contented himself with providing an antidote in the shape of a marginal note, which some later copyist transferred to the text. Obviously a man like this—a worthy and faithful but pedantic scribe—would do nothing in the way of romanticising his text. Rather may we conclude that if he felt justified in making any change, and this instance would seem to show that he didn't, he would have toned down and rationalised it.

[2] Thus giving him the kingship for a time.

aid he could gain from his followers. His sorcerer, Math-gen, would cast the mountains of Ireland on the Fomorians, and roll their summits against the ground—the twelve chief mountains of Ireland would support the Tuatha de Danann, in battling for them; his cupbearer would bring the twelve chief lakes of Ireland before the Fomorians, so that they should not find water therein whatever thirst might seize them—but drink should be provided for the men of Ireland, 'though they bid in battle to the end of seven years'; his druid would pour three showers of fire on the foes of the Fomorians, and would take out of them two-thirds of their valour and their bravery and their strength, and would bind their urine in their own body and in the body of their horses —but every breath the men of Ireland exhaled should be an increase of valour and bravery and strength to them. Then said the Dagdae: 'The power which ye boast, I shall wield it all myself.' 'Thou art the *good hand*' (Dagdae), was the cry; and the name stuck to him afterwards. Lug and Dagdae and Ogma obtained counsel and aid from the three gods of Danu, and during seven years they prepared for battle.

At length the two hosts found themselves in presence. The men of Ireland made a resolution not to allow Lug to go into the battle, as they feared an early death for him, owing to the multitude of his arts. The chiefs of the Tuatha De gathered around him, and he asked each one what power he wielded. In turn, Goibniu the smith, Dian-Cecht the leech, Credne the brazier, Luchta the wright, Ogma the champion, the Morrigan, sorcerers, cupbearers, druids, poets, and witches, vaunt their prowess. Lastly, the Dagdae declares that under his club the bones of the enemies shall be as hailstones under the feet of herds of horses. And so, when the battle raged, the weapons of the Tuatha de Danann, however much they suffered, were repaired at once by Goibniu and his comrades; the slain and maimed were restored to life or healed by Dian-Cecht and his kin. In vain did some of the Fomorian warriors sacrifice themselves to frustrate the magic wiles of their foe. But the Fomorians were mighty warriors, and the battle was desperate; 'harsh was the thunder throughout the battle, the shouting of warriors, the clashing of shields, the flashing and whistling of glaives, the rattling and jingling of quivers, the winging of darts and javelins, the crashing of weapons.' Nuada fell by Balor. 'An evil eye had Balor; never was it opened save only on the battlefield. . . . If an army looked at that eye, though they were many thousands in number, they would not resist a few warriors.' He had acquired this power thus: 'His father's wizards were cooking wizardry; he came and looked over the window, and the reek of the brew came on his eye.' He and Lug met, and Lug slew him with the cast of a sling, which carried the eye through the head, and thrice nine of his host died beholding it. The Fomorians were routed; and, as to the slain, 'they are in no wise to be numbered till we number stars of heaven, sand of the sea, flakes of snow, dew on a lawn . . . and the Son of Ler's horses in a sea storm.' Lug and his comrades captured Bres; to save his life he undertook that the kine of Erin should always be in milk, but this would not avail him; then, that the men of Ireland should reap a harvest in every quarter of the year, but this would not avail him; finally, he named the lucky days for ploughing and sowing and reaping, and for this he was spared.

THE RABELAISIAN ELEMENT IN IRISH MYTHOLOGY.

In the above summary I have simply given the sequence of the events common to this romantic tale and to the Annals, or which, at least, may reasonably be supposed to underlie the Annalistic account. The tale is told in a very confused way, offers incidents which are obviously out of place, or interpolated from other tales, and has a kind of underplot formed by adventures of the Dagdae. These are conceived in a Rabelaisian—and at times an ultra-Rabelaisian—vein, of which the Dagdae's visit to the Fomorian camp may serve as a specimen. Having asked for a truce, which is granted, he is offered his fill of porridge by the Fomorians ; the king's caldron is filled for him, five fists deep, into which went fourscore gallons of new milk and the like quantity of meal and fat. Goats and sheep and swine were put into it, and all were boiled together with the porridge. The entire mess was spilt into a hole in the ground, and the Fomorian chief threatened death to the Dagdae unless he consumed it all. The Dagdae was equal to the task ; and little wonder that at the end his belly was bigger than a house caldron. The complications which ensue are discreetly omitted by Mr. Whitley Stokes in his translation, alike on grounds of decorum and from the great obscurity of the passage. Indeed, it is noteworthy that, although on the whole the language of the tale is comparatively recent—not older, that is, than the eleventh century—and although certain portions give the impression of having been redacted perhaps a century or two later, yet, on the other hand, many passages are so archaic as to baffle Mr. Whitley Stokes, the greatest living authority on old Irish. If it be further added that the oldest portion of Cormac's Glossary—

a text that is of the tenth century—contains, *s.v.* Nescoit, an episode of our tale almost verbally the same, the reader, with Annals and romantic tale before him, will not be inclined to dispute the conclusion that the latter cannot be regarded as an amplification of the former, but must, on the contrary, be held to represent the mass of fiction out of which the Annalists extracted their dry and bald pseudo-history.   It is true that our tale, the only considerable surviving fragment of this romantic literature, is late in redaction, and has probably been considerably worked over in details, but it reproduces with substantial accuracy, I believe, the matter as well as the tone and manner of an earlier version.   In especial I regard the Rabelaisian, Aristophanesque element not as accidental and secondary, but as primary and essential, and as belonging therefore to the earliest literature in which the Tuatha de Danann mythology was embodied.   It is no chance coincidence, but is due to the essential kinship of the two bodies of mythic fiction, that this very element is prominent also in the mythology which has Dionysus for its centre.[1]

---

[1] The Rabelaisian passages which introduce the Dagdae are closely allied in style and tone to the great middle-Irish Rabelaisian burlesque, *The Vision of Mac Conglinne*.   As Professor Wollner has acutely pointed out in his Introduction to Professor Kuno Meyer's edition and translation, the Vision has come down to us in two forms : a shorter one which may go back to the eleventh or early twelfth century ; a longer one which is probably as late in redaction as the thirteenth century. The author of this second version followed the lines of the old story fairly closely, but clothed it in a form as picturesque, humorous, and masterly of its kind as anything in literature before Rabelais himself.   Professor Wollner has made it evident that neither version is a mere Irish imitation of the continental stories about the Pays de Cocagne, but represents a native development, on the burlesque side, of the fancies presented romantically in the Elysium voyages.   It may, in fact, be regarded as

COMPARISON OF ANNALISTIC AND ROMANTIC ACCOUNTS.

Now, if the Annalistic account be compared with the romantic one, it is seen that whereas the former, as befits the dignity of history, is wholly concerned with the strife in war and policy of rival races, the latter has for underlying theme the agricultural welfare of the land. The rule of Bres is marked by want and famine; his defeat is signalised by the return of material prosperity, which he is forced to guarantee, and by the institution of agriculture properly so called. It hardly needs pointing out that this element is not likely to have been introduced by storytellers of the twelfth, thirteenth, and fourteenth centuries. We possess a number of stories which may with certainty be assigned to these centuries, and which do develop the Tuatha de Danann mythology in a romantic vein, and probably without much regard for the authenticity of the traditions; but their development is on quite different lines. It is the princely, courtly, amorous, and wizard side of the Tuatha de Danann upon which they lay stress, and which they exaggerate in a manner that wearies when it does not offend. The rude and simple buffoonery of the comic interludes in the older mythic tales is, as a rule, foreign to the later mediæval fiction, which, *mutatis mutandis*, occupies in Irish legendary literature somewhat the same place that the Amadis cycle does in the literature of chivalric romance.[1]

a parody on the *genre* of mythic-romantic narrative studied in the first section of this essay. Professor Wollner states that all the elements of Mac Conglinne's vision of the land of unlimited eating belong to an early stage of agricultural development.

[1] There are exceptions—*e.g.* the story known as the Pursuit of the Gilla Dacker (*Silva Gadelica*, pp. 292 - 311 ; Joyce, *Old Celtic Romances*, pp. 221-273). But the comic element is supplied by the Fenian heroes rather than by the T. de D. wizards.

We must pause here for a moment and sum up the results of our investigation. The mythical nature of the Tuatha de Danann is proved by the fact of their preceding, in the legendary history of the race, the fabulous king to whose reign is ascribed the origin of civilisation; the story of their arrival in Ireland, of their conflict with the Firbolgs and Fomorians, of their dispossession by the sons of Mil, is thus, in the main,[1] mythology. At a comparatively early date, say in the seventh century A.D., the process of turning this mythology into pseudo-history began—a process similar in its essential spirit to that by which Euhemeros and other classic writers endeavoured to rationalise Greek mythology. The Annalistic account has preserved, however, some of the mythical features of the god clan—*e.g.* their magical power generally, and their dominion over the weather specially. The romantic fiction in which the mythology had been embodied, and from which the Annalists extracted their narrative, has disappeared in its earliest forms, but is represented with substantial accuracy by the only considerable remaining fragment of the second stage of this fiction—the Battle of Moytura. Here we find the magical powers of the Tuatha De strongly insisted upon, and likewise a connection of these beings with the agricultural welfare of Ireland, wholly lacking in the Annalistic account.

The surmise that the Tuatha De are, in part, at least, gods of growth and fertility, manifestations of the spirit of life animating in ever fresh transformations the whole of nature, is strengthened by the fact that in the legendary description

---

[1] I say, in the main, as it is not impossible that historical conflicts between the invading Goidels and the races they found in possession of Ireland may have supplied some details to the final redaction of the mythology.

of the beginning of civilisation (Tighernmas' fabulous reign), religious worship is identified with the cult of Crom Cruaich, a cult of ritual sacrificial nature, probably akin to that of which Dionysus was the object among the Greeks.

DINNSHENCHAS MENTIONS OF THE TUATHA DE DANANN.

The Dinnshenchas mentions of the Tuatha de Danann now claim our attention. In the first place, it is noteworthy that out of the 161 legends from this collection printed and translated by Mr. Whitley Stokes from the eleventh to twelfth century compilation, no less than forty-eight, or nearly one-third, are wholly or mainly concerned with the fortunes of this mysterious race. How large the proportion is must strike the student who remembers that in the literature which we can with certainty assign to the centuries preceding the eleventh, the Tuatha de Danann cycle, as such, fills a very small place. One could not wish for a more effective reminder how much of Irish mythic romance has perished beyond recovery, how unsafe must be any argument founded solely upon the occurrence in extant literature of this or that legendary theme.[1]

As a sample of the legendary matters contained in the Dinnshenchas, let us take the account of the origin of the famous fair held every third year at Carman on the first of August. 'There were three men who came from Athens and one woman with them, sons of Extinction son of Darkness son of Ailment, and their names were Violent, Black,

[1] The Dinnshenchas references are to Mr. Whitley Stokes' edition and translation of the Rennes MS. (*Revue Celtique*, vols. xv. and xvi.), of the Oxford MS., issued separately under the title *Bodley Dinnshenchas* (D. Nutt); and of the Kilbride MS., issued separately under the title *Edinburgh Dinnshenchas* (D. Nutt).

and Evil, and her name was Carman. By spells and charms and incantations the mother ruined every place. . . . So they came to Ireland to bring evil upon the Tuatha de Danann, by blighting the corn of this island upon them. To the Tuatha de Danann that seemed ill. So Ai, son of Ollam of their poets, and Cridenbel of their lampooners, and Lugh Laebach of their wizards, and Be'cuille of their witches, went to sing charms upon them, and parted not from them till they had driven the three men over sea.' Carman, left as a hostage, dies of grief, 'and she asked the Tuatha de Danann to hold her fair at her burial-place, and that fair and place should always bear her name. And the Tuatha de Danann performed this so long as they were in Ireland.' . . . 'For holding the fair, the Leinstermen were promised corn and milk, and freedom from control of any other province in Ireland ; that they should have men royal heroes ; tender women ; good cheer in every several house ; every fruit like a show ; and nets full of fish from waters. But if it was not held, they should have decay, and early greyness, and young kings.' [1]

EXPLANATION OF THE CARMAN LEGEND.

The full significance of this legend is not apparent until we recall that the first of August was a day sacred to Lug, the slayer of Balor, the master of all arts, the father of Cuchulinn, and, possibly, as we saw in the first volume, the oldest lord of the Happy Otherworld. In addition to the triennial festival at Carman, an annual festival was held at Tailltin in Meath, the institution of which was definitely ascribed to Lug. The story is thus told in the *dinnshenchas*

[1] R. D. No. 18.

of Tailtin : 'Tailtin, daughter of Magmor, was the wife of
Eochu the Rough, son of Dua the Dark. 'Tis by him the
fortress of the Hostages was built in Tara, and she was the
foster-mother of Lug, the son of the Dumb Champion. 'Tis
she that asked her husband to clear away for her the wood
of Cuan, so that there might be an assembly around her
grave. And after that she died on the calends of August,
and her lamentation and funeral games were held by Lugaid.
Hence we say Lugnasad.'[1] Keating, in his account of the
festival, remarks that the 'games resembled those calle
Olympic in Greece,' a remark far truer than he knew. F(
just as the Olympic games were at the outset the festival (
one special Greek tribe, to which circumstances gave a pai
Hellenic character, so we may judge that each Goidelic trit
celebrated its own Lugnasad, and that the same histori
circumstances which made Tara a political, made the neigh
bouring Tailltin a religious centre, and gave to its Lugnasa
a character of pre-eminence which it retained for over
thousand years at least. The natural tendency would be t
associate the god's name solely with his chief festival, and t
drop it in the mention of other festivals. But we are justifie(
in taking all the celebrations into consideration if we wish t(
form a clear idea of the nature of the festival. It happens,
too, and not infrequently, that the secondary and more
neglected examples of a rite preserve its primitive traits
better than the leading ones, to which a larger mass of
extraneous matter becomes, in the course of time, attached.
If, then, we take both legends as referring to the same festival
—the one (Carman) special to the Leinster tribes, the other
(Tailltin) common to the whole Irish race, we cannot fail to
note the predominantly agricultural character of the rite ; it

[1] R. D. No. 99 ; also Ed. D.

is connected with the discomfiture of evil powers hostile to vegetation, upon its due performance depends the welfare and increase of the soil.   That both accounts should start the festival from the death of a woman is suggestive in connection with Professor Rhys's explanation of the term Lugnasad as Lug's marriage—*i.e.* in his interpretation, the wedding of sun-god and earth, from which the life-giving produce of the soil was to spring.   This sacred marriage is, as we know, a widespread feature of the agricultural ritual studied by Mannhardt and Mr. Frazer, as underlying the polytheistic mythology of Greeks and Germans.   But just as the ritual often culminated in the sacrifice of the king-priest, the symbol or incarnation of the animating spirit of vegetation, so, too, his consort suffered not infrequently a like fate.   Such an interpretation of the legend as is here suggested cannot be regarded as assured, but it is at least plausible.

We have met with Bres, the Fomorian king over the Tuatha de Danann, both in the Annals and in the romantic tale.   The *dinnshenchas* of Carn Hui Net runs as follows : Bres, son of Elathan, died there ; 'tis he that in the reign of Nechtán Fairhand, King of Munster, demanded from every rooftree in Ireland a hundred men's drink of the milk of a hornless dun cow, or of the milk of a cow of some other single colour.   So Munster's kine were singed by him (Nechtán) in a fire of fern, and then they were smeared with a porridge of the ashes of flaxseed, so that they became dark brown.   That was done by the advice of Lugh Mac Ethlenn and of the wizard Findgoll, son of Findamnas ; and they also formed three hundred cows of wood, with dark brown pails in their forks in lieu of the udders.   These pails were dipped in black bog stuff.   Then Bres came to inspect the manner of these cattle, and so that they might be milked in his presence. . . . All the bog stuff they had was squeezed out as if it was milk. . . . The Irish were under a *geis* to come thither at the same time, and Bres was under a *geis* to drink what should be milked there. So three hundred bucketsful of red bog stuff are milked for him, and he drinks it all'![1] Little wonder that he died in consequence.

This curious legend has all the appearance of being one of those explanations of ritual which are the source of so many myths. The statement that the men of Ireland were under a *geis* or taboo to assemble at a particular place and time seems to indicate a festival of a similar character to the Lugnasad, and the remainder of the story is a description of the rites practised (passing the cattle through the fire as a substitute for actual sacrifice?) and an attempt to account for them.

At times we catch in the Dinnshenchas legends far-off echoes of a giant world, so mighty and so remote as to leave upon the mind the same thrill of uncanny wonder as is provoked by the mythical lists in Kilhwch and Olwen. 'Tuirbe's strand, whence was it named? . . . Tuirbe Fragmar, father of the Gobbán Saer, 'tis he that owned it. From that heritage he used to hurl a cast of his axe from the Hill of the Axe in the face of the flood tides, so that he forbade the sea, and it would not come over the axe. And no one knows his genealogy, unless he be one of the defectives who fled from Tara before the Master of Many Arts' (*i.e.* Lug).[2]

In this legend, which tells the power of Goibniu's father, we have not only a supreme manifestation of Tuatha de Danann dominance over the forces of nature, we have also, as Mr. Whitley Stokes has pointed out, a close parallel—the

[1] R. D. No. 46.   [2] R. D. No. 125 ; also Ed. D.

only one in the Aryan story-treasure—to a feat of Vishnu's told of in Aryan-speaking India at much the same time probably that the Goidels first landed in Ireland.

To return to the purely agricultural side of Tuatha de Danann power. This is how the Plain of Lifé got its name. 'Lifé, daughter of Cannan the Pict, wedded Deltbanna, son of Drucht. . . . Out of the elfmound of Bodb on Femen was he. South of Tara they set up, and because the plain over which she came seemed beautiful to her, she asked that her name might be in it; and Deltbanna dealt out no more liquor for the men of Erin until yon plain was called by his wife's name.'[1]

Nor is the semi-humorous element noticeable in the oldest romantic tales concerning the Tuatha de Danann absent from the Dinnshenchas. We are told that 'Gaible, son of Ethadon, son of Nuada of the Silver Hand, stole a bundle of twigs which Ainge, the Dagda's daughter, had gathered to make a tub thereof. For the tub which the Dagda had made for her would not cease from dripping while the sea was in flood, but not a drop was let out during the ebb. He hurled a cast of that bundle, and a fair wood grew thereout.'[2]

Mention has already been made in vol. i. (p. 211), of the legend known as the Conquest of the Sid, which tells how Angus, son of the Dagda, won his fairy palace of the Brugh and of its marvels. 'Great was the power of the Dagda over the sons of Mil, even after their conquest of Ireland,' says this tale. 'For the Tuatha de Danann, his subjects, destroyed the corn and milk of the sons of Mil, so that the latter were forced to make a treaty of peace with the Dagda. Not until then, and thanks to his goodwill, were they able to harvest corn and drink the milk of their cows.'[3]

[1] R. D. No. 12.   [2] R. D. No. 11.   [3] Quoted, *Cycle Myth.* p. 69.

This is perhaps the most definite statement that can be recovered from Irish mythic literature concerning the agricultural essence and potency of the Tuatha de Danann ; for this reason I have reserved it until now. The evidence previously adduced would suffice, I maintain, even in the absence of this statement, to assign to the Folk of the goddess Danu the *rôle* of protectors, fosterers, inspirers of vegetable and animal life ; and when this *rôle* is found connected with the practice of ritual sacrifice, the conclusion as to the true nature of the Tuatha de Danann seems inevitable.

HEROIC SAGA MENTIONS OF THE TUATHA DE DANANN.

But, it may be said, only one or two phases of the complex personality of the Tuatha De have been considered. Other evidence concerning these beings has been neglected. In this chapter I have adduced texts which, on the whole, deal with the Tuatha de Danann mainly, if not solely, and as a distinct group of individuals. But the many stories quoted in earlier chapters, alike from the Dinnshenchas and the Heroic Sagas, clearly show that this is not the only mode of their appearance in Irish mythic romance. Throughout the entire range of that romance, whether it tell of the Milesian kings who founded Emania, of the Ulster king, Conchobor Mac Nessa, and his knights, of Cormac, or of Finn and his band of warriors, the Tuatha de Danann appear as the friends, the protectors, the rivals, the opponents, of the mortal heroes. The story-tellers seem ignorant of any limitation of time imposed upon these wizard champions—they remain eternally wise and courteous and amorous throughout the thousands of years strung together by the chroniclers. Limitations of place, on the contrary, may be noted, especially in the later romances—the

invisible kingdom of Erin being parcelled out among the
folk of the *sid* as definitely as its outward form was shared
among the races of Niall or Owen, of Connall or of Brian.

How does the consideration of this aspect of the Tuatha
de Danann affect the estimate of their nature we have based
upon the more purely mythological texts? To rightly
answer this question we must keep steadily in view what
each class of mythico-romantic literature really is, and what
is the true import of its evidence. Comparison between
Ireland and Greece has already proved fruitful and illuminating. Resort may again be had to this expedient, and it
may prove of value not only as illustrating the unfamiliar
Irish by the familiar Greek literature, but as throwing new
light upon the latter.

COMPARISON OF GREEK AND IRISH MYTHIC LITERATURE.

We know Greek mythology on the literary side from
several sources. We have the witness of the heroic poems,
the most famous, of which, the Homeric, have come down
to us entire, whilst we have a considerable amount of information concerning the secondary and more imitative works.
This, the **epic tradition**, may be dated from the tenth to
seventh centuries B.C. The interest is primarily heroic,
only secondarily mythological. From the eighth and seventh
centuries we have the systematised, crudely philosophical
account of the mythology which has come down to us under
the name of **Hesiod.** To a somewhat later period belong the
more romantic versions of mythological episodes known as
the **Homeric Hymns.** From the seventh to fifth centuries
we have a number of scattered references in the **lyric poets,**
especially in Pindar, at the close of this period; in the
main the lyrists follow the epic tradition, but seem also to

have preserved traces of a number of local sagas which had not attained the honour of incorporation in the epic cycles. In the fifth century the **dramatists** furnish us with a great mass of new material only in part derived from the epic tradition, whilst the historian and philosopher make the first essays of critical rationalism applied to the mythology. But not until the great creative impulse of Greek literary art is long spent, not until the critical, antiquarian, **Alexandrine period**, do we get systematised surveys of the whole or definite portions of the mythology. The second century Apollodorus and Antoninus Liberalis; the first century Parthenius (imitated by Ovid), have preserved much precious material. Meanwhile, the critical philosophical spirit had been busily at work, and the mythology had either been rationalised into pseudo-history, as by Euhemeros, or refined away in a maze of metaphysical subtleties. But all this time, and for centuries longer, the practice of worship was kept up, the rites were duly performed, the personages of the ecclesiastical hierarchy recorded; and, from the mass of inscriptions and other historical texts relating to what may be called religious archæology, we derive valuable hints concerning the formal side of the mythology. So conservative were the ministers of public worship, that in the second century after Christ, **Pausanias**, travelling through the Greek world, describing the shrines *de visu*, and transcribing, where not deterred by religious scruples, the temple legends, transmitted to the modern world what is in some respects the most precious and authentic source of information concerning the myths of Hellas. At the present day the investigator of Greek religion starts, in the first place, with what may be the very latest recorded testimony—inscriptions, etc., dating possibly from the Christian period, or the evidence of Pausanias concerning the actual facts of worship; the Alexandrine compilers are often found to have an evidential value superior not only to the dramatic and lyric development of the epic tradition, but even to the very fount of that tradition—to Homer himself. The euhemeristic and philosophical interpretations are of value solely as witnesses to the existence of that which they endeavour to explain.

If we compare Greece and Ireland we see at once that the inscriptional, historic evidence by which, in the former, we can control and supplement the information derived from literature, is, in the latter, wholly lacking. Moreover, whilst the almost entirety of Greek mythic literature is earlier than, and absolutely unaffected by, Christianity, the entirety of Irish mythic literature, in its present form, is later than Christianity, and has been affected by Christian classic culture to some extent. In spite of these profound differences, comparison between the two literatures is not only possible but fruitful. The earliest Irish heroic cycles correspond to the Greek epic tradition, but it is doubtful if any Irish epic tale occupies in Irish literature the same position the *Iliad* does in Greek; rather must the Irish tales be regarded as answering partly to the latest cyclic poets, partly to the archaicising, imitative school represented in Greece by the third-century Apollonius Rhodius. The Irish Hesiod is the Book of Invasions, but unfortunately this is, of all portions of the Irish mythic record, the one which has been most deformed by the alien culture of Christianity. Luckily, a small amount of the mythology, treated euhemeristically in the Book of Invasions, has come down to us in romantic form; this may be compared with those myths preserved by the Homeric Hymns. Finally, to the compilatory, descriptive section of Greek mythological literature—Apollodorus, Antoninus Liberalis, Pausanias—correspond, though very imperfectly, the Irish compilations, known as the Coir Anman, or mythico-heroic biography, and the Dinnshenchas, or mythico-heroic topography.

Just, then, as the student of Greek myth turns to the actual details of the cult and to the literature which is most closely connected therewith, if he wishes to form a clear idea of the nature and origin of a divinity, using the poetic representation by the epic or dramatic singer as a secondary and controlling source of information, so the student of Irish myths must seek for precise evidence as to the nature of the Irish gods from the compilations rather than from the heroic sagas. The reason is evident. All forms of literature—the rudest as well as the most sophisticated—are subject to the same necessity, that of interesting the hearer or reader in the fortunes of the personages presented to him. In heroic sagas the gods can but appear as foils to or conveniences for the hero; they are not the leading characters, and it is essential that their powers or fortunes should not compete with those of the real heroes. Moreover, from the numberless incidents of the god's career known to the heroic singer, it is almost inevitable that certain ones alone should be chosen for the complex web of his narrative. Fighting and love-making are the staple of heroic saga as of all romance; it is the warlike and amatory side of the Pantheon which will be represented in it far more frequently and certainly than that which would find expression in the ritual legends.

'Tis then, I would urge, vain to seek in mentions of the Tuatha De, scattered through the Cuchulinn and other heroic sagas, aught else than, in the nature of things, we can find there—reference to the warlike and amorous exploits of these beings, presented so as to be an effective foil to the fortunes of the mortal or semi-mortal hero. It is much that we were able to recover from the heroic sagas the picture of beings pre-eminent in art magic, capable of assuming all shapes at will, lords of a land of ideal plenty in which every form of vivid, sensual, material enjoyment is present; masters of the mystery of life, by whom the perpetual flow and transformation of the animating essence (which in this world can only be maintained by bloody sacrifice and inevitable death) is so ordered and governed that neither death nor decay assail them. It would be too much to look for those myths, dependent upon and symbolising the ritual, which form the root of all the complex manifestations of the divine personality. As it is, now that analysis has led us to this point, the connection of the two conceptions we are investigating must seem natural and legitimate; the god from whose favour are sought fertility and increase, who is himself the incorporate symbol of life and growth manifest in perpetually recurring, ever varying, yet eternally similar forms, is also lord of the land in which fertility and increase find their highest expression.

DEVELOPMENT OF THE TUATHA DE DANANN MYTHOLOGY.

The development of the mythical literature connected with the Tuatha de Danann may now be briefly sketched. Originally, if we may judge from analogy, it doubtless consisted wholly of chants forming part of the ritual, and of legends accounting for and interpreting ritual acts. Out of such materials there would gradually arise a mythology—an attempt, that is to say, to represent the phenomena of the natural and social world under the guise of a divine history. Removed one degree from its primitive function of being a simple assistant and exponent of the ritual acts upon which depends the material welfare of the race, the mass of mythic legend becomes complex and plastic; its divine *dramatis personæ* acquire a wider range of attributes, supplementary, as a rule, to the primitive conception, but often transcending and supplanting it. A body of narrative comes into being, plot and incidents and personages of which are readily adaptable to that idealised representation of racial history known as heroic saga. But when the gods enter the world of mortal heroes, they must bow to the conventions of heroic legend; they insensibly put off more and more of their primitive character, and tend to approximate to the ideal standard of their mortal antagonists and interlocutors. In the case of the Tuatha De, two of their essential characteristics not only persist after their inclusion in the heroic sagas, but are developed and influence the development of the heroic epos. As holders and givers of life, the Tuatha De are alike deathless and capable of manifestation under the most diverse forms—hence their wizard might, hence, too, the attribute of deathlessness so marked a feature of themselves and their land; as bestowers of fertility and increase, they are, by their nature, liberal and amorous. Thus is formed that picture of these beings found in the oldest heroic sagas, long antedating, in all likelihood, the rise of Christianity, almost unaffected by the advent of the new faith, and persisting in literature down to this very century. The fairy loves of Etain or of Cuchulinn, the hosts of Connla or Cormac, had sufficiently sloughed off their godhead to retain their place undisturbed in the heroic romance which was loved with equal fervour by the half-pagan bard and the Christian saint. It went otherwise with the mythology properly so called. This could not but conflict with Christianity, and was only preserved under a form—the pseudo-historic—which masked its real nature, or, as in the case of the Battle of Moytura, was associated with and subordinated to the pseudo-history. To some extent the process of turning the mythology into history may have reacted upon the heroic sagas, though most of them had assumed a settled shape long before. Some modification seems to have taken place with a view of bringing them into line with the Annalistic schemes devised by the antiquary class. The fact, too, that beings, originally deathless, were assigned to definite dates, tended, in some cases, to emphasise that 'mortalising' (if I may coin the word), of the Tuatha De, which itself was a necessary consequence of their inclusion in these heroic cycles.

Pre-eleventh century Irish literature has thus preserved the outlines of the mythic narratives which grew out of the old chants and ritual legends, but only more or less disguised as pseudo-history; in the case of certain texts—e.g. the Battle of Moytura—the disguise is slight and unessential, the body of the story is genuine mythology. It has also preserved, in the narrative of the dealings between the Tuatha De and the heroes, glimpses of these beings which are but little younger in age than the purely mythological conceptions. Both forms—mythic and heroic—had passed into literature long before the Viking invasion; their substance persists in the post-Viking redactions, although the latter have certainly been affected in small details by the events of the ninth and tenth centuries. But as a whole, myth and heroic epos alike belong to the oldest and most genuine manifestations of Gaelic belief and romantic fancy.

In post-eleventh century literature, as is but natural, the

Tuatha De tend to break away more and more from their primitive mythological basis, and to develop upon lines laid down in the heroic sagas. It is possible, also, that the lateness of the date at which the great southern heroic saga, that of Finn and his warrior band, came into the hands of the professional bardic class, is responsible for the obliteration of certain mythic features of the Tuatha De in this cycle. On the other hand, it must not be forgotten that the wizard god-clan plays a far more important part in the Fenian than in the older cycles.[1] Be this as it may, the tendency in the mythic romance of the thirteenth to the eighteenth centuries is to accentuate the courtly, amorous, and magic side of these beings; to leave in the shade their original agricultural character, and to eliminate the Rabelaisian element.

It should be added that the true nature of the Tuatha De was never entirely lost sight of in Ireland. I have already quoted several passages clearly showing that Irish scribes and antiquaries recognised these beings as the gods of their ancestors, and were led astray neither by the romantic nor by the pseudo-historic presentment of their forms in the literature of the time. More remarkable still is the fact, as vouchsafed for by an entry in the Book of Armagh (*i.e.* dating at the latest from the tenth century), that the mythical belongings of these beings were correctly described; the unknown writer styles them *dei terreni*— gods of the earth.

---

[1] The reason for this is, I think, obvious. The Northern cycle was fashioned by the bards at a time when the heroic tradition was still looked upon as history; it was sung before men who claimed descent from the heroes. Hence the subordination of the immortal, the prominence of the mortal element.

I have hitherto refrained from making any use of the
fairy belief of modern Ireland. It was necessary, in the
first place, to form a clear idea concerning the nature and
development of the ancient belief with which it is connected. Historical and mythological evidence has been
adduced in support of the contention that the Tuatha De
are, in the main, deities of agriculture, and that their
worship consisted, in the main, of ritual sacrifices. We
are now in a position to examine the evidence of modern
folklore, and see if it also supports this contention.

CHAPTER XVIII

THE CONTEMPORARY FAIRY BELIEF OF THE GAELIC-SPEAKING PEASANT

Irish mythic literature in its relation to peasant lore—Parallel of Greek and Irish mythic literature in their relation to national life—The essential elements of Irish peasant lore—The conservatism of Irish social organisation—The influence of Christianity—Formal classification of Irish peasant lore—Its true nature—The fairies; fallen angels explanation; peculiar signification of the Gaelic versions — Special features of fairy lore; the agricultural festivals and their connection with the fairy world; local character of the Irish fairies; fairy love of neatness; fairy revels by night; witchcraft and fairydom; the changeling belief; Irish in relation to general European fairy lore—The Tuatha de Danann and death.

THE foregoing discussion shows us that we must be prepared to expect elements of varying origin and date in modern fairy lore, and gives us useful hints for distinguishing them. We have seen that the original basis of the Tuatha de Danann mythology is an agricultural creed expressing itself in a ritual determined by the sequence of the seasons and their relation to agricultural operations, and having for its animating principle a conception of life as something fluid and indestructible, derivable from powers which need to be sustained and placated by sacrifice if they are to perform efficiently the services which their human worshippers seek at their hands. Overlaying this

199

primitive basis, dependent upon it in its main outlines, but differing largely from it in detail and in colouring, we find a mythology which appeals to other than purely agricultural needs and interests, which is intended more especially for the warrior and governing class, which has taken account of the enlargement of religious conceptions due to the widened material and intellectual horizon of the race, and which has become plastic by having passed out of the hands of a sacerdotal class, intent solely upon preserving the formulas of ritual and their orthodox explanation, into those of a literary class intent mainly upon pleasing an audience of chiefs, champions and (to an extent which varied considerably at different periods) great ladies.   This second stage of the mythology, in all its varying forms, and developed in directions which led it far away from its original starting-point, has formed the staple of purely Irish literature from the earliest period to which we can trace it back down to its practical extinction in the last century.   By far the largest portion of that literature is heroic saga, stories about famous kings, warriors, and heroines of olden times; when these stories are examined with any care they are found to be versions, more or less altered by an admixture of historic fact or deliberate poetic fancy, of mythological tales.   In view of this fact much of the elaborate discussion bestowed upon the historic credibility of these sagas is beside the mark.   It is possible that men named Cuchulinn or Finn or Cormac did actually live at about the dates traditionally assigned to them, and were famous chiefs or warriors; it is certain that 99-100ths of what is ascribed to them bears no relation whatever to historic fact, but is simply older myth slightly humanised, or new invention on the lines of older myth. This literature, although appealing mainly to the fighting, ruling class, was yet common to the whole people ; the tradition was living and national, it was the task of the official poet or story-teller to give it voice and form, but his subject-matter was, in the main, imposed upon him, and he could not, even had he wished, depart widely from the traditional outlines. Hence there was, so far as we know, no such break between the highest literature of the time and the mass of the people as there is, for instance, in modern times, where first-class literature, save in the case of a few religious classics, is neither appreciated by nor exercises any influence upon the majority of the nation.

Thus the Irish peasant necessarily became familiar with the bardic, romantic version of the mythology ; it is doubtful if there was ever any real consciousness on his part of the changes in spirit and incident which gradually modified the old stories. The new world takes its place by the side of the old. On the other hand, although historic records represent the mass of the population as engaged as much, apparently, in fighting as in those occupations of sowing, reaping, hunting, fishing, cattle-breeding, in which the mythological conception had a serious and practical and not merely an æsthetic or historical value, yet we know that this must arise from the imperfection of the record. Raids and cattle-spoilings and expeditions to win fresh territory or to carry off desirable damsels, are more interesting alike to teller and hearer than the bare chronicle of harvests, but, after all, the folk at large must always have been engaged mainly in bread-winning, an arduous task dependent as we have seen upon the good-will of mysterious powers, to assure which definite means were requisite. So we may take it that these means were never neglected, whatever else might be, and that the antique powers, however much they may have changed in appearance and attribute, received their prescribed meed of rite and sacrifice. Thus, a portion at least of the older myth store would be preserved, and in course of time the same power would come to wear a double aspect, rustic or courtly, according as the stories concerning him belonged to the earlier or the later stage of the mythology.

Mythic Literature in Greece and Ireland.

We may again find in Greece at once a parallel and a contrast to the development of mythic literature in Ireland. Down to a certain period, alike the substance and the animating spirit of Greek literature are almost wholly drawn from the mythology, and down to that period the literature is national, accessible to, shared in, and understanded of all. The æsthetic and intellectual impulse of the race manifested itself at the set and hallowed seasons when a common purpose of worship, rejoicing, emulation, effort, intensified the energy and the sense of brotherhood of the Hellenic tribes. Then came a change; the highest minds of the race turned away from the mythology; Homer, Hesiod, Pindar, the tragedians, the heroic historian Herodotus, are replaced by Thucydides, Plato, the orators, the writers of realistic comedy. The mythology loses its import for the thinker, the man of letters, and, coincident with this loss, literature puts off its national character and becomes the interest and occupation of a class. But all the while the practical side of the mythology maintained itself in full vigour; the antique rites were performed in the prescribed manner, the business of religion was carried on as before. In Ireland there is nothing corre-

sponding to the great break at the close of the fifth century
B.C. between the Greek thinker and artist and the traditional mythology; the Irish man of letters never outgrew
his archaic ideal.   But the practical, the business side of
the mythology, was revolutionised by the introduction of
Christianity.   In Greece the poet and philosopher came
to disdain or ridicule the myth, whilst the priest still performed the rite with slavish accuracy.   In Ireland the
myth, with a modicum of change, lived on in the poet's
heart and brain, the rite had to yield, to disappear, to
hide, or to disguise itself before the alien faith.   Down to
the introduction of Christianity the Irishman was in the
position of the Greek to whom participation in the Thar-
gelia, or the rites of the Eleusinian mother, and the public
reading of the Homeric poems, the recitation of the epi-
nician odes, the performance of the crowned tragedy, were
all acts of kindred nature having the like intent and
sanction.   After the introduction of Christianity his rude
substitutes for Homer, the ode, or the drama, still retained
their sway over him, but his Dionysus, his Demeter, had
to creep back to the peasant's hut, their earliest home, to
forfeit the pomp and circumstance of kingly and sacerdotal display.

THE ESSENTIAL ELEMENTS OF IRISH PEASANT LORE.

A priori, then, we might postulate certain things about the
belief of the Irish peasant.   After all, strive as may kings
and priests, change as may modes of government and faith,
man, equally with all animated nature, must eat and breed,
and grow and decay and die.   It is only amongst a comparatively small section of humanity that the true nature of
such influence as man can exercise over the great recurrent

manifestations of natural life is recognised and acted upon.
For the vast majority of the peasant class the proper mode
of compelling the essence of life to manifest itself as we
wish is what the cultured style a supernatural one, by
means of rite and spell or charm.   The peasant is alike
credulous and sceptical, tenacious of old custom and
largely tolerant to anything that appeals to his sense of
logic.   He will grant the efficacy of the Christian rite,
especially when it is presented to him under the quasi-
mythological guise of saintly influence, but he will not
renounce the older practice; in dealing with powers so
capricious as those of Nature, the wise man accepts all the
help he can get; the saint may fail here, the fairy there,
the witch in a third case, and where the one fails the
other may succeed.   And the older powers he cherishes,
in spite of priests and saints, are not the gods whom the
imagination of poets and the ambition of priests had
glorified, rather their ruder prototypes to whom all along his
worship had been paid.   When, bereft of their trappings,
shorn of their splendour, Dionysus and Demeter creep
back to the peasant's hut, he is conscious of little sense of
degradation, they are not suddenly unfamiliar to him as
they are to priest and bard who had embodied in them
the highest ideal of the race.   So the ancient rite, little
changed it may be from its earliest inception, lives on
fairly harmoniously (save in cases to which we shall allude
presently) by the side of the newer ones.   Bread must
be won, and man must have his proper machinery for
influencing and controlling the life that quickens and dies
in the bread.   But man does not live by bread alone.   He
has a fancy to be charmed, an intellect to be satisfied.
The new faith has much for both needs, but here again

the old faith retains its power. And whereas in every other European land the ministers of the new faith were as bitterly opposed to the fanciful as to the business aspect of the older creed, in Ireland it is the saint who protects the bard, the monk who transcribes the myth, whilst the bird flock of Faery, alike with the children of Adam, yearn for and acclaim the advent of the apostle.

THE CONSERVATISM OF IRISH MYTH.

Thus the imaginative part of the mythology lived on little influenced by the new order of things, subject only to the natural development which accentuated the courtly and amorous side of its personages. True, a new imaginative literature in the shape of saintly legend and apocrypha claimed the ear of the folk, but it differed too much from the older tales to influence or be influenced by them to any appreciable extent. What is noteworthy is, that after the introduction of the new faith, literature, whether Christian or non-Christian, remained in the main national. The organisation of court bards and story-tellers was maintained, the great social gatherings, such as the fairs of Carman and Tailltin, the Irish equivalents of the Greek Olympic festival, were kept up, the mass of the people continued to share in the intellectual and artistic life, such as it was, of the higher classes. Until native Irish society was finally broken up, until in the course of the seventeenth and eighteenth centuries the higher classes attained a higher level of culture, foreign in essence and form, which effectually separated them from the remainder of their countrymen, this state of things continued—Gaelic Ireland, even down to the time of Michael Comyn and the

last bards of the eighteenth century, possessed a homogeneous culture, a common literary convention.

The Influence of Christianity.

We may discern in the lore of the Irish-speaking
peasant two elements, the one practical—for use ; the other
imaginative—for pleasure.   Either element is partly derived
from Christianity, partly and to a much greater extent from
pre-Christian conceptions.   In both cases the non-Christian portion has been somewhat influenced by Christianity,
but in greatly varying measure.   The imaginative element
has only suffered outward unessential changes in the rare
and secondary instances in which it has been changed at
all.   Not so the practical, work-a-day element   Here there
was direct possibility of conflict with the Church's claim
to control and guide the operations of nature to the advantage of her faithful sons.   Even if the priest did not
himself care to listen to stories of Finn and the Tuatha de
Danann, he could indulge his flock in their chief intellectual pastime provided mass was duly attended and
the homily duly listened to.   It was otherwise when belief
in powers that interfered at every moment in the peasant's
life was concerned ; it was the Church's prerogative to
bless harvest and herd, to make intercession for shower or
sunshine, to be the recognised intermediary for praise and
thanksgiving.   It is curious to see how the inevitable
rivalry affected the older faith.   The Church did not as
a rule contest the reality of the adverse powers, but it
stamped them with an unholy brand—they were demons,
or the neutral angels, whatever might was theirs in the
present they were bereft of all hope of future bliss.   Here

too there was discrimination; the more potent the efficacy
of the pre-Christian rite, the more it would arouse the
opposition of the Christian priest as tending to draw away
the peasant from the true path. Much was indifferent,
harmless even, it could not be approved, there must attach
to it a vague sense of the uncanny, the unallowed, but
still it might be tolerated, passed over with indulgence.
Much, on the other hand, in the older faith was in itself
fierce, monstrous, obscene, though in using these words
we must recollect that they convey to us a sense of reprobation which was totally lacking at the time. The bloody
sacrifice, the frenzied and orgiastic spring and harvest festival,
were expressions of religious fervour as were, to cite similar
instances, the sacrifice to Moloch and the midnight worship
of Dionysus. It is these intense and awful rites that are
really potent, it is to them, when the milder agencies of
Church or fairy prove of no avail, that the peasant has
recourse. The Church cannot tolerate or even ignore
them, it must oppose and thunder against them. And
so in the peasant's mind the natural horror of certain
conceptions and certain rites is intensified by the fact
that they essentially are the forbidden thing. Whether
this does not in a measure tend to heighten his appreciation of the potency attaching to them is another matter;
it may fairly be argued that by branding as unholy and
malign certain features of the older faith, the Church has
in reality kept them alive, it may be asked whether witchcraft be not largely a product of the attitude taken up by
adherents of the higher towards the most archaic and
savage features of the lower faith. In any case, the varying attitude of the Church—tolerant, mildly censorious,
fiercely antagonistic—towards varying portions of the

peasant creed might be expected to react upon and influence their development.

FORMAL CLASSIFICATION OF IRISH PEASANT LORE.

If we classify peasant lore from a somewhat different
point of view, we may divide it into practices which presuppose, more or less, the existence and activity of certain
extra-human powers, into sayings about these powers, and
into stories of which they are the *dramatis personæ*, the
first two classes forming what I have styled the practical,
the third, the imaginative element of the lore. In the
first class we may have features of immemorial antiquity,
dating far beyond the period in which druid and bard
elaborated a Gaelic Pantheon and a Gaelic mythology out
of the ruder powers of growth and renovation, we may
have features belonging to the period of druidic and bardic
ascendency, we may have features due to the influence of
Christianity exercised in varying measure upon the older
creed, and finally, we may have features wholly Christian
in their origin, but distorted in the peasant's mind, accom-
modated to his level of intellect and fancy. In the second
class, the sayings about the powers, all will probably be
derived from the druid and bard, as far as the pre-
Christian element is concerned, from the priest as far as
the Christian element is concerned, with some adjustment
to ruder conceptions in the first case, with much distortion
and transposition to a different plane of thought and feeling in the second case. The third class, the stories of
which extra-human powers are the *dramatis personæ* belong
in the main to the secondary and tertiary stages of the pre-
Christian mythology, although the amount of stories purely

Christian in origin is fairly considerable; in the mutual action and reaction of pre-Christian and Christian mythic romance it is at least possible that the latter is the weaker, that the peasant's ideal of the saint is influenced by and assimilated to that of the champion and wizard rather than that the contrary operation takes place.

In these general *a priori* considerations, as to what we may reasonably deduce concerning the Irish peasant lore of the last five hundred years from the known historical factors and conditions of the previous thousand years, I have, as will be recognised by all familiar with the subject, sketched the outlines of that lore, as extant at the present day, briefly but comprehensively. In every considerable body of belief and practices there are a multitude of primary features referable directly to the fundamental conceptions of the creed ; there are, furthermore, a number of features due to the normal, but nevertheless highly differentiated, development of those conceptions ; there are features, mostly secondary, due to abnormal development caused by the intrusion of alien conceptions; there are, finally, features which cannot be explained at all, a fact due either to the imperfection of our knowledge, or to that element of purely individualistic fancy which plays in psychological evolution the same part that the tendency to 'sports' does in physiological evolution. Leaving this very small residuum of the inexplicable out of account, I think I may venture to assert that nearly the whole of Irish fairy lore can be interpreted by aid of the historical factors and conditions I have mentioned—an agricultural ritualism out of which has grown a romantic mythology, opposed by, mingling and harmonising with, an alien ritualism and an alien body of romance.

I do not propose to essay here a methodical exposition and interpretation of Irish fairy mythology upon the lines indicated above. Such a task would require at least three or four hundred pages, and it would, in a large measure, be a simple repetition of the admirable essay prefixed by Jacob and William Grimm to their translation of Crofton Croker's Fairy Legends and Traditions of the South of Ireland, which appeared at Berlin under the title *Irische Elfenmärchen* in the year 1826, and was translated, most excellently, by Crofton Croker in his third volume, published in 1828. Indeed, much that I have advanced in the foregoing pages of this chapter had already been stated, definitely or conjecturally, by the brothers Grimm, and if I am able to carry the elucidation of the subject beyond the point at which they left it, this is simply because I have access to sources of information, the pre-eleventh century literature of Ireland, which had not been opened up in their day. As regards the actual peasant lore, scanty and questionable in form as were the facts upon which they had to work, their interpretation is nearly always as sound as it is illuminating. I propose, then, rather to emphasise certain elements, the importance of which seems to me to have been overlooked, and to suggest an agricultural connection for others which have hitherto been explained differently or left unexplained. Moreover, as is obvious to any well-informed student now, as it was to the brothers Grimm in 1826, the mass of Irish fairy lore is akin to that found among the peasantry of every European land. Any general principle of interpretation must be applicable to Teutonic or Romance, as well as to Celtic peasant lore. But the latter has its *differentia*; these, if the foregoing considerations have any validity at all, should find their explanation in the historical conditions which have separated the Celtic world so markedly from the rest of European Christendom. I shall endeavour to show that where Irish fairy belief differs from that of the rest of Europe, the difference is due to causes familiar to the reader of the foregoing pages, to the same causes which have determined the special evolution of Irish culture generally.

THE FALLEN ANGELS EXPLANATION OF THE FAIRIES.

The Irish peasant shares the belief common to all European peasantry, that the fairies are either the fallen angels who for some reason have escaped the nethermost pit, or those who, remaining neutral, and retaining their more than mortal powers, were punished by denial of access to that bliss which is open to every mortal if he believe in and practise the true faith. This wide-spread belief was an almost inevitable outcome of contact between two systems of faith, each of which held as firmly as the other the objective reality of the fairy powers, and one of which, and that the dominant one, regarded them as hostile, or at least suspicious. But its existence has never, to my knowledge, been properly utilised for the history of fairy mythology. The fallen or neutral angels play no important part in the purely Christian scheme, nor is their influence and activity as natural a development from early Christian doctrine as is for instance the intercessory, propitiatory power of the saint; it is, therefore, unlikely that the Christian missionary would have introduced the legend unless he was confronted by beliefs, and what seemed to him facts, which he could not account for in any other way. On the other hand, we know exactly how he did account for the official gods of paganism to whom an organised worship was paid—he described them as devils, their worship as devil-worship. Thus, whilst the wide spread of the legend testifies to the equally wide spread of the existence of the belief to explain which it was framed, the difference between the attitude of Christianity towards it and towards official paganism, testifies to a strongly-marked difference between the two—in the eyes, that is, of the first Christian missionaries. For *we* must not exaggerate the difference or misapprehend its nature. It was a matter of outward and visible form rather than of inward spirit. In the one case the Christian priest was confronted, often bitterly opposed, by a rival sacerdotal organisation, in the other case he had to deal with peasants willing enough to accept his organisation, provided he did not interfere too rudely with their beliefs and practices. Small wonder if the supernatural power worshipped by the pagan priest became a devil in the Christian's eyes, whilst for the peasant divinities the fable of the neutral angels was sufficient reprobation.

Now in Ireland this story, which belongs, as I have said, to common European folk-lore, is told with details found nowhere else, and which reveal its true nature. In 1879, an old woman at Askeaton, near Limerick, told Mr. David Fitzgerald that 'Crom Dubh, St. Patrick's servant, was asked by the fairies to put the following question to his master, "What time will the Slánagh Sídhe go to Paradise?" "Not till the Day of Judgment, for certain," answered the saint. Before that the Good People used to put the sickles in the corn and the spades in the ground, and spade and sickle used to be seen working for men without visible assistance; but thenceforward the Sídhfir would do nothing. The question was put on the last Sunday in July, and ever since, that day (or the first Sunday in August it sometimes is) is called in Ireland Crom Dubh's Sunday.'[1]

It would be difficult to find a more terse or pregnant historical myth. Prior to the advent of the new creed, the ancient powers had controlled and directed the growth of cereal and pasture, they had worked unseen and in mysterious wise, but now their reign was over, the priest had come, and they would do nothing. The psychology and history of two religions are summed in the old wife's tale. This is the most striking instance of the conception known to me, but it finds varying expression all throughout Ireland. Another of Mr. Fitzgerald's informants tells us that when the fairy heard the saint's answer he said, ' If that's so, we'll do good and bad (before that they had done nothing but good).' Again, a Donegal variant makes the questioner none less than Mananann Mac Lir; the question is put to Colum Cille, and when the answer is returned, ' There is no forgiveness to be got,' Manannan exclaims, 'Woe is me! for years I've helped the Catholics of Ireland, but I'll do it no more, till they're weak as water.'

In the latter instance, the name of the anxious questioner shows his connection with the old mythology, a connection still more marked in the Askeaton story. For Crom Dubh, Patrick's servant, is, there can be little doubt, identical with the Cromm Cruaich, before whose image, set up on the plain of Mag Slecht, the folk of Ireland, as we have already seen, were wont to sacrifice a third of their offspring.

---

[1] *Revue Celtique*, iv.

The legend told how the saint had broken the power of the life-thirsty idol; he touched it with his crozier, and the image bowed itself before him, Crom Dubh became Patrick's servant. It is significant that the day sacred to him corresponds closely in point of time to that of the great harvest-festival, the Lugnassad, which was celebrated throughout all Celtdom in the first week of August. Mr. Leland Duncan found that in Leitrim, on the last Sunday of July, known as Garland Sunday, the young folk dress the wells in their neighbourhood with garlands of flowers.[1] Here there is but little trace of the ancient Lugnassad, but at Kilmanahan, a Meath parish, in the early part of this century, the Sunday was devoted to horse-racing and dancing, whilst the previous eve was given up to worship at St. Bridget's well;[2] this is quite in keeping with the practice of ancient Ireland, where religious rites and popular sports were as closely associated as they were in ancient Greece.

Thus, upon a story about the fairies, itself a product of the contact between the fairy belief and Christianity, light is thrown by a custom which has likewise felt the influence of the younger faith and is now no longer connected with the fairies, whilst both story and custom only assume their full significance when they are compared with the myths and rites of pre-Christian Ireland. The special value of Irish evidence lies in the continuity of the record which enables us to definitely connect the modern practice and fancy with those of the earliest historic times. Had only

[1] *Folk-Lore*, iv. 182.

[2] Mason, *A Stat. Account of Ireland*, 3 vols. 1814-19, i. 494, reprinted *Folk-Lore Journal*, ii. 211. Mason's informant gave him the name of the day as Garlic Sunday, probably a corruption of Garland Sunday.

the ancient record been preserved and no modern folk-lore collected, it would yet be safe to assert that the latter must still exist, or have existed quite recently; had the ancient record perished, we could surmise its contents with tolerable accuracy from extant folk-lore. The folk-lorist has frequently to be content with thus restoring the chain from one or two links; in Ireland nearly all the links have been preserved.

SPECIAL INCIDENTS OF FAIRY LORE.

As a rule, stories about the fairies throughout Europe are episodic; details of the faith took the popular fancy and formed the subject of popular story-telling; comparatively little is to be found applicable to the fairy class as a whole, and from which the psychological basis of the creed may be inferred. This is the case in Ireland as elsewhere, though to a less extent. Stories are still told there which imply an appreciation of fairy nature, and which sum up in concrete form the history of fairy faith. Thus, Mr. Duncan found the following tale widely spread throughout Leitrim: The fairies challenged the giants to fight in harvest time, and chose a cornfield for the battle. When the giants arrived the fairies made themselves invisible, and set to work to fight with the butts of the sheaves. The giants stood this for some time, and then, finding it impossible to return the blows of their assailants, they turned and fled.[1] This vivid little myth gives in brief the hope and faith which the peasant has embodied in the fairy creed. Against the giants, the huge wrecking forces of storm and flood and drought, enemies of orderly in-

[1] *Folk-Lore*, v. 178.

crease, of periodic growth, he seeks the aid of invisible allies, nor is his search a fruitless one; the sheaf of corn, however frail a weapon it may seem, is strong to overcome the opposing powers; struggle as they may, the giants must at last turn and flee.

The Agricultural Festivals.

Just as all over Europe the peasant tells stories about the fairies, so all over Europe he has preserved an ancient ritual, the agricultural nature of which has been fully set forth in the works of Mannhardt and his school. But, as a rule, this ritual no longer stands in any close or precise connection with the fairy creed. This is understandable. The practices in question were held by the peasant essential for the prospering of seedtime and harvest, for the welfare of flock or herd; he would cling to them at all costs. They might, however, be put under the patronage of the new religion, or at least the antique powers this ritual was designed to placate might be discreetly ignored. The bonfires of St. John's Eve or Hallowe'en would still be objectionable to the Christian priest, but less so than if the Fairy power of Life were directly invoked and recognised. For the most part the Church has contented itself with this ignoring process, the result being that all over Europe we find rites which are obviously not Christian, but which in their present form are divorced from any definite anti-Christian or pre-Christian doctrine, and thus lack any effective sanction save that of tradition. The Christian peasant continues to do what his pagan forefathers did before him. But *that* had a clear and precise meaning which has largely died out of the modern usage which may be likened to a cathedral service performed by a congregation of ignorant atheists. Curiously enough the rite has at times been retained with greater fulness when definitely associated with a personage of the new faith, the holiness of the saint atoning in the Church's eye for the heathenishness of the practice. Thus the parish of Clonmany in Meath is under the guardianship of Columkill. On the festival day, the 9th of June, the following customs were observed at the beginning of this century :—'Certain places were ceremoniously circumambulated, certain prayers, deified by the saint, being repeated the while. Men formerly drove down their cattle to the beach on that day and swam them in that part of the sea into which ran the water of St. Columb's Well.'[1] Here the intervention of the saint has probably been no less efficacious in preserving a pre-Christian rite than was his known intervention in support of the bardic class when that ancient repository of Irish myth and romance was threatened with suppression at the close of the sixth century.

As a rule, then, in Ireland as elsewhere, the extensive body of rites traditionally practised at the great Spring, Summer, Autumn, and late Autumn festivals is brought into no very close connection with the fairy creed. True, that in Ireland, as elsewhere, fairy activity is commonly believed to be quickened and intensified on such days as St. John's Eve or Hallowe'en. In Ireland now, as nine hundred years ago, when the tale of Nera's Journey to the Otherworld was in all probability written, ' Demon women appear always on the night of *samhain*' (All-hallows)[2] though the fact that the oral tradition is not edited by a

[1] *Stat. Account*, i. 185 ; reprinted *Folk-Lore Journal*, ii. 40.
[2] See *ante*, vol. i. p. 207.

monk, as was the romantic tale, prevents the application of the uncomplimentary adjective. But this would not be sufficient in itself to stamp the seasonal ritual as belonging to the world of Faery. Just, however, as in Ireland the tales told about the fairies, although closely paralleled elsewhere, yet reveal their true nature and origin more than do their non-Irish analogues, so we also find tales which undoubtedly take their rise from the observances connected with the great agricultural festivals, and which at the same time have for their *dramatis personæ* the denizens of fairy land. One such may be quoted :—Near Loch Guir, in Munster, the enchanted lake of Earl Gerald, is a hill known as Knockainy, 'Ainé's hill, ' Every St. John's Night the men used to gather on the hill from all quarters. They were formed in ranks by an old man named Quinlan whose family lived on the hill in 1876 ; and *clíars*, bunches that is of straw and hay tied on poles and lit, were carried in procession round the hill and the little moat on the summit. . . . Afterwards people ran through the cultivated fields, and among the cattle, waving their *clíars*, which brought luck to crops and beasts for the following year.[1] . . . One St. John's night it happened that one of the neighbours lay dead, and on this account the usual *clíars* were not lit. Not lit, I should say, by the hands of living men ; for that night such a procession of *clíars* marched round Cnoc'-'Aine as never was seen before, and 'Ainé herself was seen in the front, directing and ordering it. On another St. John's Night a number of girls had stayed late on the hill, watching the *clíars* and joining in the games.

[1] Precisely such a rite as is presupposed for ancient Greece by the ritual of the Eleusinian mysteries. Cf. Dr. Jevons' account in his *Introduction to the History of Religion*, p. 365.

Suddenly 'Ainé appeared among them, thanked them for the honour they had done her, but said she now wished them to go home, as *they wanted the hill to themselves.* She let them understand whom she meant by *they*, for calling some of the girls she made them look through a ring, when behold, the hill appeared crowded with people before invisible.'[1]

Here we have the antique ritual carried out on a spot hallowed to one of the antique powers, watched over and shared in by those powers themselves. Nowhere save in Gaeldom could be found such a pregnant illustration of the identity of the fairy class with the venerable powers to ensure whose good-will rite and sacrifice, originally fierce and bloody, now a mere *simulacrum* of their pristine form, have been performed for countless ages. Many are the tales still told of 'Ainé in South Ireland; she is ' the best-hearted woman that ever lived.' She was, as often happens to the dames of Faery, mastered by a mortal lover, a Fitzgerald, to whom she bore the famous magician earl, and the oldest families of the district around Knockainy are proud to claim descent from her. Among other traits of her good heart may be cited her gift of a luck-bringing sheep which she bestowed one night on a family near Knockainy. Her domain is a rich and fertile one now, but it was not always so. Once, Earl Gerald ' came to visit his mother, and looking round on the bare soil he said, It is long since barley was winnowed here, 'Ainé. Next morning when he looked at the hill it was all planted with pease, set by his mother during the night.'

[1] *Revue Celtique*, iv. 190. D. Fitzgerald, *Popular Tales of Ireland.* The traditions about 'Ainé were collected by Mr. Fitzgerald in County Limerick during the year 1876.

These local legends of which 'Ainé is the heroine illus-trate another feature special to Irish fairy lore. As a rule throughout Europe the fairy is anonymous and conceived of by the peasant collectively rather than individually; it is the exception outside Ireland to find a definite name and personality assigned to members of the fairy world, still more so to find them associated with special places or tribes, with which their activity is bound up, and away from which they are unknown or at least unheeded. Extra-human beings special to given localities or connected with particular families are of course common enough, but they have generally, outside Gaeldom, become differentiated from the fairies. In Ireland the possession of a distinct individuality and of a clearly defined domain is frequently met with in the living fairy lore. As a rule name and domain correspond to those associated with the Tuatha de Danann chiefs and heroines in the romantic tales of the last six or seven centuries, and many incidents still related of the fairy class may likewise be found in those tales. It is thus the romantic rather than the practical side of Irish mythology to which we must refer this trait of Irish folk-lore. But, as in 'Ainé's case, legends survive which do not seem in any way due to the romances; the personages they celebrate, the incidents they chronicle are unrecorded there. We must rather turn for an explanation of their sur-vival to the persistence of the tribal system in Ireland down to comparatively recent times. Whilst religious conceptions, and the rites in which they were embodied, were in the main common to all Gaels, each tribe or clan doubtless had its special form of the rites, its special name for the powers worshipped, its special version of their fortunes. It was, we must believe, from this mass of local saga that the romance writers (that is, the official story-telling class) drew much of their material ; worked up in their hands it would spread throughout Gaeldom and enrich the common stock of mythic narrative ; much, however, was certainly never thus worked up, and has either perished or is only recoverable in the shape of local tradition. Whether derived from the common Gaelic storehouse of mythic romance, or from local saga, the presence of names, of personalities, of distinctive groups of narrative connected with those personalities, gives a body, a reality, to the fairy world of Ireland lacking elsewhere.

Thus alike in story and local rite the true nature of the Irish fairy is still easily apparent, nor, indeed, does the point require demonstration as far as the Irish peasant is concerned. He fully appreciates what the fairy can do for him, what it is he has to hope for or fear at fairy hands. As one of Mr. Curtin's informants winds up the story of Tom Connor and the fairy cow :—'From that out Tom Connor's cows had two calves apiece, and his mare two foals, and his sheep two lambs every year, and every acre of land he had gave him as much crop in one year as another man got from an acre in seven. At last Connor was a very rich man, and why not, when the fairies were with him ?' [1]

FAIRY LOVE OF NEATNESS.

Stress has already been laid upon the fragmentary, episodic nature of the extant fairy creed. It was an inevitable consequence of its compromise with Christianity, and so much of modern culture as filtered down to the present,

[1] Curtin, *Tales of the Fairies*, p. 126.

that certain portions of his antique faith should become divorced from their contact, and thereby susceptible of independent development. Some elements too offered more chance than others to the romantic, story-telling instinct of the folk ; these would survive though often greatly altered. But the change, however great, should not entirely conceal the real nature of the incident. Let us examine some of the most widely spread items of the fairy creed, and see if they betray their origin. To quote Mr. Curtin : —' A striking trait in the Irish fairy tales is the number of observances caused by the presence of fairies, rules of ordinary living, so to speak. For instance, nothing is more pleasing to fairies than a well-swept kitchen and clean water. A dirty kitchen and foul water bring their resentment.'[1] This love of neatness, this insistence on certain observances, are of course not peculiar to Irish fairies ; they characterise the fairy clan throughout Europe, and are strongly marked in the oldest lengthy and connected account of the fairies we possess, that recoverable from English writers of the sixteenth and seventeenth centuries. Why this should be so has not, to my knowledge, been satisfactorily determined. Obviously, we must ask, not, why do the fairies like this or that, but, why does man, the creator of the fairy, attribute to him this characteristic? In other words, we must seek for a psychological reason, and for one the validity of which is likely to be apparent in other domains of thought and fancy. Such a reason is furnished, I conceive, by the known tendency of the craftsman, at a particular stage of development, to attach a religious value to precise and rigidly determined order in the performance of his craft. The history of religion itself—

[1] Curtin, p. 178.

and one factor of religion was the conception of it as a most potent craft for securing definite material ends—is full of instances ; to this very day every jot and tittle in the ritual of even the most spiritual creeds is guarded with a reverence which is, in the proper sense of the word, superstitious. The allied craft of law furnishes kindred examples, from the formalities upon the due fulfilment of which depended the legality of sale among the Romans down to the practice of our courts at the present day. There exists a ritual which must be carried out to the letter, or the transaction, spiritual or legal, is invalided. Now, agriculture is not only one of the oldest crafts, it is one in connection with which the organised religious spirit manifests its existence earliest. Its ritual must have been of a particularly rigid and inflexible nature. But when the ritual was partly emptied of its animating conceptions by the advance of Christianity, partly replaced by Christian observances, partly transformed to meet Christian exigencies, it would become disorganised, broken up, its significance would be obscured, distorted. What would subsist would be a vague but ineradicable conviction that so and so must be done or the powers would be displeased, and in especial, an abiding belief in the conservatism of these antique beings, a distrust of innovation, an assurance that the fairies know best, and that man must not meddle with them. It is in keeping with what we know of other early forms of religion, *e.g.* the Hebrew, that many of the observances should in themselves be useful and reasonable.

If I am right in this conjecture, the widespread and long-continued existence of stories in which the fairies are represented as the jealous guardians of definite rural and household observances testifies to their having at one time been the objects of a ritual worship in which the peasant class was deeply interested, and the rites of which were ineffaceably impressed upon the peasant mind. But no other ritual save that which aims at increasing and regulating the life of nature for the benefit of the peasant class, answers the requirement.

THE FAIRY REVELS BY NIGHT.

The peasant who holds tenaciously to certain practices, although he could give no other reason save that he trod in his forefathers' footsteps, is also firmly convinced that fairy life belongs in the main to the night side of nature. For him, as for the poet,—

> ' The weaker, holier season wanes,
> Night comes with sorrows and with sins,
> And in all forests, hills, and plains
> A keener, fiercer life begins.'

The classic manifestation of the fairy folk is their dance by moonlight, in wild and desert places, which, if the belated mortal sees, and seeing is drawn by an irresistible spell to share in, ensures him centuries of unalloyed bliss compressed within the semblance of a night, or dooms him to a fate from which not even Christ's vicar may save him, according as the legend has been more or less modified by Christianity. Some realistic basis there must be for this story told wherever reigns the belief in fairydom. A psychological reason may be sought in the opinion that night is essentially the time for growth, vegetable or animal. Increase is practically imperceptible during the day, yet it takes place, and must therefore take place at night, when the Powers of Increase must be active and strenuous. But this reason would only explain why night is assigned to the fairy, it would not account for the special form in which the fairy loves to manifest himself. That, if I mistake not, is due to traditional reminiscences of the ritual, midnight, frenzied, orgiastic, in which throughout the rest of Europe, as in Greece, the Power of Increase was invoked, his aid demanded, his support assured. We have seen reason to hold with Professor Rohde that this ritual had effects and consequences little dreamt of in all likelihood by those who first practised it; it created and perpetrated a psychological state out of which was developed, together with other conceptions, that of a god's land of unalloyed delight, a land the denizens of which are free from the shackles of time, locality, and personality imposed upon them in this world. It is, therefore, significant that the legend of mortal participation in the midnight fairy dance should be characterised by the loss of all sense of time on the mortal's part, and, though less frequently, by his access to a wonderland of joy and riches. Reminiscences of the ritual would thus form the framework and supply the details for the legend, but the true reason for its persistence lies elsewhere than in the fact of its perpetuating the memory of rites which impressed the imagination of the peasant class. There is, as we saw, a psychological justification for the beliefs which sprang out of and embodied themselves anew in the ritual. The participant in the frenzied rites was actually, as it seemed to him, delivered from the bonds of sense, did actually pass into a wonderland of ecstatic joy where time and space were not. All this is summed up in terse dramatic form by the legend of the fairy revellers and their mortal visitor, and the legend lives because it symbolises the psychology as well as the history of a worship.

Witchcraft and Fairydom.

If the witness of living tradition be required in defence of this interpretation, I may cite again the story of 'Ainé leading her fairy host in the torchlight procession and other midnight rites, by which herd and crop are hallowed and protected. On the historical side there is a fair amount of evidence that in districts now occupied by Celtic-speaking peoples, rites akin to those of the Dionysus cult were practised. This evidence has been discussed by, among others, Mr. Hartland (*Science of Fairy Tales*) and Mr. Gomme (*Ethnology in Folklore*), and I need only refer to what they have said, and to my remarks on the festival of the Namnites priestesses described by Strabo and Pomponius Mela (*ante*, ch. xvi.). But I must dwell a little upon another set of romantic fancyings to which the ritual of the Powers of Increase has given rise in popular imagination. It is evident that even as the rites themselves fell more or less under the ban of the new faith, and were, as the case might be, tolerated as harmless, mildly denounced, or thundered at with every missile of the Church's artillery, so the resulting stories may be expected to reveal every gradation of the struggle between Christianity and pre-Christianity. This is so even if we restrict ourselves wholly to fairy-lore. There is nearly always something uncanny in the fairy revel, but in numerous stories there is something distinctly unholy and malign. One such story, which has passed through the hands of a poet who gave it a distinctive Christian colouring, who accentuated the unholy side of Faërie, is the Legend of the Knight Tannhäuser. If we compare it with its closest analogue (perhaps its immediate prototype?), the story of Thomas the Rhymer and the Fairy Queen, we find the Christian note more pronounced, though in the latter it is far more insistent than in the vast majority of living folk-tales. Between the Tannhäuser legend at one end of the scale, and at the other many a tale picked up in this century, in which the mortal visitor to Faëry is the object of admiration and envy rather than of reprobation, every shade of man's feeling towards the invisible world may be noted. But there exists a group of stories and traditions in which that world is wholly malign, its denizens wholly evil, its mortal ministrants stamped with loathsome and hideous horror. I allude of course to witchcraft, and to the stories and traditions to which it has given rise. In popular tradition the most striking features of witchcraft are perhaps the witch's power over animal and vegetable produce (in nine cases out of ten the witch exercises her malign influence by preventing butter 'coming,' by inflicting barrenness, or by blasting crops), her ability to assume animal shape, and the fact that she receives and renews her power in assemblies of an initiatory and sacramental character. It is this assembly of witches and wizards, the *sabbat*, to use the technical term, which forms the hellish counterpart of the fairy dance. Such at least is the Brothers Grimm's opinion: 'Die Reihen auf dem Brocken, die Tänze um die Johannisfeuer waren sicher nichts anders, als Feste der Lichtelfen, sie haben sich in greuliche, teufliche Hexentänze verkehrt.'[1] In my opinion

---

[1] *Irische Elfenmärchen*, cxxiii. 'The dances on the Brocken, those around the fire on Midsummer Eve, were nothing more than festivals of the Elves of light; they have been transformed into hideous, devilish dances of witches' (Crofton Croker's Translation, 142).

the inevitable results of the shock between Christianity and the older faith it superseded, are sufficient to explain all the varying forms which the phenomena of that faith have assumed in folklore, including those of witchcraft. As we saw just now, the priest denounced the pagan god as a devil, whilst he contented himself with styling the peasant's deity a neutral angel. The one was a potent and influential rival, the other could, as a rule, be disregarded or even brought within the Christian fold. But there were elements in the peasant faith which could not be overlooked, with which no compromise was possible. It was precisely these elements which were the most potent; recourse would be had to them in cases of emergency, when the ordinary resources of the ritual had failed. The horror of the Christian priest at practices which he could not but deem bloody and obscene would naturally be intensified by the thought that his flock were resorting to them because *he* had failed; ordinary fairy observances which could be carried on simultaneously with the Church's rites might be tolerated, but not usages in which was concentrated the fiercest spirit of the old faith, the last remains of organised sacerdotal opposition to Christianity. These considerations seem to me to justify the view expressed by the Brothers Grimm. A different view has, however, been urged by Mr. Gomme in the most suggestive and stimulating of his works, *Ethnology in Folklore.* According to him 'witchcraft is the survival of pre-Aryan aboriginal beliefs from aboriginal sources, fairycraft the survival of beliefs about the aborigines from Aryan sources.'[1] I shall discuss this theory later. It is only indirectly connected with the question discussed in the foregoing paragraphs, the question, namely, whether

[1] *Op. cit.* p. 63.

fairy revels and witches' *sabbat* can be traced back to the midnight festivals of those antique divinities of growth, who on Irish soil became the Tuatha de Danann, and the prototypes of the modern fairy.

THE CHANGELING BELIEF.

If the fairy is characterised by a love of orderly neatness, and a conservative fondness for old ways, if he shows himself chiefly to mortals in the midnight revel, the practice by which he comes in closest and more frequent contact with humanity is the toll he levies upon human life. The new-born child, so be he is healthy and vigorous, the young and prolific woman, are especially exposed to his attack. But the fairy does not take as does death, he admits and acts upon the principle of a life for a life ; true, the exchange he makes with the mortal is an unfair one for the latter, who receives a worn-out, peevish, ailing existence in return for the new and vigorous one of which he has been robbed. No incident of fairy intercourse with mortals is more commonly recorded, none has a wider range of distribution, none is believed in more implicitly than the substitution of changelings for human beings. We can only, in my opinion, explain the practice if we recognise in the fairies representatives of the antique lords of life and increase, of the powers to whom man looked for the periodical outburst of new life, and whom he strengthened in their task by sacrifice. This is substantially the theory of the Brothers Grimm : ' Wie etwa Homer von den Geistern erzählt, dass sie Blut begierig einsäugen, um das Gefühl des Lebens zu erlangen, so scheinen diese geisterhafte Wesen ihren Kreis durch die geraubten jugendlichen Menschen zu erfrischen oder wieder herzustellen, welches in Wales wirklich Volks-glaube ist.'[1]

There are two ways in which, as it seems to me, the sacrificial worship which we know to have been current in pre-Christian Ireland may have given rise to the changeling belief. The sacrifice of 'one-third of their healthy offspring,' though it may have been accepted as necessary, *must*, even when the creed was most firmly believed in, have weighed as a heavy burden upon the people. After the triumph of Christianity, and the consequent abolition of human sacrifice as a normal feature of the ritual, the practice may well have assumed in the eyes of the people the aspect of raids carried out by an unhuman upon human society. If this view be correct, the belief would be the outcome of natural horror felt for sacrifice by the victim's relations, reinforced by the reprobation of Christianity. The practice of the fairies would come to be looked upon as altogether detest-able, the gist and point of the stories which narrated it would be supplied by the human ingenuity or courage which outwitted fairy malice. It is, however, conceivable that the changeling belief may be older than the change effected in the popular mind by the introduction of Christianity. What was the root-conception of the antique agricultural worship?—that the Powers invoked were the lords and depositories of life; this they would dole out to

---

[1] *Irische Elfenmärchen*, civ. 'Almost in the same manner as Homer relates of the spirits that they eagerly sucked blood to imbibe a sensation of life ; these beings seem to renovate or replace their circle by their youthful prey, which is in fact a popular superstition in Wales' (Crofton Croker's Translation, p. 119). I don't know Grimm's authority for the last statement, and I can find no definite mention of such a superstition in later writers.

their human worshippers, but on conditions; nothing is given for nothing, and if the Power of Life and Increase is to manifest himself, he must be fed, hence the necessity for sacrifice; but the stated, periodic, ritual feeding of these powers may, on however liberal a scale it is calculated (and, if we believe the *dinnshenchas* of Mag Slecht in Ireland, there was nothing niggardly in this respect), be insufficient, in which case they have to forage for themselves, and what more likely than that they should anticipate their dinner hour and carry off likely morsels between-times? I have purposely used crude, brutal terms for putting this theory, in order to emphasise the brutally practical nature of these antique faiths, the rigorous logic which boggled at no con- clusion however revolting. Another strand of thought may also be disentangled. It is now a commonplace of our studies that sacrifice was reckoned efficacious in proportion to the vitality of the victim; hence the sacrifice of the king, the representative of the source of power, or rather the depository for the time being of that power. Life was hoarded up in him so as to be available for emergencies. By a similar train of reasoning, youth, vigour, beauty, free- dom from blemish, have at divers times and places been requisites in the victim. It is at least possible that the sickly and ailing would be rejected when the time came for each family to supply its quota of victims, and this might easily translate itself in the folk-memory into the statement that the fairies had carried off the healthy and left in ex- change the sickly. Of these two explanations the second is the more adventurous, and I should hesitate to put it forward otherwise than tentatively, but it accounts for the changeling better than does the other. In either case it should be noted there exists some justification, realistic and psychological (the psychology is false, but that doesn't matter) for the peasant belief. It is a fact that the healthy and vigorous die unaccountably, that the sickly and ailing live on, but it is a fact which the peasant cannot consider natural, and for which he must therefore seek an extra-natural cause.

I have now, I trust, made it probable that the fairy creed of modern Ireland, connected historically as it is with the romantic mythology of which the Tuatha de Danann are the *dramatis personæ*, is the living representative of an ancient cult paid to the powers of life and increase; it has been modified and distorted by Christianity, certain elements, in themselves fierce and horrible, have been rendered still more detestable, thanks to the attitude Christianity has taken towards them, but on the whole the dominant conceptions, in which are expressed man's relations to nature, have remained substantially unaltered. In especial, the most popular incident of the fairy cycle, the changeling story is found to be connected with the antique conception of life and sacrifice; how potent is the belief finding expression in this story may be gauged when we remember that only two years ago it induced a father, a husband, and half-a-dozen cousins (all of them, save the husband, average representatives of their class, the small Irish peasant) to slowly roast an unfortunate woman to death because they suspected her of being a changeling.[1] Again I repeat that I make no attempt to account for every detail of fairy-

---

[1] The essential facts of the Clonmel so-called 'witch-burning' case may be found *Folklore*, vi. 373 *et seq*. There can be little doubt that whilst the husband wanted to get quit of his wife, her father and cousins believed, more or less strongly, that it was a fairy substitute they were torturing.

lore. I have endeavoured to lay bare the broad lines, the ruling conceptions of the creed, and I do not think I have gone far wrong.

IRISH AND GENERAL EUROPEAN FAIRY-LORE.

Comparison with the general mass of European fairy-lore will be found, I think, to place the above conclusions beyond reasonable doubt. That lore is substantially the same to-day elsewhere in Europe as it is in Ireland; if we may judge from the fact that the attitude of Christianity towards it has been everywhere of much the same nature, its sameness was as great fifteen hundred or eighteen hundred years ago as it is now. Hence the beliefs and practices from which it derives, and to which it testifies, must have been of such a nature as to appeal most strongly to the peasant classes, of such a nature indeed as to rigidly determine their practical action, whilst summing up expressively their view of the relations between man and nature. No other set of beliefs and practices save those connected with breadwinning (I use the word in its widest sense) answers, unless I am mistaken, to these requirements. The peasant's belief is everywhere of much the same character, because everywhere his mode of life, his interests, are very similar; these have changed little since the earliest time, hence the comparatively slight change in his beliefs.

On the other hand, the differences, such as they are, between Gaelic and non-Gaelic fairy-lore are easily explicable by known historical conditions. Gaeldom remained comparatively unaffected by Rome, hence the survival down to recent times of the tribal system, which has preserved much local mythology, hence the continued existence of a mythological romance, uninfluenced by the classic mythologies, thanks to which the Irish fairies have kept name, attribute, and personalities. England shared, through the Arthurian romance, in the ancient stock of Celtic mythic narrative, and the connection between the peasant's lore and the fairy world of romance was never wholly lost sight of here as elsewhere; because of this, English, alone of the great modern literatures, has given a place of honour to the fairy, has sought for and found some of its most exquisite effects in the land of illusion and fantasy.[1]

The Tuatha de Danann and Death.

There is one aspect alike of the Tuatha de Danann and of the fairy clan, which I have hitherto left unnoted, but which deserves mention, especially in a volume which discusses the Irish conception of life-transference, viz. their connection with death, their possible identification with the spirits of the dead. We find a traditional association of the Tuatha de Danann with prehistoric monuments, which examination reveals to be of a sepulchral nature; in texts which are at least 900 years old this association is emphasised, and the sepulchral nature of the monuments is insisted upon.[2] Moreover, certain traditions (*e.g.* those cited on p. 183 *et seq.*) connect the origin of the great festivals with burial ceremonies. Again, modern folklore frequently fails to distinguish between fairy and ghost; traits, incidents,

---

[1] I have dealt fully with this point in my presidential address to the Folklore Society for the Session of 1897 : ' The Fairy Mythology of English Literature ; its origin and nature ' (*Folklore*, March 1897).

[2] The material, archæological and literary, has been brought together and discussed by Mr. George Coffey : ' The Tumuli and Inscribed Stones at New Grange, Dorset, and Knowth ' (*Transactions of the Royal Irish Academy*, November 1892). Cf. my remarks, *Folklore*, iv. 370.

attributes ascribed to the one are ascribed to the other; and the churchyard is almost invariably a favourite haunting place of the fairies.[1]

Against these facts we have to recognise (1) that nothing in the recorded mythic romance in which the Tuatha de Danann play a part connects them with ancestor-worship in the strict sense of the term, and (2) that the oldest witness to their connection with the great sepulchral mounds of the lower Boyne valley is furnished by texts which belong to the euhemerising period, when the Tuatha de Danann were transformed into an ancient race of kings, conquered and dispossessed by the invading Milesians. If the Tuatha de Danann were not historical personages, the eighth-tenth century statement that they were buried between certain mounds cannot be true, and may be only an anti-quarian fable.   On the other hand, how in that case is the modern folklore to be accounted for?   It cannot be traced back to romantic tales of the last seven or eight centuries. These, it is true, insist strongly upon the association of the Tuatha de Danann with the great sepulchral monuments, which according to eighth-tenth century texts were their favourite burying-places, but they assign no sepulchral character to them.   The Irish peasant who listened to tales about Angus of the Brugh, would never learn from them that the Brugh was at one time regarded as the grave of the Dagda, Angus' father; nor would anything in these tales give him the faintest idea that sepulchral sites generally were the haunt of Angus' kindred.   No, the connection must lie deeper than any antiquarian guesswork of the

---

[1] Mr. Curtin's already quoted work (*Tales of the Fairies*, etc., London, 1895) gives full and precise witness to the confusion actually existing in South Irish folklore between ghost and fairy.

period when Irish mythology was euhemerised, or any influence upon the official story-telling class which the antiquaries may have exercised. It is, I think, a natural and inevitable one. In the first portion of these studies we saw that the idea of a Happy Otherworld, although possibly prior to and certainly independent of that of a Hades, *i.e.* a world to which all men go after death, forcedly coalesced with, influenced, and was influenced by it. In the same way the conception of Powers of Life inevitably suggests that of Powers of Death; the mere fact that the former are kept in working order, so to say, by sacrifice, establishes a connection between them and the something which, whilst we live, is ourselves, and when we cease to live must go elsewhere. The theory that life is a fixed quantity, that to obtain possession of it we must give its fair equivalent, necessarily leads to the conclusion that departed life, which but a moment ago we saw in full and vigorous manifestation, and has now gone—somewhere—has gone to reinforce the stock upon which we essay to draw when we approach the Powers that hold it with rite and sacrifice. But if a portion of the universal vital essence lately animated some one dear to and revered by us, to whom we looked up as a protector and counsellor, why should its disposition or its capacity change because it has gone elsewhere? As a community let us appeal to the Powers of Life with the proper ritual; the advantages we hope for will be shared in equally by all the individuals composing the community; but as individuals why should we not make the most of any private interest we have among the Holders of Life, and as prudent individuals let us keep alive this interest by rite and offering. In such a way, I take it, ancestor-worship would graft itself in a natural and inevitable manner upon the cult of the Powers of Life. In its earlier form it probably preceded the patriarchal family, and it would forcedly suffer far-reaching modification in communities the organisation of which was based upon that institution. It is known to us chiefly from the practice of such communities, and our current theories respecting it are naturally coloured by this fact. A far more altruistic reason is thus usually assigned for the institution than seems at all likely; it is explained by the desire to ensure the comfort and well-being of the departed—but early man, we may be sure, did not trouble himself about the welfare of his dead, unless he thought he could gain something by his solicitude; the dying man might be firmly convinced that *post mortem* offerings would be essential to his comfort, the survivors would not have acted on this conviction unless there had been in their own minds an equally strong conviction that the game was worth the candle.

There may possibly be a yet earlier connection between the dead and the Powers of Life. It has been urged, in this country by Mr. Grant Allen alone to my knowledge,[1] that, as growth manifests itself more freely in the immediate neighbourhood of the dead body, the grave is in reality the ultimate source of all mythical conceptions connected with the origin and the essence of life. I shall return to this view in the next chapter. Here I need only call attention to it.

The sepulchral association alike of Tuatha de Danann and of fairy is thus an early and, so to say, a natural element of the worship paid to these powers. Even if, as Mr. Grant Allen claims, that worship was not originated by burial practices, it could not but develop a connection

[1] *The Attis of Catullus*, London, 1892.

with beliefs concerning the dead and their activity. This development must have taken place, no matter what the special burial customs of the ancient Irish might be. It seems immaterial, therefore, to the present inquiry to examine the archæological evidence respecting the disposal of the dead in Ireland. As a matter of fact, the same perplexing duality of practice is to be found there as elsewhere in Europe, and notably in Greece.[1] The body is sometimes burned, sometimes buried; the two modes of disposal overlap each other in locality and in time, indeed there are tombs in which remains of burnt skeletons are found in company with entire ones.[2] No satisfactory hypothesis has been worked out on the basis of the archæological evidence as to differences in race or in religion among the dwellers in pre-Christian Ireland. The record of the monuments does not enable us to progress beyond our deductions from early myth and living folklore. It is upon the validity of these deductions that I must rest my case.[3]

[1] Cf. Cecil Smith, *Folklore*, December 1892.

[2] Coffey, *op. cit.* p. 18.

[3] A different view of the Tuatha de Danann has been urged by M. d'Arbois de Jubainville in his *Cycle Mythologique*. I have thought it best to set out my theory rather than to polemise against his, the more so as the difference of view arises in part from the fact that we consider the beliefs at different stages of evolution.

CHAPTER XIX

SUMMARY AND CONCLUSION

Summary of preceding investigation—Statement of results (*a*) as regards
the Aryan world generally; (*b*) as regards Greece; (*c*) as regards Ireland
—Objective and subjective elements in the primitive agricultural cults,
their diverse fortunes in the development of mythology—Possible non-
Aryan origin of the cult, Mr. Gomme's views discussed and criticised
—Dr. Jevons' views concerning the development of the Elysium and
Re-birth themes in the Greek world discussed and criticised—Con-
clusion.

I DO not propose to carry the special lines of investigation further, and it is time to sum up the results, and
to endeavour to draw some conclusion. We started from
the consideration of an Irish romantic tale belonging,
substantially, to the eighth century of our era at the latest.
Embodied in it are two main conceptions : (1) that of a
land of unending joy to which mortals may penetrate
without dying, but from which they may not return to
earth under penalty of death ; (2) that of extra-human
beings who can unite themselves with mortals and beget
offspring, into whom they transfuse some of their extra-
human capacities and attributes. In itself this tale is only
one, and not the most important, of a group presenting
similar features. Attentive consideration of the entire
group shows that the second conception is also found in
the form of the god's assumption of manhood, sometimes
simultaneously with the manifestation of his extra-human

personality, sometimes with temporary abeyance of the latter; in other words, god-incarnation occurs by the side of god-parentage. Furthermore, both conceptions are found, at an early stage, heroicised—the personages of the tales have more than human strength, courage, and beauty, their adventures transcend the ordinary experiences of humanity, but they are not, by definition, extra-human; the world in which they move, however magnified, with whatever romantic colours endowed, is man's world, not gods' world. Obviously secondary, these stories attest by their early appearance in extant Irish literature, the age of the primary class of stories out of which they have developed, a class represented by those tales in which some of the personages distinctly retain their extra-human character. A presumption is thus created of great antiquity as far as the latter are concerned, a presumption strengthened when we consider that both conceptions have their analogues in the new faith which in the fourth and fifth centuries of our era profoundly modified the religious, whilst it affected but slightly the social, organisation of ancient Ireland. The Irish Land of Women and Youth has analogies with the Christian Paradise and Heaven, the Irish incarnation stories with the Incarnation of Christ. In both cases the analogy proves, upon investigation, to be independent of any direct influence exercised by Christianity upon pre-Christian Irish paganism. Unless, therefore, a simple coincidence, it must be due to something in the elements which Christianity absorbed into its complex being from the older classical world, and which it profoundly modified. In the case of the Happy Otherworld conception, this 'something' proved to be the Greek vision of Elysium, which, equally with the Greek vision of Tartarus, was taken over by Christianity. Tracing this vision back as far as we can, to the Homeric poems and to those statements of Hesiod and the mythographers, which, although younger in point of record, belong to a stage of Hellenic myth as early as, nay even earlier, perhaps, than the Homeric poems, we detect a most striking similarity to the Irish tales. Although from fifteen hundred to two thousand years separate the earliest recorded Greek and Irish utterances in a form, substantially speaking, that extant, yet both stand on much the same stage of development, save that Ireland has preserved, with greater fulness and precision, a conception out of which Homeric Greece had already emerged. Examination of the mythologies due to other Aryan races, or rather, to prejudge nothing, to peoples speaking Aryan tongues equally with the Greeks and Irish, reveals the remarkable fact that Greeks and Irish alone have preserved the early stage of the Happy Otherworld conception in any fulness. The Vedic mythology of the Aryan immigrants into Northern India, the Avestic mythology of the Aryan immigrants into Northern Persia, the Eddic mythology of the Scandinavian Teutons, all present an eschatology as advanced as, or in certain respects more advanced than, Greek eschatology of the sixth, fifth, and fourth centuries B.C. Ireland, if we may judge from existing native records, had not reached the eschatological stage prior to the introduction of Christianity. Greece has preserved very clear traces of its pre-eschatological stage, and in the range and continuity of its mythic record we are enabled to trace how the eschatological conceptions of the Otherworld grew out of the pre-eschatological. At the same time Vedic India, Avestic Iran, and Eddic Scandinavia, show sufficient traces of the pre-eschatological conception to warrant the assertion that amongst these Aryan-speaking peoples the course of development, although we cannot follow it, must have been the same as among the Aryan-speaking Greeks, where we can.

At this point of the argument we must revert to the Irish tales. The connection between the two conceptions (Happy Otherworld and Reincarnation), although persistent, does not, at first blush, seem primary or essential. There is no apparent necessity why the story of Manannan and Mongan should be associated with that of Bran's passing to the Land of Women, no apparent necessity why Cuchulinn, the re-birth of Lug, should visit Faery, no apparent necessity why Etain should be re-born as a mortal and wooed by a lord of the Happy Land. If we consider the tales simply as independent tales, either mythical or romantic, if we isolate them from other elements of Irish culture, there is no justification, either mythological or artistic, for the association of the two conceptions. Its great age is thereby demonstrated. Ideas and themes are not connected without reason, and if no reason appears on the face of extant texts, it can only be because these have lost features and elements they once possessed. As a matter of fact the Greek evidence furnishes the desired clue. In Greek mythology, as in Irish, the conception of re-birth proves to be a dominant factor of the same religious system in which Elysium is likewise an essential feature. Thus in Greek religion the two conceptions are associated persistently and reasonably, whilst in Irish mythic fiction they are associated persistently, but not, on the face of it, reasonably. In Greece, the re-birth conceptions centre around Dionysus and develop with his cult. Turning back to Ireland, we note another connection beyond what may be called that of mere juxtaposition between the two conceptions; the same clan of supernatural, extra-human beings figures in both, and forms, in fact, the desired link between the two. Something, then, in the essence and personality of these supernatural beings, the Tuatha de Danann, should account for their lordship of the Happy Otherworld, for their capacity of transformation, of incarnating themselves in divers shapes. The comparison, which at once suggests itself, with Dionysus makes it probable that the Tuatha de Danann are Powers of Life and Increase, like the Greek god, a probability confirmed by examination of the scanty extant records of the cult paid to them, and of the older mythology in which they figure. Modern fairy-lore, allowing for the inevitable changes brought about by Christianity, is found to be of the same nature, to involve the same conceptions, to rest upon the same basis, as the pre-Christian Tuatha de Danann mythology.

Such are the main results of the inquiry stated in the logical order of their deduction from the facts, an order differing somewhat from that followed in the foregoing investigation, which considered either conception separately. We can now essay a reconstruction of the historical development, points and phases of which have been clearly discerned or deduced with reasonable certitude. At the outset we postulate communities largely if not mainly dependent for their support upon the produce of the soil and of domesticated animals. We only know of these communities from Aryan sources, and we must conclude that as far back as our records carry us (say to the fifteenth or eighteenth century B.C. in the case of the

Greek or Vedic Aryans) they were largely if not mainly Aryan. A prominent if not the chief object of their religion was the worship of the Powers of Life and Increase. This consisted chiefly in periodic ritual festivals the purpose of which was to induce these Powers to manifest themselves for the benefit of man, and to strengthen them in the due fulfilment of the task upon which depended man's welfare; sacrifice being the means adopted to accomplish this end. The philosophical basis of the worship was furnished by the conception that the vital essence is of unending persistence and of infinite variability, and by the principle that nothing is to be had for nothing, that to gain life we must give life. Freedom from mortality and decay, or rather, an infinite capacity for entering into new forms and assuming new shapes of life, is thus an inherent attribute of the Lords of Life and Increase. As soon as a mythology grew up—as soon, that is, as the Powers worshipped by man took upon themselves shape and individuality, and became the subject of stories (subject in their turn to the fundamental laws of artistic composition)—the beings who were to grow with the progress of the community, to acquire all the attributes and capacities which material, intellectual, and moral development made it inevitable for men to bestow upon them, were stamped with certain ineffaceable characteristics. Develop and change as they might, they retained to the last the marks of their origin. Other attributes and characteristics seem due to the effect produced upon the participants in the sacrificial rites; some at least of these passed into a state of ecstasy in which they shared the capacities and partook of the joys belonging to the Powers they invoked; life entered into them in a larger, more intense measure, they became free of the god's land. The picture of this must go back to a comparatively early stage; its lineaments and colours are of a simple description, betraying little if any sign of advanced material civilisation. The vision to which man had access in the exaltation of worship derived its form and colour from natural phenomena, and its material equipment from the social life familiar to the visionary. The close connection of the sun with the development of life in nature must have been noticed early in mankind's career; the Sun-god was necessarily an ally of the gods of growth. That the sun as he sank every evening to rest amidst the flaming beauties of the western sky, was proceeding to a land of more than earthly radiance must have been among the first of definitely constituted myths. He may sink into the earth or into the sea according to geographical position; hence the varying accounts of his wonderland, now beyond the western main, now within the hills bounding the western horizon. As the tribes shifted from inland to seashore, or worked their way inland from the coast, different versions would arise to be harmonised later by thinkers and poets.

Of the two aspects of the ancient worship of the Powers of Life and Increase, the secondary, dependent upon the subjective feelings of the worshipper, was necessarily the most capable of expansion. The objective purport of the cult, the increase of fertility, was bound to remain the same, and as the end in view was a serious and practical one, little departure could be allowed from the rigid ritual upon which success was supposed to depend. Moreover, as the needs and capacities of social man were widened, so the ancient craft of agriculture was menaced by other forms of human activity which appealed to the bolder, more adventurous spirits of the race. On its objective side the agricultural worship tended to become that of the least progressive portion of the community. Not so on the subjective side. The spirit of life entering into the ecstatic visionary was liable to all the change, all the progress of which its inmate was capable; the rude and antique vision of the shape-shifting god in his simple wonderland may thus become enriched with all the radiant imagination of a Homer or a Pindar, may be translated by the moral fervour of a Pythagoras or an Empedocles into an Elysium, or subtilised by the philosopher into an allegory of man's origin and destiny.

In Greece we can in a large measure trace this evolution, especially if the great differences in the culture level between the various parts of the Hellenic world are borne in mind. The oldest monuments of Hellenic genius, the Homeric poems, belong to a society removed by ages from the simple communities in which the worship of the Powers of Life and Increase had its rise, yet this worship was preserved in a comparatively primitive form in other parts of the Hellenic world for ages after the composition of the Homeric poems. On the whole, despite the existence of such local cults as that of the Eleusinian Mother, it may be said that the objective side of this worship comes before us as a survival in the Greek world; if it seems a living reality in certain districts or at certain times there is reason to suspect the intrusion into the main citadels of Hellenic culture of ruder, more primitive elements from outlying regions where it retained its full vitality. The perplexing history of Dionysus worship is apparently best accounted for in this way; the fiercer, crueller features had been shed or softened down among that section of the Greek race to which we owe Homer, they survived elsewhere and forced their way in an archaic form to the surface of the Greek world at a later period. Yet their remoteness and strangeness were felt, and Greece imagined fables which told of their alien origin. Alien in one sense they were, just as the beliefs of the poor wretches who tortured Bridget Clery to death at Clonmel two years ago would be alien if they claimed expression in our present-day worship and literature.

On the subjective side the influence of conceptions derived from the antique cult was deep and enduring in the Greek world. From the worship of Dionysus sprang the Drama, its outward form reproducing, its inmost spirit expressing the mutability and variety of social life, even the worship was based upon and symbolised the mutability and variety of natural life. Again, the close connection between Dionysus, Lord of Growth, and Apollo, Sun-god and Fosterer of Life, which is such a marked feature of both cults, and which, if I am right, goes back to almost the earliest stage of mythological fancy, enriched the religious possibilities of the Dionysus cult. In connection with Apollo, Greek religion touches in some ways its highest level; Apollo's comrade shared the ever-widening sphere of beauty and significance occupied by the sun-god. Whether Professor Rohde is right or no in wholly deriving the remarkable religious movement of the sixth century B.C., in which are blended ascetic and metaphysical elements, from the simple naturalistic worship of Dionysus, and in asserting its independence of any outside influence of an advanced type— whether, in fact, Orphic Pythagoreanism is, in the main, a regular product of the Greek genius working up native elements of immemorial age, or, on the contrary, a recent Greek adaptation of conceptions which had previously reached a high level of religious development elsewhere, is a problem I do not attempt to solve. I have stated Professor Rohde's view, and I have shown, I think, that the development postulated by him finds a partial, but striking parallel in Irish mythology; I shall state presently the opposed view, last advocated, with signal ability and wide knowledge, by Dr. F. B. Jevons. As a result of the foregoing investigations, I venture, however, to claim that even if Orphic Pythagoreanism have to be referred in part to outside non-Hellenic sources, yet that nevertheless the Dionysus cult is at once genuinely Greek, and did from the outset contain those elements which appear in the sixth and fifth centuries B.C. under a moral or philosophical guise:—the conception that life can pour itself, as it were, out of one vessel into another, outcomes of which were the doctrine of metempsychosis and the ascetic-metaphysical ideal of existence which it produced; the conception of a god's land, the outcome of which was an Elysium reserved for the just, with the corresponding Tartarus for the unjust.

In Greece we can trace this evolution wholly in pre-Christian texts and monuments. In Ireland we possess nothing that is entirely unaffected by Christianity; for Celtdom generally we have, it is true, a few scattered notices of the pre-Christian period, but they come to us through Greeks and Romans, and we cannot be certain how far they faithfully reproduce Celtic ideas. Another great distinction between the two bodies of evidence lies in the fact that whilst one is furnished by the most advanced group of the Aryan-speaking peoples, the other comes from a group holding, together with the Germans, a midway position in the Aryan scale, less advanced than Italian, Vedic,

or Iranian, more advanced than Lithuanian or Slavonic
Aryans.   Alike the necessary imperfection of the record,
due to its preservation by Christian hands, and its inevitable meagreness (even if we had it complete), due to the
less advanced condition of the group, forbid us to look in
Gaeldom, as revealed by extant texts, for a close parallel to
Greek development.   In Greece the Powers of Life and
Increase, worshipped by the primitive agriculturists, are
but one element in the completed Hellenic Pantheon, and
this has been subjected to so much change, to such enlargement and glorification, as to be wellnigh unrecognis-
able.   In Ireland, to judge by extant native texts, these
powers must have constituted the predominant element of
the Pantheon, and cannot have departed very widely from
their primitive form.   Yet here we must bear in mind the
imperfection of the record due to its transmission through
Christians; it is the more highly organised members of
the Celtic Pantheon, those who reminded the Christian
missionaries, as centuries before they had reminded classic
observers of the classic gods, who would naturally be boy-
cotted by the monkish scribes.   Allowing fully for this,
and allowing also for the fact that the Continental Celts
would, as they came in contact with the higher civilisation
of Greece and Rome, assimilate their own deities to those
of the classic Pantheon (why should they not? the god of
the Celt, the god of the Greek or Roman, were after all
cousins, if cousins who had got on in the world unequally),
and thereby increase the likeness which enabled the fusion
of the two systems of worship after the Roman Conquest, I
still think the statement just made concerning Irish mythology likely to be fairly accurate.   In the main that mythology had for its *dramatis personæ* the agricultural Powers

of Life and Increase, in the main it was made up of stories of which the ultimate essence and significance were agricultural. At what date it became heroicised, that is to say, entered as an element, a subordinate element, into tribal traditions of famous chiefs, warriors, or wizards, it is impossible to say. Heroic saga is everywhere the product of shock and stress; as soon as a tribe shifts its quarters, comes into contact with other tribes, is affected by marked alternatives of victory or defeat, it develops heroic saga, and this, all the world over, is compounded of scenes and situations which have already done duty in the mythology. All we can say is that from the eighth to the third century B.C. was a period of unrest, conquest, empire building and empire decay for the Continental Celts; it is safe to claim that Celtic heroic sagas must have grown up during this period. What earlier sagas there may have been we know not, because we know nothing of earlier history.

In considering the history of Greek religion, I distinguished between the objective and subjective elements of the primitive agricultural faith, and urged that the latter immensely outweighed the former in interest and importance. When Greece first comes before us, she had passed out of the purely agricultural stage, and its positive elements survived either as local cults or as folklore, *i.e.* as the creed and practice of the less advanced, in contradistinction to the creed and practice of the more advanced sections of the community. In Ireland we naturally expect and find a different state of things. If we may judge from the *dinnshenchas* of Mag Slecht, the ritual of the Irish gods remained agricultural in essence and intent down to its supersession by Christianity. The object of worship was to promote increase, the theory of worship was—life for life. Some allowance, it may be urged, should in this case be made for the imperfection of the record. Pre-Christian notices of the cult do not exist; what we possess may possibly describe the emergence of ruder, primitive elements of the faith after Christianity had destroyed its higher manifestations. It is as if Christianity should annihilate Mahometanism, and then describe as typical of Islamism a Bedouin rite, practised perhaps centuries before Mahomet's day, and surviving the religious system he founded. The mention of Crom Cruaich, the definite association of the cult with the mythical first king, negative to my mind such a possibility. We are entitled, I think, to take the testimony of the Mag Slecht *dinnshenchas* as it stands, and to say that in ancient Ireland worship retained down to the introduction of Christianity its primitive intent, and the primitive mode of compassing that intent.

Irish evidence is silent as to any development of the subjective element of the antique faith among the Celts; neither a metaphysic nor an ethic can be recovered from the Irish texts. The pantheism of the Amairgen poems is, I believe, if the word pantheism be used in its ordinary sense, the result of reading into these undoubtedly ancient texts the conceptions of a later age. The utmost they show is that ancient Ireland had advanced some steps in the path trodden by Vedic India, the path which led to the conception of the priest or devotee as inherently equal to his god, and as capable of attaining that equality by certain definite means. If this is so, it would be another of the significant points which Ireland shares with Vedic India to the exclusion of other Aryan-speaking peoples, and the testimony of which must be weighed in any attempt to determine the order and chronology of Aryan migrations.

In other respects the incarnation conception has a purely romantic significance in extant Irish mythology, it has originated no philosophic or moral doctrine.

On the Continent the case seems different. Many classical observers testify to the existence among the Southern Celts of a philosophic doctrine taught by the priests, and exercising a practical influence upon the ideal and conduct of life. Sacrifice, which in Ireland retained its original purport, that of promoting increase of crop and herd, seems to have been practised by the Southern Celts, with a view to acquiring and controlling life as manifested in man; the priests of the tribe were thus able to defeat death, and to assure to their tribesmen a continuance of existence. The effect of the doctrine was to intensify the fighting spirit of the tribe, to exalt the powers of a warrior and priestly aristocracy.

This is apparently the high water mark of advance in this direction among the Celts. The virtuous man (taking the word virtuous in its etymological sense) was assured of renewed existence, thanks to the practices of his creed; but this existence would seem to be passed in this world. I say 'would seem,' for some of the later classical testimonies, notably that of Lucan, support an opposite interpretation. But if we consider the classical evidence as a whole the balance inclines, I think, to the view that whilst the Southern Celts utilised the incarnation conception for religious and social purposes, they did not so utilise the Happy Otherworld conception; they reached the idea that the virtuous would live on, they did not reach the idea that they would go to a heaven. They probably, nay, almost certainly, possessed in common with the Irish the germ of a heaven in the shape of stories about a god's land, to which favoured mortals might penetrate; they did not develop the germ, or work it up into an essential component of their creed. As regards the Irish, I do not think either conception was utilised save in romance; on the philosophic and moral side neither was developed in such a way as to raise the social and religious ideals of the community beyond their primitive level.

The later history of these conceptions among the Celtic-speaking communities is comparatively plain. On the Continent the Celtic tribes came in contact with the rich and highly organised Græco-Roman mythology, and discarded their own mythic romance. In the British Isles Celtic mythic romance escaped the destructive influence of Rome, was spared by Christianity, and served, almost down to the present day, as a backbone and rallying centre to the peasant lore about the fairies, which is substantially the old agricultural faith, preserved in rude and crude form, and partly reshaped by the fierce opposition or the insidious patronage of Christianity. Gaelic peasant lore only differs from that of other parts of Europe, because Gaeldom has preserved, in a romantic form, a portion of the pre-Christian mythology. Thanks to the fact that this mythology enters largely into the Arthurian romance, the literature of modern England has retained access to the fairy realm, and has been enabled to pluck in the old wonder-garden of unending joy fruits of imperishable beauty.

We may here fitly consider the relation of the antique agricultural faith, which has been described to the totality of Aryan beliefs and institutions. It is held by distinguished scholars to be pre-Aryan, due to races which occupied Europe before they came under Aryan domination, and which still, after three to four millenniums of Aryan overlordship, form a large part of the whole population, and the major part of the agricultural population. The Aryans are, it is said, the tall, fair-haired, blue-eyed men, shepherds, hunters, poets, warriors, who subdued the short, dark tillers of the soil, imposed upon them their language and social organisation, and accepted from them, in part, their religion.

That Europe, viewed solely from the standpoint of physical anthropology, contains different races, is certain ; that in the earliest monuments of Aryan literature the Aryans did describe themselves as fair-haired and light-eyed is also certain ; that there is implied throughout the early literature of Aryan-speaking peoples a standing opposition between the fair and dark races may again be granted ; that Aryan institutions, as they come before us at the dawn of history, are based upon ancestor-worship, and the patriarchal family may be conceded, though more doubtfully. Again, the existence of short, dark races in the very earliest past, and at the present day, is beyond doubt ; nor can the survival of numerous practices and beliefs, which seem inconsistent with ancestor-worship and with the patriarchal family, and all the patriarchal family involves, be denied. It is more especially with the latter argument that I am concerned. In a work from which I have already quoted, *Ethnology in Folklore*, Mr. Gomme ascribes much of existing folklore, in especial agricultural folklore, to the men who preceded and were subdued by the Aryans. The advanced culture of the conquerors arrested the development of the beliefs and practices of the conquered, and these have remained stationary and archaic. He points out that in India, which we know to have been invaded by Aryans who partially brought under their sway short, dark races, savage agricultural rites are practised which the Brahmin priesthood, the representatives of the conquering Aryans, tolerate, but which cannot be explained from Vedic and post-Vedic Hindu religion, nay, which are inconsistent with it. Fragmentary survivals of similar rites occur in Britain, and can be reconstructed by comparison with the living Indian form. The one rite has certainly originated among, and is practised by, non-Aryans, under partial Aryan supervision; was this not also the case with the other?

Mr. Gomme's argument, based upon wide knowledge of the facts and urged with extreme ingenuity, demands careful attention. I have no prejudice against the theory of pre-Aryan survivals, but it strikes me as being sometimes used to account for facts that can be explained more simply otherwise, and it is, I think, vitiated by the implication that the development of Aryan-speaking peoples cannot be traced back beyond a certain stage. It is quite true that a well-defined series of institutions and beliefs, which, for convenience sake, may be styled patriarchal, can be recovered from the records of Greeks, Romans, and Vedic Indians, and that many customs, testified to in antiquity and still surviving, seem inconsistent with it. But this inconsistency does not necessarily imply the presence of alien racial elements. There have been, apart from the introduction of Christianity, mighty changes in the Aryan world since the patriarchal type of social organism studied by Fustel de Coulanges and Hearn predominated. There may have been changes of an equally far-reaching character in the unrecorded past of the Aryans.

To leave generalities and come to Mr. Gomme's special instance, I would point out that the history of the Aryans in India does reveal changes, religious, social, philosophical, of the most striking character. The Brahmin of to-day represents the Aryan of three thousand years ago scarce more faithfully than does the Christian priest; can we argue from his attitude to that of his ancestor who entered the valley of the Indus some three thousand five hundred to four thousand years ago? Again, it may be argued that if similarity of rite between aborigines of India and Britain proves them to be both non-Aryan, it also proves them to be non-Aryan in the same way, *i.e.* to be racially akin? Mr. Gomme would, I feel sure, demur to this conclusion; but if it be held, and rightly held, that identity of rite cannot prove identity of race between the peoples practising those rites, it follows that difference of rite does not necessarily betoken difference of race. The analogy of the Semitic world is instructive in this connection. There too the institution of the patriarchal family flourished in historical times, but along with it there subsisted more archaic institutions; there too we meet a highly organised mythology and worship, but they rest upon, or, by the survivals imbedded in them, presuppose an earlier cult of the Powers of Life and Increase, a cult of much the same nature, expressing itself in much the same way as the proto-Dionysus cult in Greece, as that of the Tuatha de Danann in Ireland. Are the Semites also a conquering aristocracy superposed upon a subject rural population, and were these pre-Semitic tillers of the soil akin to the hypothetical pre-Aryans?

In general I am disinclined to rely upon differences in religious ideas and practices as a means of discriminating race. And in this special case I can but note that even if the conceptions and rites we have studied in the foregoing pages had their origin among pre-Aryan-speaking races, yet we know of them from Aryan records, we investigate them in connection with Aryans, they have been assimilated by Aryans and become Aryan for all purposes of historical inquiry. Their ultimate origin is a matter of comparative indifference. But I cannot refrain from expressing my opinion that although Aryan records are mainly either the history of chiefs and warriors or mythic romance designed to please them, yet large masses of the population, as truly Aryan in blood (if there be any Aryan blood at all) as the chiefs and priests, had to till the soil, and that their beliefs and practices must have resembled those of other tillers of the soil. I cannot, therefore, but regard as doubtful the theory of my friend Mr. Gomme, that the beliefs respectively grouped together as witch-lore and fairy-lore are derived from different races, and may be used for racial discrimination.[1]

I have set forth a hypothetical development of the worship of the Powers of Life and of the secondary conceptions derived from it, which assumes that both worship and con-

[1] Whilst this chapter was passing through the press, Professor Karl Pearson's *Chances of Death and other Studies in Evolution* appeared. In the second volume is a remarkable group of articles: 'Woman as Witch'—'Evidences of Mother Right in the customs of Mediæval Witchcraft'—'Ashiepattle; or Hans seeks his luck'—'Kindred Group Marriage'—in which the author argues with great ability and success in favour of the thesis that early Aryan culture was matriarchal. Professor Pearson's evidence is mainly drawn from the word and custom store of the Teutonic branch of the Aryans; this is significant in view of the fact that the Teutons were the last of the great Aryan races to migrate, and that the substitution of patriarchalism for matriarchalism seems to be essentially a product of the migration period when the older forms of society were broken up and when the strength of the man became a more important factor than the skill of the woman.

R

ceptions belonged to at least two Aryan-speaking peoples—
Greeks and Celts—as far back as we can trace their history,
and that they grew independently among either people. As
far as the worship is concerned there would not be much
opposition to my thesis. It has not been contended as yet,
even by the straitest advocate of transmission, that the
Celts assisted at some Thracian festival of Dionysus and
transplanted what they saw to Ireland. It is otherwise
with the secondary conceptions : Re-birth and Happy Otherworld. These have found expression in myth and romance,
and an influential school holds that myth and romance are
nothing but a series of borrowed reproductions from one
original. The similarity between Greek and Irish myth is
sufficient for this school to prove dependence of the one
upon the other. Other scholars, while not holding this
extreme view, would yet suspect my hypothesis because it
involves vast stretches of time, because it carries back
certain conceptions to the period before the differentiation
of the Aryan-speaking peoples. This is enough for them
to brand the hypothesis as 'unscientific.' I venture to
think that this attitude is unscientific, is indeed mere prejudice. We have no right to assume the long continued
existence of institutions or conceptions concerning which
we have no direct historical testimony, if we can account
for them satisfactorily otherwise, but if we cannot, the
mere fact that centuries or even millenniums are involved
does not constitute a valid objection. Especially is this the
case in dealing with Celtdom ; we can trace back its history
for over two thousand years, and we detect a remarkable
persistence of social institutions, of literary ideals and conventions. Yet the Celts, although to a less extent than
almost any European people, have been subjected to violent

and far-reaching changes in historical times. If they have shown such conservatism during the last two thousand years, are we not entitled to assume equal conservatism during the previous centuries of which we have record? I venture then to disregard all purely *a priori* objections based upon the inadmissibility of referring to a prehistoric period a conception known to us only in comparatively recent historic times. But I cannot disregard any attempt to establish a different order of evolution for the phenomena I have noted. Such an attempt has been made in a work of which the signal ability, the wide and penetrating scholarship, have won instant recognition, Dr. F. B. Jevons' *Introduction to the Science of Religion.* In finding myself at variance with a scholar of Dr. Jevons' attainments I cannot conceal from myself the likelihood that he must be right, I wrong. At the same time, I cannot but maintain opinions which are the result of such intelligence and power of study as I possess. I purpose therefore to set forth Dr. Jevons' views, and state my objections, and then to let the matter rest for the decision of scholars. According as his view or mine is correct the question of the ultimate relations of the conceptions of Elysium and Re-birth, alike to the older cultures of the East, and to savage culture in general, appear in a different light and claim a different answer. It seems best to settle firstly what is the true place of these conceptions in the Aryan world before discussing their relation to the pre-Aryan and non-Aryan worlds. If I consider Dr. Jevons' work alone and disregard statements of other scholars which conflict with my hypothesis, it is because Dr. Jevons has used the material I brought together in the first volume of this work, and has taken up a definite position towards the problem

I set out to solve if I might. Discussion is more likely to be fruitful when the disputants are in full possession of each other's views.

Dr. Jevons describes, explicitly, the various factors, sociological, mythological, moral, which enter into the concept of savage religion, and traces, implicitly, their evolution up to the establishment of Christianity. He is concerned alike with the forms of religion discernible among races of a low stage of culture and with their development among the most gifted and progressive of the Aryan-speaking people, the Greeks. He is thus led to examine the remarkable religious movements which characterised the Hellenic world in the sixth and fifth centuries B.C., and which resulted in a highly organised eschatological system and in a doctrine of metempsychosis. In thus essaying to account for the new prominence given to the joys and penalties of the next life, to the new importance which the mysteries assumed among the Greeks during these two centuries, he attacks from the standpoint of general religious history problems which I have discussed solely in so far as they involved, proximately or remotely, the Irish evidence.

DR. JEVONS' EXPOSITION OF THE DEVELOPMENT OF RELIGION.

Savage religion starts when the savage, having learned to discriminate among the energies which surround him—to recognise some as natural (*i.e.* which he can control), some as supernatural (*i.e.* which he cannot control)—selects, as it were, certain of these energies, essays to enter into friendly relations with them, to win their favour and assure their support. In thus acting, he was determined by the conception that certain things are forbidden, and that to do the forbidden thing entails dreadful consequences—a conception formally expressed in the world-wide institution of taboo, which, according to Dr. Jevons, lacks all realistic or experiential basis, and is in its essence spiritual, the product of a 'feeling that sense experience is not the sole source or the final test of truth.' The energies, manifestations of supernatural life and activity, with which savage man first sought to establish relations were mainly animal, and the relations he did establish make up the series of institutions known as totemism. Savage man, bound by blood kinship to his fellow-clansman, binds himself by the same tie to his totem, his animal god, and thus obtains among the supernatural powers an ally upon whose aid he can rely in extraordinary circumstances as confidently as in ordinary circumstances he relies upon that of his human kinsmen. In both cases the connection is ultimately the same, hence the mode of initiating or renewing it was of the same character—by the blood-covenant. The totem, the animal god, was sacrificed to induce him to remain at the altar on which his blood was smeared. What remained over of the body was consumed by the worshipping kinsmen : at first it was wholly eaten ; in later times the eatable portions alone were used as food, the bones, offal, etc., were burnt. Sacrifice was thus originally an act of communion, establishing or renewing between man and his god the blood-kinship, the only form of alliance upon which man could count. Changes in the social conditions of the community effected corresponding changes in the institution of sacrifice. From being a communion it became a tribute or an expiation. Expiation presupposes human transgression ; hence the substitution of a human victim as a more potent and reasonable form of atonement. To this secondary development of sacrifice—tribute or expiation in the place of communion, human in the place of animal victims—corresponds the rise and establishment of ancestor - worship. Here, too, we find human sacrifice, the wife or the slave being slaughtered on the chief's tomb. The original purport was to provide society and service to the deceased in the life after death. But the sacrifice came to assume the same expiatory, piacular character as ordinary sacrifice, with the result of accentuating the likeness between ancestor and god.

By this time man had formed an idea concerning the next life. It was passed in a far-off land, the remoteness of which was proved by the unfrequent visits of its inmates to earth ; the land itself might be underground, a natural deduction from burial customs. It might be differently conceived of by different peoples. Among the Greeks it was at first figured as a dreary, bloodless, shadowy realm, the Hades to which Odysseus penetrates. Burial customs testify to the belief that life was continued on substantially the same lines as in this world, and in their turn led to the idea that the survivors could, by appropriate rites, influence the well-being of the departed. The increasing definiteness with which Hades was located underground did not obliterate the impression that the dead might also go to a far-off land ; but this was relegated to a far backward of time, and if, of old, men went there, it was because there were heroes then, deserving of a better fate than the gloomy underground realm, the lot of most mortals. But this heroic otherworld still existed, beyond the rays of the setting sun, reserved for the mortals whom the gods specially favoured. In Greece this conception would seem to be an alien one, partly borrowed from Egypt. The Egyptians, too, pictured the next life as the continuation of this one, but they pictured it at first under fair and smiling colours, and the fertile plains of Aalu seem to have given the hint of the Greek Elysium. From the Greeks this vision of a happy Otherworld—not the ordinary Hades to which men at large went, but an old-time wonderland for those favoured of the gods—spread to the Celts and originated the romantic narratives of which the *Voyage of Bran* is the type.

The existence of a double otherworld, one of which was pictured under far more attractive colours than the other, yielded the germ of the retribution theory. Man went to one or the other after death according to his deserts in this life, his deserts varying, of course, with the social and moral ideals of the period. The Egyptians would seem to have developed the conception before other peoples; at all events the monuments and texts of the Middle Empire (*i.e.* at latest 1500-1000 B.C.) show a definitely constituted hell, to escape from which by favour of and union with Osiris, was the ardent preoccupation of the Egyptian devotee. Here again Greece would seem to be debtor; but along with the retribution theory, its heaven and corresponding hell, she borrowed the doctrine of metempsychosis.

In the totemistic stage, man speculating as to his lot after death would naturally aspire after assimilation to his totem god. Egypt, which presents so many traces of totemism, has preserved the record of à time when change into an animal was a normal post-mortem desideratum. The later development of belief in the fertile plains of

Aalu did not destroy the old conception, but relegated it to the vulgar, stamped it with inferiority, and ultimately branded transmigration into an animal as the evil to be avoided at all costs. It was under this form that it was introduced by Pythagoras into the Greek world.

The impulse to borrow, alike with the borrowed material, came from without. The evolution of sacrifice—from an act of communion to an act of tribute—had been determined by the evolution of society from a nomadic, pastoral stage through agriculture to civilisation (using the word in its etymological sense) of a monarchical or quasi-monarchical character. Evolution in belief proceeded concurrently with the change and progress of material culture. But the latter might be arrested or destroyed from without. This occurred in the Northern Semitic world in the seventh and sixth centuries B.C. The communities of Syria and Palestine were overwhelmed from Assyria and Babylonia; the great empires of Assyria and Babylonia themselves went down before the Persian. Calamities so catastrophic begot profound unrest and dissatisfaction with the traditional religion. Among the loftier minds of the Hebrew people there was engendered a new moral and religious ideal; among the mass of worshippers the expiatory aspect of sacrifice became prominent, and its aspect as an act of communion with the tribal gods was revived. A natural effect was to restore to honour such fragments of archaic ritual as had survived. Hence a profound modification of worship, due partly to the rise of new conceptions, partly to the emergence of old conceptions, transformed to suit current needs. The general effect was to deepen man's sense of reliance upon his deity, to intensify his apprehension concerning his fate both in this world and the next, to urge him to seek salvation in strange rites, especially such as seemed to him to come down from the time when his god was in intimate communion with him, and not as now, estranged and displeased.

The religious spirit, thus modified, blew from the East to Greece. It must have begun to act as early as the seventh century B.C. Solon's legislation provides for the existence of θίασοι—religious associations based upon the voluntary principle instead of on that of blood-kinship, the only bond of common worship known to earlier times. As early as 596 B.C. solemn purificatory rites were resorted to by the Athenians. Throughout the sixth century the movement grew. As in the East, so in the West, it drove men back to archaic rituals, which had lived on among the ruder, more backward elements of the population, and which now had new meaning, added significance, read into them. Hence the emergence of the rustic Dionysus cult, in itself of the same nature as the imported Eastern cults, and easily identifiable with them; hence the importance assigned to the Eleusinian mysteries, an agricultural festival first thrown open to the Athenians in the fifth century, and eagerly resorted to by them as the truest type and fount of antique lore concerning the mysteries of life and death ; the ancient ritual was retained, but new conceptions were read into it, and a new mythology arose to account for its perplexing features. The outcome was the establishment among the Greeks of the retribution theory, with all its consequences, moral and philosophical, and the ' concep- tion of a religious community, the bounds of which were not limited by those of any political community, and the members of which were knit together, not by the tie of blood or a common citizenship, but by the bond of spiritual fellowship.'

So far Dr. Jevons. It would be easy for me to minimise certain points of difference between his views and those which I have set forth in this work. Thus with regard to sacrifice, I might point out that there is no necessary incompatibility between his account and mine. I do not profess to trace the conceptions I have studied beyond the agricultural stage of culture. But Robertson Smith, and Dr. Jevons who adopts his theory of sacrifice, work back to a pre-agricultural stage, and both admit that by the time agriculture had become the basis of social organisation, the institution had modified its character, and from being wholly an act of communion, had become almost entirely an act of tribute. Indeed, this modification is an essential element of Dr. Jevons' reconstruction of religious evolution; it is the dissatisfaction felt with the gift-theory of sacrifice, the reversion, in outward form, to the earlier communion theory, enriched as this was, in inward spirit, by all the material and intellectual conquests of the community during the intervening centuries, that constitutes the great religious movement of 700-400 B.C., the necessary precursor of the greater religious movement of 1-400 A.D. It is, however, far from my wish to minimise points of difference, and I would express my conviction that important as is the communion element in sacrifice, it was not at the outset the sole and primary one, to which, at a later stage, the gift- and atonement-theories of the institution were added, but that the first men who practised sacrifice had a clear idea they were to get something definite in exchange for what they gave. The bargain element, the theory of life for life, is, I believe, as old as the communion element, and sacrifice was, from the first, bloody—purposing to feed the Holders of Life, which have their home in the earth, or fiery—purposing to feed the Fosterers of Life, who have their home in the sun.

Apart from this general divergence, there is specific divergence in our way of accounting for the development of other-life and other-world conceptions among the Aryan-speaking peoples.

POINTS OF DIFFERENCE.

For Dr. Jevons this development is due *mainly* to foreign influence ; for me it is due *mainly* to the natural working of native conditions. I italicise the word mainly, as Dr. Jevons would not deny that the Aryan-speaking Greeks had carried the conception of the other-life to a certain point, nor should I deny the possible, or even the probable, influence alike of the eastern world upon Hellas, and of the Hellenic world upon Celtdom. It is all a question of degree. According to Dr. Jevons, the Greeks did not carry the conception of an other-world beyond the stage of a gloomy and bloodless Hades ; a blissful other-world, an Elysium, they had to borrow from the Egyptians, passing it on in their turn to the Celts. Although he speaks less positively upon this point, he would doubtless regard the conception of a Tartarus, of the other-world as a place of punishment, as equally borrowed. Indeed, whatever positive evidence there may be for the Egyptian origin of Elysium, is slight compared with that in favour of the Egyptian origin of Tartarus. Again, Dr. Jevons describes the metempsychosis known to the Greeks of the sixth and fifth centuries B.C. as wholly derived from Egypt. I, on the other hand, would regard the ancient agricultural worship, based on sacrifice, the existence of which I have postulated among Greeks and Celts, as pregnant with all the possible developments of either the Elysium or the Re-birth conception, and I would only call in the aid of foreign influence where its existence is indisputably proved by historic record, or where it is absolutely necessary to account for singularities in the process of evolution, which would otherwise be inexplicable.

M. Foucart's Theory of the Eleusinia.

Up to a certain point, Dr. Jevons and I are at one.   He admits the existence of agricultural cults among the Greeks. The worship of Dionysus, of the Eleusinian Mother, are in his eyes Greek in their origin, although they were transformed in historic times under the influence of alien conceptions.   In this he differs from another advocate of the foreign origin of certain Greek rites and myths, M. Paul Foucart, who, in his *Recherches sur les Mystères d'Eleusis*, distinguishes two periods of borrowing by the Greeks from Egypt.   Originally, say in the seventeenth-sixteenth centuries B.C., 'colonists or fugitives from Egypt brought the cult of Isis and Osiris to Argos and Attica.   The indigenous Pelasgi probably worshipped the earth among other natural objects, but only in a rude and impersonal way.   The Pelasgic Earth-goddess was absorbed by Isis, who was not only a chthonic deity, but also the giver of agriculture and civilisation.   As Osiris was closely associated with Isis, the oldest form of the Eleusinian cult included a god as well as a goddess; and in historic times this god, who was at first known by the simple title of θεός, continued to exist as Zeus Eubouleus, Pluto, and Dionysus.   Originally, the worship of the Eleusinian Demeter was merely a form of the general

worship of Isis-Demeter or Demeter-Thesmophoros, which
was adopted by all the Hellenic tribes before the Dorian
tribes. . . . In the seventh century B.C., the Greeks became
better acquainted with Egypt, and borrowed the doctrine
of a future life, as taught in the religion of Isis and Osiris.
This idea of a happy state, reserved for the initiated after
death, was not a natural outcome of the old worship of
Demeter καρποφόρος and θεσμοφόρος, but was thus a later
addition to the original debt.'[1]

This theory has a more rounded and logical aspect than
Dr. Jevons'. It gets over the difficulty I have just hinted
at, for the French scholar does not, like the English one,
allow the Greek origin of certain institutions, and then
imply that the Greeks were incapable of developing them
as freely as the Egyptians, *ex hypothesi*, had done; he
boldly traces the entire institution, root and branch, to the
outside. But this thorough-going solution of the problem
raises as many difficulties as it lays. As Mr. Sikes has well
pointed out: 'the Eleusinia and Thesmophoria arose from
agrarian ritual; and M. Foucart will hardly contend that
agriculture in general was introduced into Greece by the
Egyptians.' The critic then goes on to enumerate the
historic difficulties: ' it has yet to be proved that the
Egyptians had any direct intercourse with the Greeks on
the mainland from the seventeenth to the thirteenth century B.C. . . . there is no evidence of any relations between
early Greeks and the Egyptians, except through the medium
of Phœnician traders and colonists.' The main reason for
rejecting M. Foucart's theory, in so far as the prehistoric
introduction of Egyptian agricultural rites is concerned, is

[1] I have preferred to give Mr. Sikes' summary of Foucart's theory
(*Classical Rev.* Dec. 1895).

furnished by Dr. Jevons in his brilliant and convincing exposition of the Eleusinia in their primitive aspect and significance.[1] In so far as certainty is possible in these questions, it is certain that the Egyptian ritual, known from texts of the fifteenth-tenth centuries B.C., could not have originated the Eleusinian and allied rituals. The question I have raised thus subsists : why, if the existence in Greece of agricultural rituals be admitted, should the Greeks, by implication, be denied the capacity of developing them without foreign aid? This, it may be said, is an *a priori* argument, but, then, so is the argument of foreign influence, and one that derives all its validity from the fact that the Egyptian development is recorded at an earlier period of the world's history than the Greek. This is true, but it only proves the possibility of influenee, and in no sense constitutes an argument in favour of its existence. That must be supported by facts, and up to now the facts upon which the theory of Egyptian influence upon Greek religion before the year 1000 B.C. is based reduce themselves to two : the similarity of the words Aalu and Elysium, and the statement in the Odyssey that Menelaus heard in Egypt Proteus' prophecy concerning his rapture to the isles ruled over by Rhadamanthus.[2] To my mind this is insufficient.

EGYPTIAN INFLUENCE ON GREECE.

On the other hand, in the period 700-500 B.C., there are marked signs of Egyptian influence in the Greek religious movement. Dr. Jevons has argued with great ability in favour of the traditional dependence of Pythagorean upon Egyptian metempsychosis, whilst M. Foucart's brilliant con-

---

[1] *l.c.* Chapter xxiv.　　　　[2] Jevons, *l.c.* p. 313.

jecture that the inscribed tablets which the Orphic devotees had buried with them correspond to the copies of the whole or portions of the Book of the Dead, which invariably accompanied the Egyptian dead to act as a guide and talisman in his journey through the otherworld, has won an assent denied to his theory as a whole. In either case it should be noted that what the Greeks borrowed was a doctrine, or a practice involving a doctrine of an advanced character, the alien aspect of which, as regards Pythagoreanism at least, was at once recognised, perhaps even exaggerated, by themselves. It is difficult to see what support these instances give to the general theory that Greek religion was revolutionised in the seventh-sixth centuries B.C. by movements originating in the Northern Semitic area, and having for their animating principle a revival of the archaic theory of sacrifice. For Egypt is not Syria, and Egyptian eschatology had long before passed beyond dependence upon sacrificial theory. It may, indeed, be urged that the North Semitic movement was a ferment which induced far more rapid development of native Greek religion than would otherwise have been the case, and that when the Greeks, thanks to its introduction, passed in a relatively short space of time through phases of development which in Egypt had lasted throughout millenniums, they, in the latest stages of the movement, naturally turned to the older land, and took over conceptions and practices wholesale. Thus restricted, there is less ground of objection to Dr. Jevons' theory; all that can be said is that the positive evidence is really very slight, and that no light is thereby thrown upon the development of religion among the Aryans who invaded India and established themselves there. Vedic and post-Vedic religion, undoubtedly, reached the conceptions of a future life and of metempsychosis. Did they possess the germs of these conceptions when they entered India, and did they develop these germs independently? In this case, why should a like possibility be denied to their Greek kins- men? Or were they too affected by the hypothetical religious movement, which had its rise in the Northern Semitic area in the eighth-sixth centuries B.C.? There is, I believe, not a scintilla of evidence to support such a contention, and Indianists would, I fancy, demur to it vigorously. I wish to insist upon this point. The problem of religious development among the Greek Aryans cannot be solved in entire independence of like development among the Indian Aryans.[1] If certain mythological and ritual factors are sufficient for solution in the one case, we ought, at least, to admit the possibility of their sufficing in the other. As a simple matter of fact, metaphysical systems of the utmost complexity and subtlety were elaborated alike in Greece and India independently of each other, and, if we may believe the most eminent

---

[1] For this reason I demur to my friend M. Gaidoz' criticism of vol. i. (in *Mélusine*) that I acted unmethodically and unscientifically in using Vedic and post-Vedic literature to elucidate the Celtic and Greek Elysium vision. This is to commit the unpardonable sin of 'compara- tive mythology.' I must plead guilty, and I am an impenitent sinner. I believe that if a trait is common to Greek and Vedic mythology an ex- planation must be one applicable in both cases. The scientific method to be pursued is thus, I maintain, to compare the myth and rites of the Aryan-speaking peoples generally, before discussing the relation of a particular Aryan religious system to those of non-Aryan peoples. This canon of investigation, of course, only applies when the origin and nature of the particular rite or myth are obscure. But this is the case with the greater part of any mythology. And where foreign influence has been at work its presence is generally unmistakable.

experts, in independence of foreign influence. The races capable of achievements such as these were surely capable of elaborating the religious conceptions that confront us in the Orphic systems.

If the instance of Indian religious development affords sound reason for hesitating to ascribe every peculiar feature in Greek to outside foreign influence, the Celtic evidence is, to my mind, of yet greater weight. It will not have escaped the reader's attention that the mass of Greek evidence concerning the ancient agricultural worship and its derivative conceptions of life, although far more extensive than meets us in Ireland, is less consistent and homogeneous. This is what might be expected on my hypothesis. I postulate a set of rites and beliefs, originally similar, among Celts and Greeks, which the former developed to a slight extent only, whilst the latter completely outgrew their primitive aspect, modifying them to meet material, intellectual, and moral requirements of the most advanced nature. What the Celts have preserved is scanty indeed, but it is nearer the source, less changed by the admixture of new or foreign elements. In particular, the conceptions of Elysium and Re-birth maintain their connection with a persistence utterly inexplicable on the face of our scanty evidence. Would this be the case if the Elysium visions were simply a borrowed piece of alien romance which happened to strike the fancy of the literary class? And when could this take place? Evidently before the Greeks became acquainted with the idea of metempsychosis, as by that time their Elysium had reached an eschatological stage, had become a heaven. Where, then, did the Celts get the re-birth conception? Did they develop that themselves? And if so, why should they be held incapable of developing the Elysium vision? Chronology, too, has to be considered. We know that Celts dominated Southern Central Europe from the Rhine to the Black Sea throughout the seventh-third centuries B.C. Contact with Greek ideas during this period is, to say the least, possible, but why should the result of that contact be limited to one particular feature of their mythology (a feature specially characteristic of its most archaic and conservative aspect), that based upon the worship of the powers of life manifested in vegetable and animal growth? We know little, and we are, unfortunately, never likely to know much, of the Celtic Pantheon. Were new sources of knowledge to be opened up, I, for one, should wonder little if it showed traces of Greek influence. I can understand the less advanced race adopting or copying the outward machinery and trappings of the higher cult. I have expressly asserted my belief in the possibility of such a process, when the Southern Celts were in fairly close contact alike with the Romans or Romanised North Italians, or with the Greeks of Massilia, in the century and a half preceding the Roman Conquest. What I credit with difficulty is that the less advanced race should pick up bits and snatches of the most obscure and neglected portion of the higher creed, or forthwith work them into coherent connection with their own more archaic beliefs. I do not assert that the process is impossible: I simply urge that it is in the last degree improbable, and that we ought not to presume its existence if we can explain the facts in any other way.

I rely, then, upon the mode of occurrence of Elysium and Re-birth conceptions in Irish mythic literature, upon their essential and intimate connection with the oldest portions of their ritual and mythology, as proof of their native development, uninfluenced from without, and I urge their independent existence among the Celts in a form singularly close to that recoverable from the Greek evidence, as an important argument in favour of their independent exist- ence among the Greeks. The latter developed them to the full extent of their capacity, and the last stages of their development may well have been hastened and modified by outside influence. It is precisely these last stages of which we find not a single trace among the Celts, and this despite the fact that after their attainment by the Greeks, the latter people were during several centuries in a position to influence their Celtic kinsmen, and did actually influence their material culture in important respects. If no such influence was exerted during the centuries when we know that Greeks and Celts were fighting and trading with each other, why should we postulate its existence, as does Dr. Jevons, at a period when we know nothing concerning the mutual relations of Greeks and Celts, when, possibly, the Celts had not even reached the stage of a racial individuality.[1]

One argument which seems to have weighed with Dr. Jevons in deciding against the possible pan-Aryan character of the Elysium conception is based upon its absence among the Romans. I confess it does not impress me. The Aryan-speaking peoples have developed the most diverse gifts and capacities, and the failure of one branch to elaborate root-conceptions, which amongst the others have borne abundant fruit, need not surprise us. We are entitled

---

[1] *i.e.* If the Greeks borrowed Aalu from the Egyptians about 1200 B.C., it is possible that there were, properly speaking, no Celtic peoples in existence to which to pass it on.

to judge the prehistoric Roman in the light of his historic record. Be the reason what it may, he displayed throughout the whole of his history an absolute incapacity to invent in the domain of mythic romance and imaginative literature generally. Well-nigh all the stories that Rome has ever told are borrowed stories ; not only has she contributed scarce one single new story to the treasure-house of the world's imagination, she has contributed no new mode of expressing that imagination in literature or plastic art. Compare her in this respect with Celtdom. Latin literature is one of the greatest and noblest the world has ever known ; for force, dignity, adequacy of thought, and expression it is, perhaps, unrivalled. It has dominated and recast European expression as Rome dominated and recast Europe. Celtic literature is scanty in bulk, meagre in thought, primitive in expression. Yet it has an originality, a power of invention, alike of incident and of literary form suited to the effective presentment of that incident, wholly denied to the immeasurably greater literature. Why should we wonder because the Celts were sensitive to the romantic capabilities of a mythic theme which the Romans left fallow? The two peoples had different gifts. The ultimate origins of Roman and Brehon law are the same, yet how diverse their growth, how immeasurably diverse the outcome of that growth. If the Romans, intent upon their own work, utterly neglected to elaborate their mythology, that is no reason for denying the Aryan nature of Greek, Vedic, or Celtic myth.

Here I leave the question. It is, I trust, set forth clearly and unambiguously. It is important, involving, as it does, the larger one, whether the religious beliefs and practices of our Ayran-speaking forefathers are, in the main, a product of the same intellectual, artistic, and moral capacities which have given to the world Greek poetry, philosophy, and art, Roman law, Indian religious metaphysic, or whether they must, in the main, be assigned to the influence of other races, of alien cultures. The correct answer to this question is found to turn, in a large measure, upon the weight and import of evidence afforded by the myths and customs of peoples, who once dominated these islands, and who still form a most important element, alike physical, intellectual, and artistic, of our mixed population.

The few pages which follow must be regarded as supplementing the Chronological Table at the end of vol. i. Whilst I am not blind to the hypothetical nature of my dates and periods, I believe them to be, at least, as near the mark as those elaborate reconstructions of the past in which the 'scientific' archæologist delights.

SUMMARY AND CONCLUSION.[1]

Circa 2500-2000 B.C. This is the earliest date to which we can carry back any Aryan-speaking community with reasonable certitude. An agricultural stage of culture had been reached, possibly an independent Aryan development, possibly taken over from subjugated populations. Influence from the great civilisations of the Nile and Euphrates valleys should not be assumed; they had probably passed through a similar stage of culture, but had outgrown it, and any contact between them and the Aryans of Central and Northern Europe could not possibly have produced the

---

[1] I have put these propositions in a definite and absolute form, but it will of course be understood that I only regard them as probable.

social and religious conditions the existence of which we are entitled to postulate among the latter.

Sociologically speaking this hypothetical early Aryan culture was, in all probability matriarchal; its religion was based upon a theory of sacrifice in which the element of bargain was at least as prominent as that of communion; its mythology had hardly progressed beyond the individualisation of certain Powers of Life manifest in vegetable and animal growth; a rude eschatology may have been elaborated on the supposition that vitality, after leaving man at death, joined and reinforced the Powers of Life, and may have resulted in supplementing the public worship addressed to the Powers generally, by private worship addressed to the departed kinsman; the dead were probably buried, and burial rites may have been influenced by and have influenced agricultural rites; a rude philosophy held all life to be one kind, manifesting itself in divers shapes—control of this vital essence was the god's attribute *par excellence.*

But for the prehistoric migrations which scattered Aryan-speaking communities from the Ganges valley on the one side to Westernmost Europe on the other, and from Greece to Scandinavia, this primitive stage of culture might have lasted on unchanged. Indeed it did persist, with comparatively little change, among the less advanced Celts and Teutons down to the Christian era, among the Slavs and Lithuanians down to the Middle Ages, and, as a matter of fact, it still furnishes a very large part of peasant custom and belief throughout Europe.

Some time after 2000 B.C. began the migrations, which settled Aryan-speaking communities in Greece, Italy, Iran, and North-West India by 1500 B.C. at the latest. Matriarchalism gave way to patriarchalism; the nature and import of sacrifice were modified; an increasingly complex ritual and mythology kept pace with the increasing complexity, alike material and intellectual, of the community. In the case of the Greek Aryans mythology may have been enriched and developed by loans, direct or indirect, from the older civilisations of the Nile and Euphrates valleys. But the evidence is by no means so conclusive as certain scholars assert, and it should be remembered that the religious development of the Vedic Aryans, which does not seem to have been affected by either Babylonia or Egypt, was as rapid and as remarkable as that of the Greek Aryans. The migration period probably substituted the practice of burning the dead for that of burial, and this may have given to the dead a bloodless shadowy character. Burial and its accompanying rites persisted, however, and kept alive belief in the continued activity and power of the dead.

As regards the conceptions studied in the present work, the ideas of a god's land of delight, and of interchange of form between extra-human and human beings were early deductions from the phenomena of ecstasy which accompanied the primitive sacrificial rites. Both ideas took shape before they were brought into connection with a doctrine of what happens to man after death. This possibly originated among the Greek Aryans after contact with Egyptian civilisation. But the direct evidence is meagre and weak, and there is no reason why the Greeks should be denied the capacity for an evolution similar to that through which Egypt had passed centuries before, and through which Vedic India passed from about 1200-800 B.C.

The development of eschatological doctrine seems to have been rapid and marked in the Greek world during the

seventh-fifth centuries B.C. It is questionable if the phenomena confronting us during these centuries are really as
novel to Greece as they appear to be ; still more questionable if they are due to religious movements originating in
the Northern Semitic world ; on the contrary, what evidence
exists in favour of outside influence points to Egypt as its
source. If the origin and development of the movement
are obscure, the result is plain enough—the constitution of
an ethico-philosophical doctrine respecting the relation of
this to the other-life. Again, let me note that momentous
as were the after consequences of this Greek movement, it
was in itself neither so extensive nor so revolutionary as
the parallel movement which among the Vedic Indians culminated in Buddhism.

About 1000-800 B.C. began in all probability the migrations of the Celtic Aryans. Starting later than either
Greeks or Vedic Indians, the Celts occupied lands less
adapted to hasten and intensify their development ; they
came, too, less in contact with more advanced civilisations
than did the Greeks. Hence when they emerge upon the
field of history they had departed infinitely less from the
primitive agricultural stage of culture. Matriarchalism on
the whole had given way, especially among the Southern
Celts, whose material evolution was more varied and
intense ; they, too, seem to have changed the theory of
sacrifice retained in its original purity among the Irish.
Mythology became fairly complex, and the rudiments of
an eschatology may possibly be discerned among the
Southern Celts whilst they are altogether lacking in
Northern Celtdom.

The features common to Greek and Irish mythology
belong to the earlier known stage of Aryan mythical evolu-

tion, and are not the result of influence exercised by the more upon the less advanced race. Survivals in Greece, they represent the high-water mark of Irish pre-Christian development; hence their greater consistency and vividness in Ireland. Fragmentary as may be the form and distorted as it may be by its transmission through Christian hands, we thus owe to Ireland the preservation of mythical conceptions and visions more archaic in substance if far later in record than the great mythologies of Greece and Vedic India.

FINIS

APPENDICES

APPENDIX A.

Scél Túain maic Cairill do Finnén Maige Bile inso sís.[1]

1. Iar tudecht[2] do Finnén[3] Maige Bile cosint śoscélu i tír nÉrend i crích Ulad,[4] luid[5] dochum láich saidbir[6] and 7 nísrelic[7] isin les cuci, corothroiscset[8] aci fo domnach.[9] Nírbu maith a chretem ind láich. Asbert Finnén fria muintir: 'Doforficba fer maith nobdídnoba[10] 7 innisfid[11] dúib senchas Hérend.[12]

2. Iarsin dosfic sruith clérich[13] arnabárach matain[14] moch, feraid[15] fáilti friu. 'Táit lim-sa dom' dísiurt,' ol sé, 'is dudchu[16] dúib.' Lotar[17] leis 7 dogníat ord[18] in domnaig[19] etir salmu

---

R. = Rawl. B. 512, fo. 97b, 2–98b, 1. *H.* = H. 3. 18, fo. 38a. *U.* = Lebor na Huidre, pp. 15a – 16b. *I am indebted to Prof. Strachan for lending me his transcript of H.*

[1] *om R.* [2] dudecht (=dtudecht) *U.* [3] du Finnien *R.* [4] ant[ś]ainriudh *add. R.* [5] ant[s]a[i]nriudh *add. R.* [6] doluid *H.* [7] nislece *R.* sidhen *add. H.* [8] corothroiscset *U.* [9] 7 *add. UR.* [10] nobardidnoba *H.* [11] innisfes *RH.* [12] orocétgabad cusindiu *add H.* [13] cleirech *H.* [14] iarnabarach matan *R.* [15] feraid *R.* [16] duthcha *RH.* [17] iarsin *add. R.* [18] ort *R.* [19] ann *add. R.*

Incipit Imacallaim Tuain fri Finnia.

L. = Laud 610, fo. 102a, 2 – 103a, 2.

1. Iar tuidecht do Finnio cosint soscelu lais hi tír nHéirenn hi crich nUlath, luid do thig láich sommai and. Nisreilc side hi tech cucci. Docinet lais fo domnach, fobith ni bu maith a chreidem in láich. Asbert Findia fria muntir: 'Doticfa fer maith nobdidnabthar 7 adfíí duib senchasa inna Héirenn file o cetagabath.'

2. Tosfic sruith cleirech [sic] arnabárach mattin, feraith failti friu. 'Toet limsa, ol se, dom disiurt, is duthchu duib. Lotar lais

7 precept 7 offrend. Ro-íarfaig Finnen a slonniud de.[1] Asbert friu : 'De Ultaib dam-sa,' ol se. 'Túan mac Cairill[2] mesi, maic Muredaig Mundeirc.[3] Rogabus for orbu[4] m'athar a [5] n-dísert sa.[6] Túan[7] mac[8] Stairn maic Sera, mac bráthar do Partholón, rob é mo ślonnud tall ar thús.'

3. Ro-íarfaig[9] Finnén de imthechta Hérenn .i. aní[10] forcoemnacair inti ó amsir Partholóin maic Sera. Ocus[11] asbert[12] Finnén ná airbértais[13] bith aici coro-innised dóib senchasa Érenn. Asbert Túan fri Finnén: 'Is[14] ansu dún cen bréthir n-Dé[15] atchúad-su[16] dún ó chíanaib[17] do imrádud.'[18] 'Is cet duit-siu tra,' ol Finnén, 'th'imthechta féin 7 imthús[19] na Hérenn[20] do[21] innisin dún coléic.[22]'

4. 'Cóic gabála ém,' ol sé, 'rogabad[23] Hériu[24] íar ndílind 7 nísragbad íar ndílind corochatéa[25] dí bliadain déac ar tríb cétaib.[26] Is íarsein rosgab[27] Partholón mac Sera. Doluid for longais cetheora[28] lánamna fichet. Nírbo[29] mór amainsi cáich[30] díb

---

1 om H Finnien de a slonnud R. 2 acairillius [sic] R. 3 munderg UR. 4 forba R. 5 itaisiu add. H. 6 ind R. 7 immorro add. R. 8 immorro add. H. 9 rofiarfaigh R. 10 indni R, indi H. 11 om R. 12 Atbert R. 13 hairbertais R. 14 fri-Is om. H. 15 dé U. 16 atchuadasu R. 17 om. UR. 18 imrarud U. 19 imtusa H. 20 nErenn R. 21 du R. d' H. 22 om. U. uait R. 23 rogabh H. 24 rogabsat Erind R. 25 corochaithtea RH. 26 di bliadain ar mile RH. 27 rogab UH. 28 cethora U. 29 nibo R. 30 caigh R.

---

dogniat hurdu domnaig etir ŝalmu 7 procept 7 offrend 7 celebrad. Imchomaircith a ślondud. Asbert friu: 'Di Hultaib damsa hi sund .i. Tuan mac Cairill mo ainm. Rogabus for orbu mo athar a Itha cussan disert n-isin do bennaib Bairche.'

3. Rosiacht Finnia coibsena fair do himthechtaib Héirenn, aní forcoemnacair o hamsir Parthaloin maic Agnomain. Asbert Findia nad n-airberdis bith chucci. Asbert Tuan fri Finnía : 'Nammuiregar-sa immin lessin, is diliu dund briathar Déi adcois dun do imradud.' 'Is cett dait dano,' ol Finnía, [fo. 102b, 1] 'do imthechta fadéin 7 imthechta Heirend do innisin dún coléic.'

4. 'Cúic gabala ém rongabath Hériu cossin n-amsir sea. Ni ragbad ria ndile 7 ni ragbad iar ndíle, cotormalta di bliadain ar míle fás iar ndul na dilenn din tír. Is iarum rogab mac Agnomain maic Starbuí, do Grégaib a chenél. Dolotar for longais cetheora lanamna fichet, ar is

fri araili. Trebsat Hérinn co mbátar cóic míli día síl and.
Dosánic[1] dunebad etir dá domnach co n-erblatar[2] uli acht
óenfer nammá,[3] ar ní gnáth orgain[4] cen scéola[5] do ernam esi[6]
do innisin scél dara n-ési. Is mesi da*no*[7] in fer sin,'[8] ol
séseom.

5. ' Bá-sa íar*u*m o dingnu do dingnu 7 o aill do aill ocom'
imdítin ar chonaib altaib na dí blia*dna* ar fichit robái Hériu
fás. Dolluid crіne[9] chucum-sa 7 sentath[10] 7 robá i n-allaib 7 i
n-díthrubaib 7 forémed imthecht 7 nobítis úama irdalta ocum.[11]

6. 'Rosgab[12] íarum Nemed mac Agnom*ain* bráthair athar
dam-sa 7 atachím-sea a hallaib 7 bá-sa for a imgabáil[13] 7 mé
mongach ingnech crín líath nocht tróg[14] immnedach. Bá-sa
aidchi and íarum im' chotlud co n-aca mo[15] dul i richt oiss
allaid. Bá-sa i suidiu 7 mé óc, 7 ba maith lim mo menma.
Iss[16] and rorádius-[s]a na bríathra sa sís.

> Amnirt indiu mac Senbath,
> arroscarad re thendrath,
> ní fo degblad co nirt núa
> atá mac Senbath senrúa.

---

[1] Dosfanic *R*. [2] erbaltatar *H*. [3] .i. *tantum add. H*. [4] orcuin *R*. [5] sceolai *H*.
[6] dar a heisi *H*. [7] *om H*. [8] int æn sin *H*. [9] crini *U*. [10] sentu *H*. [11] acum *U*.
[12] rogab *RH*. [13] incabáil *U*. [14] trog*h* nocht *R*. [15] mu *R*. [16] *From here to end
of verses om. RH*.

---

már amainse cáich díb fri araile. Trebsit Hérind co mbúi míle dia
chlaind. Dosnic duneba etir dá domnach conidapthatar acht œnfer.
Ar ni gnáth dígail no horgain cen sceolu n-éisi do innisin scel dara
n-éisi. Is messi in fer sin.

5. ' Basussa iarum o dangun do dangun 7 o aill do aill ocom ditin ar
chonaib altaib di blia*dain* ar trichait rombúi Heriu hi fás. Doluid
críne form assennath 7 addró im thecht. Roba i n-aldaib 7 dithribib 7
nobítís húama aurdalta lim.

6. 'Rosgab mac Agnomin iarum, brathair athar damsa. Attac*in*
innsidi [sic] a hallaib 7 básu fora n-ingabáil, os me mongach ingnech
crín nocht tróg imnedach. Básu aidchi n-and im' chotlud conacca,
lodsa hirricht huiss allaid. Bássu hissuidiu iarum, bássu hoc, maith mo
menma lim.

' Na fir sea thecait anair
cona rennaib rúamnait gail,
nimthá lúd hi cois *ná* il-láim
do thecht fora n-imgabáil.

' Starin, is tairbech in fer,
atágur Scemel scíathgel,
nímmain Andind cia dágind,
mád bé Béoin, nísnagsind.

' Cía rom[f]ácbad Beothach beó,
Cach*er* is garb a garbgleó,
Britán doní da gaib gus,
atá fræch ferci ar Fergus.

' Atát chuc*u*m, a comdi cain,
cland Nemid maic Agnom*ain*,
trén atát for ti m' fola
do chosnam mo chétgona.

' Rocóraigit d*u*a trém' chend
dá beind for trí fichtib rend,
co filim garblíath ir-richt
ar cǽmchlód áisi a bamnirt. A.

7. ' Bá-sa thóisech-sa do almaib Hérenn íar sudiu ó robá
ir-richt sétha, 7 bói alma mór do ossaib alta imm*u*m cach
conair nothégind.[1] Dor*u*malt-sa iarom m'amsir[2] amlaid sin[3]
fri hamsir Nemid 7 fri amsir a claindi.[4] Intan íarom tánic
Nemed doch*u*m na Hérenn a m*u*rchoblach, cetheora bárca
trichat[5] a lín 7 tricha in cech báirc, conosrala[6] in muir for
sechrán fri ré bliad*na*[7] colleith for muir Chaisp, 7 robateá[8]

[1] Ba thoisech do almaib (alltaib *H*) Er*enn* 7 do-imchellaind Er*inn* 7 alam mor di
(do *R*) ossaib immum *RH*. [2] m'aimsir íarsin *R*. [3] *om. RH*. [4] 7 fria claind dara
heisi *R*. [5] Ar intan dolluid Nemed dochum n*Erenn* cetheora barca ar trich*ait RH*.
[6] conisrala *R*. [7] bli*adain R* sechran bliad*na H*. [8] robaitea *R* robaittea *H*.

7. 'Ocus bassa hurræ alma 7 doimchellind Heirind 7 ala*m* mór di
hossaib immom. Dorrumalt tra in n-aimsir sin fri hamsir Nemed [sic]
7 fria hamsir a gabala dia chlaind. Ar intan doluith Nemid [sic]
dochum Heirenn cetheora bárca ar trichait allín 7 tricha fer in cach
[fo. 102^b 2] bairc, immusrala muir bliadain 7 leth robaitea 7 atbathatar

íarsin 7 atbáthatar di¹ gortai 7 d'ítaid,² acht cetheora lánamna
nammá³ im⁴ Nemed. Roforbair⁵ a síl-som íarsin 7 rochlan-
naigistár⁶ corrabatar cethri míli ar trichait lánamna⁷ and.
Atbathatar side da*no* uli.⁸

8. 'Dolluid íarom críne 7 sentatu form-sa⁹ 7 bá-sa for
teched¹⁰ re n-dóinib 7 conaib altaib.¹¹ Bá-sa fechtas and i
ndorus m'úama,¹² cuman lim beus¹³ 7 rofetar techt asin¹⁴ richt
i n-araili.¹⁵ Lud-sa íarom i ndeilb thuirc allaid.¹⁶ Iss¹⁷ and
asbert-sa :

> 'Glasreng¹⁸ mé indiu etir cúanaib,
> am tríath trén co robúadaib,
> domrat i ndubi ndecair
> rí na n-uli i n-ilrechtaib.

> 'Matan robá-sa ac dún Bré
> oc comrac fri sensruthe,
> ba cǽm mo churi dar lind,
> lenad ócbad áibind sind.

> 'Mo churi robtar dathi
> etir fíannaib i n-aithi,¹⁹
> fogertis mo gai 'masech
> for ócaib Fáil for cech leth.

> 'Intan nobimmís 'nar [n]dáil
> oc cocert breth Partholáin,
> ba bind fri cách 'na canaind,
> ba síat briathra fírthadaill.

¹ do *R.* ² 7 d'ítaid *om. RH.* ³ *om. RH.* ⁴ vm *R.* ⁵ Fororbart *R* roforbrisit *H.*
⁶ a sil 'sin Er*inn* *R* a sil-sen a nErinn *H.* ⁷ cetheora lanamma trich*at* ar cetheoraib
milib lanamnan *R.* ⁸ *om. RH.* ⁹ Doluid crine formsa 7 sentath (sentu *H*) *RH.*
¹⁰ teicheth *R.* ¹¹ alta *U.* ¹² mo uama *R.* ¹³ *om. RH.* ¹⁴ as cech richt *R.*
¹⁵ beos *add. H.* ¹⁶ alltaid *R.* em *add. H.* ¹⁷ *From here to end of verses
om. RH.* ¹⁸ .i. torc *U.* ¹⁹ inait*h*bi *with punctum delens over* b *U.*

___

[di] gorta acht cetheora lanamna im Nemeth. Fororbairt a síl sin for
Herind corrobatar cetheora míli ar trichait lana̱mna and im Nemed.
Dorroibtatar da*no* huile iatside.

8. 'Doluid crine formsa asennath 7 bássu for techud ria ndóinib 7
chonaib altaib. Bássu aidchi and i ndorus huaime, cuimen lim 7
rofetar dul asin richt inn-araill. Lotsu i ndeilb tuirc allaid.

' Ba bind mo chocert áni
etir andrib co n-álli,
ba segda mo charpat cǽm,
ba bind mo dord dar dubrǽn.

' Ba lúath mo chéim cen fordul
hi cathaib oc imforcum,
ba cæm mo drech, robói lá,
indiu cíarsam glasreng-sa.   Gl.

9. 'Bá-sa ém,' for sé,[1] 'hi sudiu isiu delb sin[2] 7[3] mé óoc 7 ba[4] maith lim mo menma 7 bam-sa[5] rurech do thrétaib torc Hérenn 7[6] do-imchellainn mo dúrais béus intan ticind hisin crích sea Ulad i n[7] -amsir mo chríne 7 mo thróge. Ar is i n-óenmagin doclæmcloind-sea[8] na delba sin[9] uli. Is airi sin nothathigind-sea in n-inad sin béus do idnaidi ind athnugthi.[10]

10. 'Gabais Semion mac Staríath[11] in n-insi sea íarsin.[12] Is díb-side[13] Fir Domnand 7 Fir Bolc 7 Galiúin.[14] Ocus rothrebsat side in n-insi sea fri ré. . . .[15] Dolluid críne 7 sentatu form-sa íarsin[16] 7 ba torsech lim mo menma 7 forfémmedus[17] cach rét dogníind remi do dénam.[18] Acht bá-sa i n-úamannaib dorchaib 7 i n-allaib díamraib m'óenur.[19]

11. 'Lud-sa íarsin dom'[20] dúrais dilis[21] dogrés. Cuman lim cach richt irrabá ríam.[22] Ro-áinius[23] mo thredan amal dogníind

<hr>

1 *om. R.* 2 *om. R.* 3 is *R.* 4 *om. R.* for sé-ba *om. H.* 5 bam *R.* 6 doimgabainn 7 *add. H.* 7 *om. U.* 8 noclaechlainnsea *RH.* 9 sa *R. om. H.* 10 *RH. omit this sentence.* 11 stainn *H.* 12 *om. H.* 13 dib *RH.* 14 7 Galiúin *om. RH.* 15 *something omitted here in U.* rotrebsat : nEir*inn add. H.* side—ré *om. R.* 16 Dollud crine formsa 7 sentath *R.* 17 uaremedh*us R.* baremidus *H.* 18 dogníind —dénam *om. RH.* 19 i n-uamaib 7 allaib am oenar *RH.* 20 do*n R.* 21 *om. RH.* 22 *om. RH.* 23 roaines *R.*

<hr>

9. 'Eím lim ón da*no* 7 maith lim mo menma 7 bássu hurræ do trétaib torc nEírenn 7 dohimchellind Heirind 7 robúi dúras lim beós d'athigid issin crich sea Hulad inn-amsir mo críne 7 mo thróge. Ar is i n-oenmagin nomchloechlaind na delba so huili dogres.

10. 'Gabais Semion mac Stairai in n-insi so 7 is dib Fir Domnand 7 Fir Bolg. Trebsat side Héirind. Doluid crine formsa 7 ba toirrsech mu menma 7 ba réimdius comaitecht na torc 7 na trét, acht bássu i nhuamaib 7 i n-allaib imm' œnur.

11. 'Lothsa dom' durus dogrés. Cuman lim [cech richt] irraba.

dogrés.[1] Nímbái cumang cena.[2] Lud-sa íarsin i ndeilb segi móri .i. murrech adbul.[3] Maith lim ón da*no* mo menma.[4] Ba fortail mé for cach rét.[5] Ba sirthech[6] imtholtanach[7] da*no*.[8] Noluinn[9] dar Erind, rofindainn[10] cach rét.[11] Is[12] and atbert-sa :

' Seig indiu, glasreng indé,
ingnad alaig utmaille,
ansu lim ar ca*ch* ló de
Día in cara romcruthaige.

' Is sochaidi cland Nemid
ca*n* réir r . . ech ríg demin,
úathad indiu síl Sera,
ní fetar cid fotera.

' Etir trétaib torc robá,
cíatú indiu etir énelta,
rofetar-sa 'na mbía de,
bíat-sa béus ir-richt aile.

' Ingnad ro-ordaig Día dil
mesi ocus clanna Nemid :
síat-som ac réir demain Dé,
mesi is Día mo chomar-se. Seig.

12. ' Gabais Beóthach mac Iarboneoil[13] fátha[14] in n-insi sea forsna cenéla[15] robátar inti.[16] Is díb-side[17] Túatha Dée 7 Ande[18] doná fes bunadas[19] lasin n-æs n-éolais, acht ba doich[20] leo ba

[1] amal-dogrés *om. RH.* [2] *om. RH.* [3] segha .i. muiriach (*nó* muirrech) mor *RH.* [4] mo menma *om. RH.* [5] ba fortaill (fortail *H.*) lim (da*no R.*) mo menma *RH.* [6] siratech *U.* saithech *H.* sirtech *R.* [7] vmtoltach *R.* [8] *om. RH.* [9] noluid-hinn *H.* [10] 7 nofindaind *R.* [11] re*cht* nobidh uile *H.* [12] *From here to end of verses, om. RH.* [13] Iardonel *UR.* [14] *om. H.* ma*ic* Nem*id add, R.* [15] cinela *RH.* [16] innte *R.* [17] dib *RH.* gailioin 7 *add. H.* [18] andea *RH.* [19] bunad *RH.* [20] doigh *R.*

Ro-æin*us* mo thredan cen biad. Ni[m] búi cumac. Lothso i ndeilb muirfeich mair. Maith on lim da*no*. Ba fo*r*otrèn [sic] mo menma, basa saithech imtholtanach. Noluind dar Héirind, nohinnaind cach ret.

12. ' Gabais Beothecht mac Iordanen in n-indsi so forsna cenélu batar and 7 is diib in Galiuin 7 Tuatha Dea 7 Ande, cenela cosnafes bunadus

din[1] longais dodechaid de[2] nim dóib, ara n-engnaigi 7 ar febas a n-eólais.[3]

13. 'Bá-sa tra amsera móra i ndeilb int sega sin[4] co tom-altus[5] na cenéla sin[6] uli rogabsat[7] tír nErend. Gabsat da*no* maic Míled in n-insi seo for Túaith[8] Dé Danand[9] ar écin. Dobá-sa[10] da*no* and-side i ndeilb inna séga sin ir-rabas[11] co mba hi cús craind for sruth. Toirsech lim mu menma acht cia luienn. Ataighin eona uile dom arccuin.[12]

14. 'Ro-áinius nómaid and-side[13] 7 rothuit cotlud form 7 lód-sa ir-richt iaich[14] abæ[15] and-aide.[16] Domchurithar Día isin n-abáinn íarsin[17] co mba inti.[18] Maith lim ón da*no* 7 ba-sa setrech saithech 7 ba maith mo ṡnám 7 no-elaind as cech[19] gábud 7 as cech[19] airceis[20] .i. al-lámaib línaige 7 a crobaib segæ[21] 7 ó gaib íascaig,[22] co filet a[23] crechta[24] . . .[25] a cech ái díb[26] indium beos.[27]

15. 'Fecht n-æn[28] ann tra[28] tan rob am[29] la Día mo chabair[30] 7 robátar bíasta icom' ingr*e*m 7 nofindad cach línaige[31] in cech

---

1 don *RH*.   2 dond R.   3 ara-eólais *om. RH*.   4 *om. R*.   5 corormoltsa *R*.
6 cinela sa *R*.   7 rogabustar *H*.   8 túathaib *RH*.   9 donann *R*.   10 Dollodsa *R*.
lotsa *H*.   11 iraba *RH*.   12 Toirsech-arccuin *om. UR*.   13 Roaoines nomaide ann
i cus craind *R*.   14 iaic *U*.   15 .i. bratan *add. R*.   16 *om. RH*.   17 *om. RH*.
18 and *RH*.   19 gach *U*.   20 as cach airceis *om. R*.   21 seabhac *H*.   22 iascaire *RH*.
23 a *om. R*.   24 *Here U ends*.   25 *A word illegible in R. om. H*.   26 a-díb *om. H*.
27 *om. H*.   28 *om. H*.   29 intan robo mithe*ch H*.   30 sa *add. H*.   31 romfinnad in
cach lin:idhe *H*.

---

lasin n-óes n-eolach, acht ba doich [fo. 103 a 1] leo bith don longis dodeochaid do nim.

13. 'Básusa tra amsera mára i ndeilb int ṡégæ cotormalt na cenela so huili rogabsat tir nEirend. Gabsat maic Mileth for Tuatha Dea in n-indsi se ar héicin. Lothso fecht i ndeilb int ṡega irraba co mba hi cuas chraind for sruth. Tuirsech mo menma. Addro luamain 7 addagin eónu aili.

14. 'Rohainius nomaidi and 7 lotso i ndeilb ind íaich abæ. Dom-chuirethar Dia isin n-abaind. Amræ lim ón da*no* 7 basa setrech da*no* saithech 7 bása hurræ snáma. Adluinid [sic] as cach gabud allamaib linaige 7 a crobaib séga 7 a gaaib línaigi, co filet a crechta indum.

15. 'Fecht and antan roba mithig ra Dia mu chobair-sea 7 rombatar biasta oc mo ingreim 7 romfinnad cach línaighi in cach lind, dombert

lind, domairthend tra línaigi Cairill ríg an tíre sin fecht ann 7
dombeir lais do mnái Cairill forraibi mían éisc.[1] Cuman lim
ón da*no* 7 domrat in fer inn-indeoin [2] 7 romimain [3] 7 rommían-
aig [4] in rígan [5] 7 romithenn a hóenur co mbá-sa ina broinn.
Cuman lim [6] da*no* in airet robá ina broinn 7 aní noráided cách
frie [7] isin tig 7 a ndorónad ind-Erinn ind airet sin.   Cuman
lim da*no* am*al* domáinic labrad [8] am*al* cech nduine 7 rofinnaind
cech rét doníthea i nÉrinn [9] 7 robsa [10] fáith 7 dobreth [11] ainm
dam .i. Túan mac Cairill.   Cotáinic íarom Pátraic co cretem [12]
dochum Érenn.[13]   'Aes mór dam-sa isuidiu 7 rombaitsed 7
rocreiteus [14] imm' óenur [15] do [16] ríg na n-uili cona dúilib.'[17]

16. Doníat íarom celebrad 7 tíagait ina proinntech [18] Finnian
cona muinntir 7 Túan mac Cairill íar n-aisneis na scél sa dó [19]
coléir dóib 7 anait [20] sechtmain ann imalle [21] ic imaccallaim.
Cach sench*as* 7 cach genel*ach* fil ind-Érinn is ó Túan mac
Cairiall a bunad*as* int senchais sin.[22]   Ronaccaillestar Pátraic

---

[1] linn, domber linaide fecht ann do mnái Cairill ri in tire seo *H*.   [2] for in
indioin *H*.   [3] *om. H*.   [4] rommianaigestar *H*.   [5] ben *H*.   [6] on *add. H*.   [7] fria
céle *H*.   [8] labraid *R*.   [9] doniathai *R*.   [10] robsam *H*.   [11] dobretha *R*.   [12] lais
add. H.   [13] *om. H*.   [14] romcreitius *R*.   [15] a oenur *R*.   [16] *om. H*.   [17] na ndule
cona duil *H*.   [18] proinntig *R*.   [19] *om. H*.   [20] sium *add. H*.   [21] *om. H*.   [22] int-sin
om. H.

---

línaigi and do mnái Chairill rí in tiri sea.   Cumen lim da*no* codomber
in fer 7 fonuid me 7 nomhithend in ben a hóenur co mba inna broind.
Cumen lim da*no* ind airet romba inna broind 7 rl. 7 an-noráided cach
ria chéile isin taig 7 a n-doronad ind-Eíre ind eret sin.   Cumen lim
da*no* om-thanic labrad am*al* cach nuidin 7 rofinnaind cach rét dogníthe
i nHére 7 ropsam fáith 7 dobreth ainm dam .i. Túan mac Cairill.
Cotanic iarum Patraic co creitem [fo. 103 a, 2].   Aésmar da*no* hissuidiu
7 rombaisted 7 rochreides imm' oenur ríg na nhuili cona dúilib.'

16. Dogniat iarum celebrad 7 tiagait hi praintech Finnía cona muntir
7 Tuan.   Arutngither colléir doib.   Anaitt sechtmain hissuidiu occ
immacallaim.   Nach senchas 7 nach genelach fír i nHére, is o Thuan
mac Cairill a bunadus.   Attraglastar Patraic riasindi-seo attuaid dó
7 atraglastar Colum Cille 7 atchuaid faitsine ndó in tíre 7 torgaid
Finnía commaid fris nobeith a phort 7 ni hétas fair-som.   'Bith
huirdnidu do loc so,' ol Tuán.   Tuán fuit in forma uiri centum annis

rempu¹ 7 atchúaid dó² 7 ronaccaill³ Colum Cille 7 atchúaid Finnian dó i fíadnaisi lochta⁴ in tíre 7 targid⁵ Finnian dó comad ris nobeith a port 7 nir étad fair-sium.⁶ ' Bid oirdnidiu do tech-sa co bráth ' ol Túan ar. . . .⁷

¹ rompo Patric *H.*   ² iartain add. *H.*   ³ ronacaillestar *H.*   ⁴ lucht *H.*   ⁵ tar-gaigh *H.* tartid *R.*   ⁶ innisin *add. H.*   ⁷ *Here R. ends abruptly.* do loc-sa ar Túan ni maith Finit. *H.*

---

i nIIéri iar Fintan. Fiche blia*dan* in forma porci, *octoginta* anni in forma cerui, centum anni in forma Aquilae, *tricha* blia*dan* fo lind in forma pi[**s**]cis. Iterum in forma hominis co sentaith co haimsir Finnio m*aic* húi Fiatach. Finit.

Tuan mac Cairill's Story to Finnen of Moville here below.

1. After Finnen of Moville had come with the Gospel to Ireland, into the territory of the men of Ulster, he went to a wealthy warrior there, who would not let them come to him into the stronghold, but left them fasting¹ there over Sunday. The warrior's faith was not good. Said Finnen to his followers : ' There will come to you a good man, who will comfort you, and who will tell you the history of Ireland from the time that it was first colonised until to-day.'

2. Then on the morrow early in the morning there came to them a venerable cleric, who bade them welcome. ' Come with me to my hermitage,' said he, 'that is meeter for you.' They went with him, and they perform the duties of the Lord's day, both with psalms and preaching and offering. Thereupon Finnen asked him to tell his name. Said he to them : ' Of the

¹ Here *L* has the rare word *docinet*, 'they fast,' of which the infinitive occurs in LU. 84a, 31 : *hi toichned .i. hi troscud*, and in Laws I. 122, 11 : *toichned rí* ' withholding his food-tribute from a king.'

men of Ulster am I. Tuan, son of Cairell, son of Muredach Red-neck, am I. I have taken this hermitage, in which thou art, upon the hereditary land of my father. Tuan, son of Starn,[1] son of Sera, son of Partholon's brother, that was my name of yore at first.'

3. Then Finnen asked him about the events of Ireland, to wit, what had happened in it from the time of Partholon, son of Sera. And Finnen said they would not eat with him until he had told them the stories of Ireland. Said Tuan to Finnen: 'It is hard for us not to meditate upon the Word of God which thou hast just told to us.' But Finnen said: 'Permission is granted thee to tell thy own adventures and the story of Ireland to us now.'

4. 'Five times, verily,' said he, 'Ireland was taken after the Flood, and it was not taken after the Flood until 312[2] years had gone. Then Partholon, son of Sera, took it. He had gone upon a voyage with twenty-four couples. The cunning of each of them against the other was not great. They settled in Ireland until there were 5000[3] of their race. Between two Sundays a mortality came upon them, so that all died, save one man only. For a slaughter is not usual without some one to come out of it to tell the tale. That man am I,' said he.

5. 'Then I was from hill to hill, and from cliff to cliff, guard-

---

[1] The names of the various leaders of the five invasions of Ireland have all the appearance of being made-up, learned inventions of a late age. They are either derived from the Bible (like *Semion*), or are adaptations of Latin names and words (such as *Partholón* from *Bartholomaeus*, *Míl* from *miles*), or they are simply appellative nouns made into proper names (like *Bith* 'world,' *Fer* 'man,' *Britán* 'the Little Briton,' *Beothach* 'a living creature,' etc.). Lastly, a few seem to be of Norse origin. *Starn* looks like Norse *stjarna* 'star' (can *Sera* be founded on Welsh *ser* 'sidus'?), *Stariath* also has a Norse look, and *Nél* 'cloud' might be an Irish rendering of a Norse *Nifl*. *Iarbonél* = *Iarmo-Nél* 'After-Nél.'

[2] This is the reading of *U*. The three other MSS. have 1002 years.

[3] *L* has 1000.

ing myself from wolves, for twenty-two[1] years, during which Ireland was empty. At last old age[2] came upon me, and I was on cliffs and in wastes, and was unable[3] to move about, and I had special caves for myself. Then Nemed, son of Agnoman, my father's brother, invaded Ireland, and I saw them from the cliffs and kept avoiding them, and I hairy, clawed, withered, grey, naked, wretched, miserable. Then, as I was asleep one night, I saw myself passing into the shape of a stag. In that shape I was, and I young and glad of heart. It was then I spoke these words :[4]

> 'Strengthless to-day is Senba's son,
> From vigour[5] he has been parted,
> Not under fair fame with new strength,
> Senba's son is an old . . .[6]

> 'These men that come from the east
> With their spears that achieve valour,
> I have no strength in foot or hand
> To go to avoid them.

---

[1] *L* has 32.

[2] It is clear that here and in § 8 *asendath* 'at last' is the original reading, which later scribes have altered into *sentath*, etc., 'old age.' *L* alone preserves the old word.

[3] Here *L* has the old verb *addró*, 'I was unable,' replaced by *fortmed* in the other MSS. Cf. *atroiset Liguir condesetar impi*, 'they were unable (to cross) the (river) Loire so that they sat down on its banks,' Rawl. B. 502, fo. 47a, I BB. 135a, 18, *atroi* Hib. Min. 70, 15, *atroe Coirpri Nuad*, 'C was unable to get it from him.' Bodleian Cormac s.v. Mugéme. *atroas, atrós* 'it was impossible,' *Rev. Celt.* XIII. 373, 396. LU. 98a, 21.

[4] These verses are out of place here.

[5] *tend-rath*, literally 'stout grace.'

[6] The meaning of the noun *rúa* has not yet been made out. The compound *senrúa* also occurs in *Rev. Celt.* XIII. 397, 6, and in *Silv. Gad.* I. 95, 11, where it is wrongly rendered 'old and blighted,' the translator taking *rúa* to stand 'metri gratia' for *rúadh* (II. p. 557).

'Starin, fierce is the man,
I dread Scemel of the white shield,
Andind will not save me, though good and fair,[1]
If it were Beoin, . . .

'Though Beothach would leave me alive,
Cacher's rough fight is rough,
Britan achieves valour with his spears,
There is a fit of fury on Fergus.[2]

'They are coming towards me, O gentle Lord,
The offspring of Nemed, Agnoman's son,
Stoutly they are lying in wait for my blood,
To compass my first wounding.

'Then there grew upon my head[3]
Two antlers with three score points,
So that I am rough and grey in shape
After my age has changed from feebleness.

7. 'After this, from the time that I was in the shape of a stag, I was the leader of the herds of Ireland, and wherever I went there was a large herd of stags about me. In that way I spent my life during the time of Nemed and his offspring. When Nemed came with his fleet to Ireland, their number was thirty-four barques, thirty in each barque, and the sea cast them astray for the time of a year and a half on the Caspian Sea, and they were drowned and died of hunger and thirst, except four couples only together with Nemed. Thereafter his race increased and had issue until there were 4030 couples. However, these all died.

8. 'Then at last old age came upon me, and I fled from men and wolves. Once as I was in front of my cave—I still remember it—I knew that I was passing from one shape into

---

[1] *dágind* I take to stand for *dag-find*.
[2] This characterisation of the various leaders of the invasion is a mere play upon their names : Andind, find 'fair'; Beothach, beo 'alive'; Cacher, acher 'fierce'; Fergus, ferg 'anger.'
[3] Literally, 'there were arranged through my head.'

another.   Then I passed into the shape of a wild boar.   Tis
then I said :

> ' A boar am I to-day among herds,
> A mighty lord I am with great triumphs,
> He has put me in wonderful grief,
> The King of all, in many shapes.

> ' In the morning when I was at Dún Bré [1]
> Fighting against old seniors,
> Fair was my troop across the pool,
> A beautiful host was following us.

> ' My troop, they were swift
> Among hosts in revenge,
> They would throw [2] my spears alternately
> On the warriors of Fál [3] on every side.

> ' When we were in our gathering
> Deciding the judgments of Partholon,
> Sweet to all was what I said,
> Those were the words of true approach.

> ' Sweet was my brilliant judgment
> Among the women with beauty,
> Stately was my fair chariot,
> Sweet was my song across a dark road.

> ' Swift was my step without straying
> In battles at the onset,
> Fair was my face, there was a day,
> Though to-day I am a boar.

9. ' In that shape, he said, I was then truly, and I young and
glad of mind.   And I was king of the boar-herds of Ireland,

---

[1] Dún Brea was, according to LL. 169 b, 35, *i nhtíib Briuin Cua-
lann*, ' a sept giving name to a territory comprising the greater part of
the barony of Rathdown, in the present county of Dublin and some of
the north of the county of Wicklow.' O'Don. *Four Masters*, I. p. 340,
note *n*.

[2] I take *fogertis* to stand for *fochertis*.

[3] A poetical name for Ireland.

and I still went the round of my abode when I used to come into this land of Ulster at the time of my old age and wretchedness; for in the same place I changed into all these shapes. Therefore I always visited that place to await the renewal.

10. 'Thereupon Semion, the son of Stariath, seized this island. From them are the Fir Domnann, and the Fir Bolg, and the Galiuin; and these inhabited this island for the time that they dwelt in Ireland. Then old age came upon me, and my mind was sad, and I was unable to do all that I used to do before, but was alone in dark caves and in hidden cliffs.

11. 'Then I went to my own dwelling always. I remembered every shape in which I had been before. I fasted my three days as I had always done. I had no strength left. Thereupon I went into the shape of a large hawk. Then my mind was again happy. I was able to do anything. I was eager and lusty. I would fly across Ireland; I would find out everything. 'Tis then I said:

> 'A hawk to-day, a boar yesterday,
> Wonderful . . . inconstancy!
> Dearer to me every day
> God, the friend who has shapen me.

> 'Many are the offspring of Nemed
> Without obedience . . . to the certain King,
> Few to-day are the race of Sera;
> I know not what caused it.

> 'Among herds of boars I was,
> Though to-day I am among bird-flocks;
> I know what will come of it:
> I shall still be in another shape.

> 'Wonderfully has dear God disposed
> Me and the children of Nemed;
> They at the will of the demon of God,
> While, for me, God is my help.

12. 'Beothach, the son of Iarbonel the prophet, seized this island from the races that dwelt in it. From them are the

Tuatha Dé and Andé, whose origin the learned do not know, but that it seems likely to them that they came from heaven, on account of their intelligence and for the excellence of their knowledge.

13. 'Then I was for a long time in the shape of that hawk, so that I outlived all those races who had invaded Ireland. However, the sons of Mil took this island by force from the Tuatha Dé Danann. Then I was in the shape of that hawk in which I had been, and was in the hollow of a tree on a river.

14. 'There I fasted for three days and three nights, when sleep fell upon me, and I passed into the shape of a river-salmon there and then. Then God put me into the river so that I was in it. Once more I felt happy and was vigorous and well-fed, and my swimming was good, and I used to escape from every danger and from every snare—to wit, from the hands of fishermen, and from the claws of hawks, and from fishing spears—so that the scars which each one of them left are still on me.

15. 'Once, however, when God, my help, deemed it time, and when the beasts were pursuing me, and every fisherman in every pool knew me, the fisherman of Cairell, the king of that land, caught me and took me with him to Cairell's wife, who had a desire for fish. Indeed I remember it; the man put me on a gridiron and roasted me. And the queen desired me and ate me by herself, so that I was in her womb. Again, I remember the time that I was in her womb, and what each one said to her in the house, and what was done in Ireland during that time. I also remember when speech came to me, as it comes to any man, and I knew all that was being done in Ireland, and I was a seer; and a name was given to me—to wit, Tuan, son of Cairell. Thereupon Patrick came with the faith to Ireland. Then I was of great age; and I was baptized, and alone believed in the King of all things with his elements.'

16. Thereupon they celebrate mass and go into their refectory, Finnen with his followers and Tuan, after he had told them these stories. And there they stay a week conversing

together. Every history and every pedigree that is in Ireland, 'tis from Tuan, son of Cairell, the origin of that history is. He had conversed with Patrick before them, and had told him; and he had conversed with Colum Cille, and had prophesied to him in the presence of the people of the land. And Finnen offered him that he should stay with him, but he could not obtain it from him. 'Thy house will be famous till doom,' said Tuan.[1]

[1] Here the story ends rather abruptly in *R*. *H*. adds, 'Not good. Finit.'

APPENDIX B.

The versified dinnshenchas of Mag Slecht[1]

LL. = Book of Leinster, p. 213*a*, 40 ; *B.* = Book of Ballymote, p. 393*a*, 15 ; *L.* = Book of Lecan, p. 500*a* ; *R.* = the Rennes manuscript, fo. 115*a*, 2.

    1. Sund nobíd
        ídal ard co n-immud fích
        diarbo chomainm in[2] Cromm Crúaich,
        tuc do[3] cach thúaith beith cen síth.[4]

    2. Ba trúag núin[5] !
        nonadraitis Gædil gúir,
        úad[6] nocochuingtis[7] can cháin
        a n-díl imm[8] dáil[9] domuin dúir.

[1] I am indebted to Mr. Whitley Stokes for kindly furnishing me with the various readings of *L*. and *R*. from photographs in his possession. As to the Rennes MS. see *Revue Celtique*, xi. pp. 90-91.
[2] *om. LL.* [3] in *R*. [4] tuc in cach thúaith lúth is síd *LL*. [5] Truag in rúin *BLR*. [6] uaid *BR*. [7] nocochungtis *LL*. nocuinngidis *B*. rochu-indcidis *L*. rocuinidgis *R*. [8] do *LL*. [9] a n-dail andil *L*.

3. Ba hé a n-día
   in Cromm crín[1] co n-immud[2] cía,
   in lucht rocraith[3] ós[4] cach cúan,
   in flaithius[5] búan nochosbía.[6]

4. Dó cen búaid[7]
   marbtais a claind toirsig[8] trúaig,[9]
   co n-immud[10] guil[11] ocus gáid,
   a fuil do dáil imm[12] Chromm Chrúaich.

5. Blicht is ith
   úaid nochungitis for rith,
   dar cend trín a sotha[13] sláin,[14]
   ba mór a gráin[15] is a grith.[16]

6. Is dó sain[17]
   noslechtaitis[18] Gædil glain,
   is dia adrad—ilar n-echt[19]—
   atá Mag Slecht ar in maig.

7. Tánic and
   Tigernmas tríath Temrach[20] tall[21]
   aidchi samna, lín a ślóig,[22]
   rosbói damna[23] bróin don band.[24]

8. Lúiset[25] olc,
   búailset bassa,[26] brúiset corp,
   ac cói ri[27] demon rosdæra[28]
   fertais[29] frossa[30] fæna folc.

---

[1] crich *L.* [2] imat *R.* [3] in luch amercid *L.* nocraith *B.* co n-immud armmlucht no . . . cruit *LL.* [4] as *L.* [5] a flaithis *L.* [6] nochosluad *LL.* nosbia *B.* [7] Do cheand mbuad *L.* [8] toisig *B.* toisich *R.* tosach *L.* toirsech *LL.* [9] *om. LL.* [10] imat *R.* [11] gail *B.* [12] in *B.* a *R.* [13] saotha *R.* [14] *om. LL.* [15] gair *BR.* [16] an grain 7 an grith *L.* [17] sin *B.* [18] noslectais *BR.* roslechtaidis *L.* [19] ilar echt *LL.* hilar ndrecht *R.* [20] Temra *B.* [21] thall *R.* all *L.* [22] śluaig *LL.* [23] domna *LL.* [24] banna *LL.* [25] laised *L.* luidhset *R.* [26] buad lecht bernai (!) *LL.* [27] re *BL.* ro *R.* [28] nosdæra *B.* [29] fersad *L.* [30] frasa *LR.*

9. Marba fir
   slúaig na[1] Banba cen bríg m-bil[2]
   imm Thigernmas taglach[3] túaid[4]
   d'adrad Chruimm Chrúaich ní muscin.

10. Uair itgén,[5]
    acht cethramthi[6] slúaig Gáidel[7] n-gér
    fer i m-bethaid—búan[8] in sás—
    ní dechaid cen bás 'na bél.

11. Imm Chromm Crúaich
    and noslechtaitis[9] na slúaig,
    cia dosfuc fo mebail[10] mairb,
    lenaid a n-ainm[11] don maig múaid.[12]

12. 'Na srethaib
    trí hídail chloch fo chethair,
    fri sæbad serb inna slóg[13]
    delb in Chruimm d'ór dodechaid.

13. 'O bói flaith[14]
    Herimoin ardfir[15] in raith,
    adrad robói for[16] clacha[17]
    co techt[18] Pátraic Macha maith.

14. Ord don Chrumm
    rogab ó bathis coa[19] bund,
    rodíchuir cen[20] gallacht n-gand
    in n-arracht fand robói sund.[21] Sund. no-b.

---

[1] *om. LL.* [2] co mbri mbil *L.* [3] *om. B.* [4] do glantuaith *L.* [5] Huair itger*n* (!) *B.* [6] ccathraimi *B.* cethroime *L.* cethrama *R.* [7] *om. LL.* [8] truag *L.* [9] raslechtait *LL.* roslechtadis *R.* roslectaidi (*sic*) *B.* [10] melaib *L.* [11] a ainm *R.* [12] thuaid *L.* [13] fa serb in slog *L.* [14] O bœ i flaith *L.* [15] ardfer *LL.* airdfear *L.* fir *B.* [16] forna *BL.* [17] adhrad forna clachaib *R.* [18] tiacht *BLR.* [19] co *L.* [20] con *LLBR.* can *L.* [21] intairr*echt* robai ann sunn *L.*

1. Here used to be
   A high idol with many fights,
   Which was named the Cromm Cruaich :
   It made every tribe to be without peace.[1]

2. 'Twas a sad evil !
   Brave Gaels used to worship it.
   From it they would not without tribute ask
   To be satisfied as to their portion of the hard world.

3. He was their god,
   The withered Cromm with many mists,
   The people whom he shook over every host,[2]
   The everlasting kingdom they shall not have.

4. To him without glory
   They would kill their piteous wretched offspring
   With much wailing and peril,
   To pour their blood around Cromm Cruaich.

5. Milk and corn
   They would ask from him speedily[3]
   In return for one third of their healthy[4] issue :
   Great was the horror and the scare of him.

6. To him
   Noble Gaels would prostrate themselves,
   From the worship of him, with many manslaughters,
   The plain is called Mag Slecht.

7. There came
   Tigernmas, the prince of Tara yonder,
   On Halloween with many hosts,
   A cause of grief to them was the deed.

---

[1] It put vigour and peace into every tribe *LL.*

[2] 'Over every host,' or, perhaps, 'harbour,' a common *cheville*. See LL. 191a, 4.

[3] Literally, 'a-running,' a common phrase. See LU. 115a, 4. 20. Broccan's hymn, v. 93.

[4] 'Healthy,' or perhaps 'whole,' *slán* being used in either sense.

8. They did evil,
   They beat their palms, they pounded their bodies,
   Wailing to the demon who enslaved them,
   They shed falling showers of tears.

9. Dead were the men
   Of Banba's host, without happy strength,
   Around Tigernmas, the destructive man in the north,
   From the worship of Cromm Cruaich—'twas no luck for them.

10. For I have learnt,
    Except one fourth of the keen Gaels [1]
    Not a man alive—lasting the snare !—
    Escaped without death in his mouth.

11. Around Cromm Cruaich
    There the hosts would prostrate themselves.
    Though he put them under deadly disgrace,
    Their name clings to the noble plain.

12. In their ranks (stood)
    Four times three stone idols,
    To bitterly beguile the hosts
    The figure of the Cromm was made of gold.

13. Since the rule
    Of Herimon, the noble man of grace,
    There was worshipping of stones
    Until the coming of good Patrick of Macha.

14. A sledge hammer to the Cromm
    He applied from crown to sole,
    He destroyed without lack of valour
    The feeble idol which was here.

---

[1] This line has one syllable too much. *sliaig* should be left out.

INDEX

[This Index has been compiled by Miss M. James, to whom I wish to express publicly my appreciation of the admirable way in which she has done the work.—ALFRED NUTT.]

Titles of works, or portions of works, quoted or referred to, are in italics.

INDEX

309

123, 126, 144, 153, 156, 160, 162, 175, 212, 233 ; ii. 54, 77, 92, 104, 105, 106, 107, 162, 165, 169, 238.
Archæological evidence, adverse to the Annals, i. 124 ; of the Brugh, 212 ; concerning the Dionysus cult, ii. 137, 191 ; in relation to the Tuatha de Danann, 234-238.
Archæological Review, i. 118, 128 ; ii. 97.
Arda Viraf, his Vision, i. 323.
Argos, i. 258 ; ii. 268.
Aristophanes' idea of Elysium (*Frogs*), i. 276.
Armagh, County, i. 138 ; See of, 188.
Arminius, i. 275.
Arnold, Matthew, on the Druids (*trs.* Lucan), ii. 111.
Art, of North Ireland, i. 120.
Art Oil, brother, of Connla, i. 146; called *Aenfher*, 147, 228.
Artemis, i. 261.
Artharva Veda, i. 294; its aristocratic heaven, 321.
Arthur, the name, Zimmer on, i. 139, ii. 7.
—— King, i. 140, his birth, ii. 22, 23-25, 88, wife's unfaithfulness, 22, 23, 25 ; his passing, 23, 25 ; his expedition to Annwfn, 89.
—— son of Bicor, of Britain, i. 137, 138, 139, 140 ; slayer of Mongan, ii. 7.
Arthurian legend, i. 236-7 ; ii. 11, French form of, in Wales, 18 ; as parallel to Mongan, 23, 35, possible sources, 23, date, 24, 26, chronological and topographical associations, 25; earlier analogues, 28, developments as type of Christian hero, 29; parallel to Cuchulinn, etc., 44; value to English Literature, 234, 253.
Arthurian Legend (by Prof. Rhys), quoted, ii. 48, 49, 89.
Artur. *See* Arthur, *supra.*
—— Map Petr, i. 139.
Arts and Crafts (*see* Bards, Boats, and Story-tellers)—Agriculture,

ii. 15, 212, 213, 224 ; Brass-working, 42 ; Bronze-working, 63 ; Building, 147, 174 ; Dyeing, and smelting, 161, 162, 174; Embroidery, i. 174, ii. 174; Glass-working, 47, 50; Healing and foreknowing, 148; Leech-craft, 174, 175; Natural science and astronomy, 108-110, 118. Various arts, 175, 176, 177.
Arvon, ii. 20.
Aryans, aboriginal belief, ii. 228, Asiatic elements amongst, ii. 158, influence in Europe, 159, conquest of Iran, i. 316, eschatology of, ii. 1, 143, 152, 241, 275, development, 241, 272, worship, 248, 249, 255, 258, in relation to pre- and non- Aryans, 259, 260 ; 271, 272, 275, 276 ; Evidence on agricultural communities, ii. 243, chiefly Aryan, 244, agricultural beliefs, etc., 253, 277; appearance, 254; survival of pre-Aryan belief, 255, assimilation of, 256, 257; Finn, the Gaelic representative of Aryan heroic type, ii. 88; invasion of India, i. 294, 315, 316, ii. 254; Italian Aryan lack of prehistoric myth, i. 283, ii. 275; migrations, chronology of, ii. 251, 277; in relation to religious conceptions, 277-280; mythic belief a common inheritance, i. 134, 214, compared with Irish, 196, hell of, 256, earliest and latest utterances, 294, 295-330; and the Avestic creed, 315 ; other world beliefs, 326, 329, Irish form the most archaic, 331, Greek parallels, ii. 1 ; evolution of religion, i. 330; Summary of views on Aryan culture, ii. 277, 278 ; Thracian and Celtic Aryans, i. 152-157.
Aryan Expulsion and Return formula amongst the Celts, i. 120; ii. 88.
Asceticism in Happy Otherworld ideal, i. 291, 311, 324, in India,

INDEX 337

Mag Slecht, the idols at, ii. 149, 150, 160, 161, 213, ritual of, 231, 250, 251.
Magheracloon, *or* Cluen Airthir, i. 138.
Magmor, ii. 185.
Mahabharata, the, its date, i. 323, 325.
Maheloas, King, i. 236.
Maidens' Land in the West (*see* Isle of Fair Women *and* Land of Women), i. 200.
Maile, the bard, i. 197.
Mainchenn, a Druid, ii. 62.
Mairend the Bald, ii. 82, 83.
Maistu, sid of, ii. 63.
Malthusianism in the Vendidad, i. 311.
Man, Isle of, as Oversea Otherworld, i. 213.
Manannan Mac Lir, Rider of Sea-horses, Lord of Faery. *See* Fann, Ler, Manawyddan, Mongan, etc.
—— and Bran's Voyage, ii. 242.
—— and Cormac, i. 190, 191, 217, 228, 282.
—— and Cuchulinn, i. 154-157, 159.
—— his father, ii. 16, 19.
—— his goblet, i. 191, ii. 90.
—— his prophecy of Mongan, i. 136, ii. 3, 4, 6.
—— his race, i. 160, 174, 175, 304, ii. 56, 72.
—— his realm, i. 192, 213, 217, 228, 229, 230, 237, 244, 274, 282, 288, 304.
—— in Heaven, ii. 9.
—— in relation to Women, i. 260.
—— non-Christian character of tale, i. 288.
—— parallels to, Greek, i. 292, 293, Welsh, ii. 16.
—— reborn as Mongan, i. 139, 143, 149, ii. 6, 26, 36, 89, 93.
—— ruler of sea-horses, i. 169, 199, 233 ; ii. 17, 178.
—— and St. Patrick, ii. 213.
Manawyddan, i. 129, the Welsh Manannan, i. 292, ii. 13, 14, 15, 16, 17, 18, 89.

Manes, the, ii. 110.
Mannhardt on the Dionysus cult, ii. 144, on agricultural ritual, 186, 216.
Marie de France, *lais* of, ii. 51, 56, 57.
Marriage by rape, ii. 72, 73.
—— sacred. *See* Lugnasad.
Mason, ii. 214, 217.
Massilia, ii. 118, 119, 274.
'Master of Many Arts' (*see* Lug), ii. 187.
Material character of Otherworld conceptions. *See* Cosmological Otherworlds.
Materialien zur Geschichte der Indischen Visions litteratur, i. 323.
Math, tale of, i. 129, ii. 18.
Mathgen, the sorcerer, ii. 177.
Matriarchy, ii. 75, 257, 278, 279, 280.
Matronymic used alone, ii. 74.
Maximus the Confessor, ii. 104.
Meath, ii. 49, 62, 63, 184, well-dressing in, 214, folk-lore of, 217.
Medb, queen of Connaught, i. 209, ii. 63, 64, 65, 66, 68, character, of, 70.
Mediterranean, western shores, civilisation of, ii. 127.
Mélusine, ii. 272.
Melvas, the regulus, i. 236.
Memnon, i. 261.
Menelaus, i. 258, 259, 261, 265, 267, 270, 282, ii. 8, 270.
Meriah sacrifice, the, ii. 149.
Merlin, ii. 66.
Messianic belief, i. 249, 250, 254.
Metamorphosis. *See* Shape-shifting.
Metempsychosis, i. 273, ii. 113, 114, 115, 117, Celtic modifications of doctrine, 118, 119, 129 ; Pythagoric and Platonic doctrine of, 126, 127, 264, Dionysiac cultus in relation to, 140 ; 142, Buddhist conception, 158 ; 248, Egyptian origin of idea, 263, development of, 264 ; 267, 270, 272, 273.

VOL. II. Y

Morrigan, the, or Fairy Queen, i. 211, 213, ii. 177, 227.

Morte d' Arthur, ii. 89.

Motherhood (*see* Matriarchy), importance of the phenomenon, ii. 81, 82.

Mountain and hill godlands. *See* Elysium, Hollow Hill (*under* Happy Otherworlds), Olympus, and Side.

Moylinny, sid of, ii. 7.

Moytura, battle of, i. 128, ii. 170, 171, 172, 173, 176, 178, 182, 196.

Mugain of Munster, ii. 82, 83.

Muirchertach, i. 122.

Muller, Dr. E., i. 198, 199.

Munster, i. 119, 146, 202, 207, ii. 34, 50, 58, 59, 60, 62, 67, 69, 71, 82.

Murias, city, ii. 171.

Muru of Donegal, ii. 8, 31, date, 32, 33, 35, 36.

Musæus, i. 275.

Music and song, a feature common to all other-world legends, i. 154, 155, 156, 159, 165, ale music, 169, sid music, 176, ii. 49, 181, 182, 233, the plaint of the sea, 183, 184, the music of the branch, 190, in Teigue's paradise, 203, 205, 206, of the land of Women, 221, 223, 228, 233, in later visions, 249, Greek Elysium music, i. 271, 275, 280, 282, 287, Scandinavian, 307, 324.

—— —— Amairgen's song, ii. 91, 92 ; Cuchulinn's death-song, i. 267 ; Druid magic songs, i. 145, 197, 198.

—— —— —— Mider's songs, i. 176, ii. 46.

Mysteries, their object, i. 275, 276.

NAMNITE priestesses, the, ii. 147, 226.

Nature, powers of. *See* Increase and Powers of Life.

Natural magic in Celtic literature, i. 206.

Navigatio S. Brendani, the, its results, i. 161, 162, 231, 284, 285, 328.

Neatness in fairy lore, ii. 221-224.

Nechtan Fairhand, son of Labraid, i. 160, his wife, 214, importance of legend, 215, ii. 186.

Ned Sheehy's Excuse, i. 210.

Nekyia, i. 255, 256, 271, 284, 291.

Nemed in Ireland, ii. 78.

Nennius the chronicler, quoted, i. 139, ii. 24, 25, 81, 93, 162.

—— *Vindicatus*, i. 116, 139, 180, ii. 7.

Nento-fo-hi-uscib, sid of, ii. 60, 63.

Neo-Platonism of the Avesta, i. 313, ii. 104, 106, 129.

Neo-Pythagoreanism, ii. 129.

Nept, i. 215.

Nera, in the Otherworld, i. 209, 210, 211, ii. 217 ; stories of same type, i. 213, 232.

Nescoit, reference to, ii. 180.

Ness, mother of Conchobor, ii. 72, 73.

Net, ii. 173.

Nettlau, Dr. Max, quoted, i. 127.

New Grange, mound of, i. 211.

New Testament in relation to Irish legend, ii. 99.

Niall of the Nine Hostages, i. 121, 189, 212, ii. 33, his race, 71, 190.

Niam, i. 150.

Night, daughters of (*see* Hesperides), i. 271.

—— and increase, ii. 224, 225.

—— revels of fairies, ii. 224-226.

Nile river, civilisation of, ii. 277, 279.

Nine, the number (*see* Niall), ii. 39, 41, 148, 161, 178, 217.

Ninian, i. 156.

Noah, i. 203, 313, 315, ii. 80.

Nonnus, ii. 130, 132.

Normans, in Ireland, i. 149, in Italy, ii. 26.

Norse Eschatology, i. 295, 296, 304, 305, 307, 308, 328.

—— influence on Irish tales, ii. 81, on the Mabinogion, ii. 21.

INDEX

342

Plutarch, i. 234; on the eating
human flesh, ii. 135.
Pluto (cf. Yama), i. 278, 322, and
synonyms for, ii. 268.
Poème, le, et la Legende des Nibel-
ungen, i. 128.
Polymestor, the Thracian, ii. 140.
Pomponius Mela, on the Druids, ii.
109-111, on Thracian cultus, 147,
on the Gallizenæ, 148, 149,
226.
Pontus, ii. 115.
Popular Tales of the West High-
lands, i. 121, 167.
Poseidon, i. 292.
Posidonius, on the Druids, ii. 112,
116, 118, on Celtic ritual, 147,
148, 149, 152.
Powell, F. York, i. 298, 301, 302.
Powers of Life and Increase. See
Increase.
Pre-Talmudic Haggada, The, i.
255.
Problems of Heroic Legend, ii. 22.
Prophecies, i. 146, 189, of Cathair
Mor, 216, of Fal, the Scone stone,
187, of Proteus, 258, 259, 261,
265, 270, ii. 270, of Virgil, i. 27;
relating to Mongan, i. 136, ii. 3,
4; to Yima's realm, i. 310.
Prophet. See Tuan.
Proteus, his prophecy, i. 258, 259,
261, 265, 270, ii. 270.
Pryderi, son of Pwyll, ii. 14, 15, 16,
17, 23, 35, 89.
Pseudo-Dionysius, the, ii. 104, his
writings, 106.
Pseudo-Gildas, the, i. 237.
Psyche, the, i. 262.
Psyche: Seelencult und Unsterblich-
keitsglaube der Griechen, i. 262,
ii. 125, 137, 138.
Psychological side of Irish legends,
etc., ii. 113, 120, 146, 194.
—— reasons for association of
Elysium and metamorphosis, ii.
139, 140, 143.
—— basis of Celtic doctrine, ii. 146,
of modern fairy creed, 224.
—— reason for fairy love of neat-

ness, 222, for night revels, 224,
236.
Psychology of sacrifice, ii. 149, 152,
153, 154, 232.
Punjab, Sanskrit-speaking settlers
in, i. 316, 317.
Pwyll, prince of Dyfed, i. 129, ii.
13-18, children of, 19.
Pythagoras and his doctrines (see
Metempsychosis, and Orphic-
Pythagorean doctrines), i. 273,
origin of, ii. 107, 120, 122, 124,
125, 127, 129, 136, in relation to
Celts and Druids, 107, 108, 109,
112, 114, 115, 117, 118, 119, 122,
123, 133, 135, 136, 143, 152; and
the re-birth idea, 114, 115, 126,
140, 146; on daimones, 115; in
the Dionysus cult, 156; philosophy
of, 246, 264, 270, 271.

QUEEN VICTORIA, her unique descent, i. 187.
Quinlan, of Knockainy, ii. 218.

RABELAIS, i. 207, ii. 180.
Rabelaisian element in the Tuatha
mythology, ii. 179, 180.
Ragallach, i. 122.
Ragnarok, i. 312.
Ram Yasht, The, i. 311.
Ramayana, The, i. 325.
Rathmore of Moylinny, ii. 7.
Re-birth, or Re-incarnation (see
Metempsychosis, Phœnix Legend,
etc.), in Avestic philosophy, i. 312;
in Buddhist philosophy, i. 330,
ii. 158; in Christian-Classic philosophy, i. 330; Cycle of, i. 256, 287;
in Greek philosophy (see Æneas),
Orphic, ii. 125, 126, 135, 157, 158;
Orphic-Pythagorean, i. 256, 330;
Pythagorean, ii. 114; ethical basis,
115, 118, 126; in Zagreus myth, ii.
130, 132; in relation to Celtic
views, ii. 118, 119, 133, 135, 158;
in Irish Celtic literature and
myth, i. 142, 281, 330, 331, method
of study, ii. 2, 3, evidence of the
Mongan cycle on, 36, 37, early

Yasna, liturgy of the Avesta, i. 314.
Yellow plague in Ireland, i. 122, 140.
Yima, the Iranian Adam, i. 309, his enclosure, 310, possible Jewish origin, 311, 313, 314, 315; described, 312, 321, 325, 327.
Yonec, lai of, ii. 56.
Young Manus, Argyllshire tale, Greek analogy, i. 272, 273.
Yule-tide, i. 298.

ZAGREUS myth, the, ii. 130, 131, and the Deluge, 135; 155.
Zalmoxis of the Hollow Hill, ii. 140.
Zarathrustra, quoted, i. 312.
Zeitschrift für Deutsches Alterthum, i. 128.
—— *für Deutsche Philologie*, i. 116.
—— *für die Kunde des Morgenlandes*, i. 325.
Zeller, E., quoted, ii. 114, 124.
Zend-Avesta, le (traduction par James Darmesteter), i. 309.
Zendavesta, the, and the First Eleven Chapters of Genesis, i. 315.

Zephyrus, i. 259, 280.
Zeus, i. 215, immortality of his sons, 258, 259, 271; 260, 261, 263, 264, 270, 274, called Amphiarus, 277, and the Zagreus myth, ii. 130, 131, 132, 133, 135, in Orphic philosophy, 134, and Phanes, 134, 135, called Eubouleus, 268.
Zimmer, H., quoted, i. 116, 118, 123, his critical methods, 126, and deductions, 127, 128, 129, 135, on the name Arthur, 139, ii. 7; on Connla, i. 144 · on Cuchulinn, 156, 158, 160; on the Imrana, 161, 162, 163, 166, 167; on Etain, 175, ii. 39, 54; on the Sid belief, 177, 178, 179, 180, 276; on the Bebind story, 200; on Adamnan's Vision, 220; on the Fourfold Division of the Otherworld, 225, 226; on the Tir Tairngiri, 227, 228.
Zosimas, the Hermit, his Apocalypse, i. 251.

Printed by T. and A. CONSTABLE, Printers to Her Majesty
at the Edinburgh University Press

AUTHOR

Meyer.

TITLE

The voyage of Bran.

DATE DUE	BORROWER'S NAME

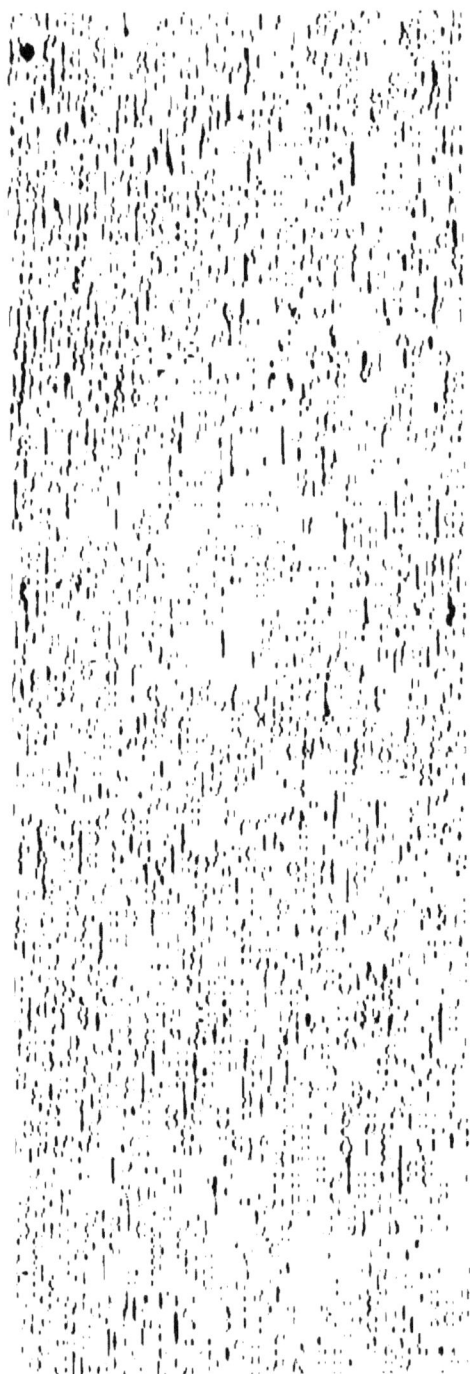

www.ingramcontent.com/pod-product-compliance
Lightning Source LLC
Chambersburg PA
CBHW030912270326
41929CB00008B/671